Hyperintelligence

Hyperintelligence

How the Universe Engineers Its Own Mind

Lars Tvede,
Jacob Bock Axelsen &
Daniel Käfer

WILEY

Registered Office(s)

John Wiley & Sons, Inc., 111 River Street, Hoboken, NJ 07030, USA

John Wiley & Sons Ltd, The Atrium, Southern Gate, Chichester, West Sussex, PO19 8SQ, UK

For details of our global editorial offices, customer services, and more information about Wiley products visit us at www.wiley.com.

The manufacturer's authorized representative according to the EU General Product Safety Regulation is Wiley-VCH GmbH, Boschstr. 12, 69469 Weinheim, Germany, e-mail: Product_Safety@wiley.com.

Library of Congress Cataloging-in-Publication Data is Available:

ISBN 9781394366095 (Cloth)
ISBN 9781394366118 (ePDF)
ISBN 9781394366101 (ePub)

Cover Design: Wiley
Cover Image: © Prostock-studio/stock.adobe.com.
Generated with AI.
Printed and bound by CPI Group (UK) Ltd, Croydon, CR0 4YY

C9781394366095_240725

CONTENTS

PREFACE

Imagine the universe squeezed into a space smaller than a grain of sand. Then, BOOM! An explosion of unimaginable power – the Big Bang – gave birth to our cosmos. In an instant, this newborn universe expands to a size that would take light-years to traverse. From the chaos emerged swirling subatomic particles, the LEGO bricks of reality. As the universe cooled, these particles assembled first into atoms, then stars, then planets. With each step, the universe, bizarrely enough, got smarter.

Fast forward to today, and we've created artificial intelligence (AI), a force evolving at breakneck speed – a trillion times faster than us!

This book charts the cosmic journey of intelligence, from the echoes of the Big Bang to the AI humming in your pocket and into a wild future. Along the way, we'll see that the universe doesn't just get smarter gradually; there are bursts and barriers. New elements or interactions trigger growth spurts where systems explore all their possibilities until they hit a wall – a "scaling barrier." Think of it as the universe saying, "Hold on, I need to catch my breath!"

Picture the universe as a giant laboratory where the forces of nature constantly experiment and evolve. It encounters challenges, like creating heavier atoms, where the formation of stars was the solution. Each time a hurdle is overcome, new, incredible possibilities open up. Interestingly, this typically happens when the density of something – atoms, cells, humans, or data – increases dramatically in a specific place, creating a whole new dynamic.

We've identified ten of these cosmic breakthroughs and growth spurts. From subatomic particles forming atoms to the birth of life to us inventing technologies, each step built on the last, creating mind-boggling complexity.

But the real game-changer? The arrival of living cells. Suddenly, the universe wasn't just complex; it was creating code – like DNA – capable of storing, transmitting, and using information to trigger action. And the most amazing part? The code started making more code. It was as if the universe had learned to write its own software, constantly upgrading and evolving.

This relentless growth is fueled by the ability to combine existing things in new ways, creating a never-ending spiral of innovation.

Right now, we're at the beginning of another explosive leap, driven by AI and a convergence of groundbreaking technologies. It's like the universe is hitting the accelerator, and things are about to get wild – in the most thrilling way.

We've mapped the universe's incredible journey toward complexity and intelligence using cutting-edge science and the AI-powered Supertrends system. Our map includes 16,000 historical innovations and 4,000 mind-blowing future predictions, including insights from 160 experts. This isn't just guesswork; it's data-driven. This is the story of how the universe got smart – and is now on the verge of becoming hyper-intelligent.

Ethics and the Dual Nature of Technology

In the initial draft of this manuscript, we included extensive ethical discussions. However, we ultimately removed them for several reasons. Firstly, incorporating a comprehensive ethical analysis would have significantly increased the book's length. Secondly, ethical considerations are not pertinent to events predating human existence; thus, adding such discussions solely for future scenarios would fragment the narrative. Finally, we believe that a narrative approach, allowing readers to draw their own ethical conclusions, is more engaging. For instance, a Hitchcock film interspersed with moral commentary on why one shouldn't stab women in showers would detract from its impact.

That said, the book does present an optimistic view of future technologies, a deliberate choice reflecting our observations. During our travels, we've noticed cultural differences in the perception of technology. In Europe, there's often a pronounced focus on technological risks, whereas in the United States and China, the emphasis tends to be on opportunities and potential benefits. Both perspectives have merit. Technology is akin to a Swiss Army knife: versatile but with sharp edges. For example, cars have revolutionized transportation but also led to accidents and pollution. Similarly, smartphones connect us yet can isolate us within digital bubbles.

Historically, technology has overwhelmingly improved our lives, elevating living standards, fostering innovation, and, after transitional periods, even promoting environmental progress. This is evident as people often migrate from less affluent to more prosperous nations. In this book, we've chosen to focus on the positive potential of emerging technologies. While acknowledging potential pitfalls – such as temporary job displacement, privacy concerns, and hypothetical risks of malicious AI – we believe it's crucial to highlight the vast opportunities these technologies present. Ultimately, focusing on potential benefits drives innovation and steers us toward a brighter future. Moreover, beyond optimistic or pessimistic views, one can adopt a realistic perspective: most technologies will evolve regardless of our preferences. The first step, therefore, is to understand them.

About Sources and Methods

This book is based on several analytical approaches. Firstly, we have naturally used a wide range of external sources. Secondly, we have identified a number of general phenomena that characterize the development of cosmic complexity. Three of these phenomena, in particular, together describe the majority of the 13.8 billion years of complexity development remarkably well. We call them "complexity cascades," "critical density," and "creative pulse," respectively, and we have simulated them using mathematical formulas.

In addition, we have drawn on the company Supertrends' research into the history of human innovation and expected future innovations.

Their database, based on approximately 75,000 AI runs and input from 160 experts, maps 16,000 historical and 4,000 anticipated innovations and shows around 200,000 relationships and dependencies between them.

You can find further information about all of this by scanning the QR code below with your phone and following the link that appears.

PART 1.

COSMOSPHERE

The Cosmosphere is the mind-bogglingly vast arena where the universe's epic drama unfolds. It's the totality of time, space, matter, and energy, a self-organizing spectacle that has conjured breathtaking complexity from the simplest of beginnings. The Cosmosphere is the kind of thing that can make anyone feel utterly small and insignificant.

But what if our universe isn't the only show in town? What if it's just one member of a cosmic ensemble, a multiverse teeming with possibilities? Let's take a closer look at our own universe's profile, a snapshot of its awe-inspiring stats and perhaps its hidden desires. . .

- **Age:** A venerable 13.8 billion years old
- **Big Bang photons per** m^3: A cool 411 million
- **Weight:** A hefty 10^{54} kg
- **Number of atoms:** A mind-boggling 10^{80}
- **Number of stars:** A dazzling 10^{24}
- **Size across:** A brain-twisting 94 billion light-years (10^{24} km)
- **Growth rate in space:** A speedy 67.5 km/s per 3.26 million light-years
- **Current volume:** A colossal $10^{24}m^3$
- **Total energy output:** A powerful 10^{48} W
- **Most energetic event (merger of two black holes):** A fleeting but ferocious $5 \cdot 10^{49}$ W
- **Desires offspring:** Well . . . maybe?
- **Born smart:** Not really, but definitely aspiring to be.

The Cosmosphere is a kingdom of endless wonders, where the universe's story unfolds on a grand scale. But, as we'll discover, even from its very first moments it held the seeds of intelligence and complexity.

I.
VIRTUALLY NOTHING

In this chapter, we witness the universe ignite with a mighty bang. Millions of years later, the first stars blaze to life, their fiery hearts becoming cosmic forges. See how stars transform simple elements into the building blocks of planets and life, scattering them across the universe in supernova explosions. We are, quite literally, made of stardust.

It's a very early August morning on the Croatian coast. As the first light creeps through the curtains in the bedroom, Maria wakes up. She's staying in a charming little family-run hotel, and beside her in bed lies her husband, John, still sound asleep.

Maria stretches, her muscles releasing the tensions of sleep. Then she slips almost silently out of bed, careful not to wake John. She tiptoes across the cool floor and puts on her favorite bikini. With a last glance back at her sleeping husband, she opens the door, sneaks out, and carefully closes it behind her. And then she walks down the seven steps to the hotel's small beach. Birds are singing out here, and the air smells of pine trees and wildflowers. Nearby, several colorful butterflies flutter among the blossoms.

The sea is glassy smooth. Maria takes a deep breath and lets a feeling of calm wash over her. It's so beautiful – the view, the sounds, the scent. Everything! She wades out into the crystal-clear water. Small fish swim playfully around her ankles in the clear shallows. A deep sense of gratitude spreads through her. All of this – the land, the air, the sea, life itself, she thinks – it's so amazing.

And then she remembers something scientists say. They say that it all arose from the void, from nothingness itself. The thought is strange.

The Strange Bang

Yes, very strange indeed. Today, there's almost universal agreement among physicists and astronomers that our universe originated from a single, enormous explosion called the Big Bang. Maria, the Earth, the ocean, the flowers, and the butterflies all came from that. This monumental event began from an incredibly tiny point, possibly smaller than a single atom. And perhaps the explosion started from nothing at all.

It's hard to imagine anything more absurd. But the scientific evidence for it is overwhelming. So even though this story seems utterly astonishing, it also appears to be true.

Another astounding aspect of the Big Bang is the incredible speed at which these events first unfolded. Most likely, this tiny speck grew to the size of Earth within less than a billionth of a second! Almost immediately after, the universe had expanded to the mighty size of the sun. And within the first full second, it may have even encompassed 10–20 light-years across – a distance equivalent to billions of kilometers. Not only did it expand much faster than the speed of light, but it grew to light-years across within an unimaginably tiny timeframe, shorter than it takes light to travel the width of an atom. This incredible first second of the Big Bang is now called "inflation."

Now imagine that during their Croatian vacation, Maria and John lie on the beach close to midnight, gazing into the clear, starry night sky. They might see the stars Alpha Centauri A and B, which are 4.37 light-years away. The distance to these is likely well within the size the universe had grown to within the first second after the Big Bang began.

Wild! But let's take the events step by step. Until about 10^{-36} seconds after the beginning, the universe was incredibly hot and dense, filled only with an immense amount of energy, so it's not really accurate to say there was nothing. Because there was a tremendous amount of energy. This energy was initially in the form of a unified "field," where all of nature's forces were completely entangled with each other. As we passed 10^{-36} seconds, the universe had expanded and cooled enough to allow the separation of the four different forces: gravity, strong and weak nuclear forces, and the electromagnetic force.

After 10^{-12} seconds, when the energy density and temperature had dropped further, some of this energy began to transform into mass through Einstein's famous equation: $E = mc^2$; energy equals "mass" (or what we call weight here on Earth) times the "speed of light" squared. This phenomenon, where energy can become mass, led to the creation of fundamental particles like quarks, leptons, and bosons. Quarks form protons, leptons include electrons, and bosons are particles like light.

In total, within one second, 17 different kinds of fundamental particles and their symmetrical antimatter counterparts had emerged, making 34 in total.

COMPLEXITY CASCADE #1

- **What?** Formation of particles
- **When?** 10^{-12} seconds after the start of the Big Bang
- **Why?** Cooling of the universe within the first fraction of a second.

Already in the first minutes after the start of the Big Bang, protons and neutrons began to combine, forming the first atomic nuclei. This process, called nucleosynthesis, continued for about 20 minutes and created a universe filled with hydrogen and helium, along with traces of lithium and beryllium.

The Red Shift and the Rumble

No matter how long anyone ponders this whole story, it will forever remain very, very strange. Despite this, the idea isn't entirely new. In fact, the Big Bang theory was first proposed in the 1920s thanks to the pioneering work of the Belgian priest and astronomer Georges Lemaître. In a groundbreaking 1927 article, Lemaître introduced the concept of an expanding universe containing an unchanging amount of matter. This article was partly based on Einstein's groundbreaking general theory of relativity from a few years earlier, which described gravity as part of a whole that we call spacetime. So, space and time are a single entity, and gravity is a curvature

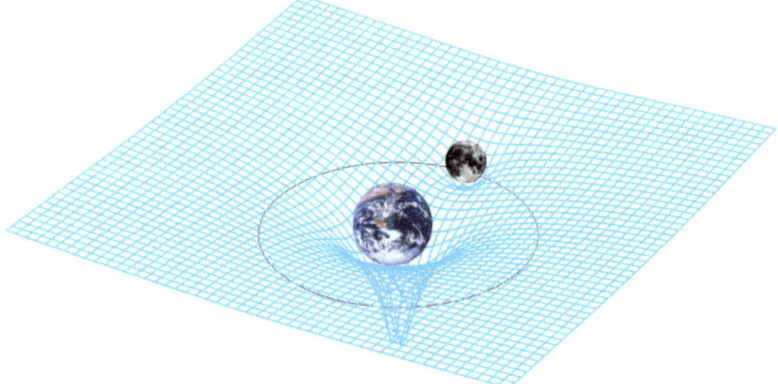

Spacetime. *Spacetime is a concept from physics that unites the three dimensions of space (length, width, height) with time as a fourth dimension. Imagine it as a kind of fabric that can be stretched and bent by mass and energy, and on which all events in the universe take place.*

in spacetime. Furthermore, Lemaître knew there were preliminary indications that stars and galaxies were moving away from each other.

But no one paid much attention to this bizarre theory in 1927. Just two years later, in 1929, however, astronomer Edwin Hubble found evidence that galaxies were actually moving away from us, with their speed proportional to their distance – a relationship now known as Hubble's Law.

This was truly significant. Imagine placing dots on an inflated balloon, each representing a galaxy. As the balloon expands, the dots (or galaxies) move further apart. In our three-dimensional universe, this expansion is driven by the vacuum – the space between atoms and particles. Hubble's observation showed that everything started in the same place, and that vacuum is constantly being produced and stretching the very fabric of space. By the way, it's a bit strange to think about an expanding vacuum. We usually think of a vacuum as nothing. But if it's constantly growing, it's intellectually a weird thing to explain.

How did Hubble measure how galaxies were moving? He built upon the so-called Doppler effect, which you can experience in your everyday life as a high-pitched tone when an ambulance siren approaches, and then a lower pitch as it moves away. Similarly, the light from distant galaxies appears to be "redshifted" due to their movement away from us. Instead of the tone of a siren, think of light shifting from blue (higher energy) moving towards us, to red (lower energy) when its source moves away from the observer. The red-shifting is, however, mostly due to the fact that space itself stretches light and thus lowers its frequency making it "redder."

To measure the distance to the galaxies, Hubble used special stars with a known brightness. By comparing their actual brightness to how faint they appeared, he could calculate how far away they were. The farther away a galaxy is, the greater its redshift. As mentioned, this indicated an initial explosion.

Many have wondered where the common starting point, the center of the universe, is. However, this question is based on a common misunderstanding. The Big Bang wasn't an explosion from a specific point in space, but rather an expansion of space itself. This uniform expansion means there's no central starting point, and therefore the entire universe can be seen as an expansion from within, effectively making every point a center for the universe's expansion. Bizarre perhaps, but all observations support this.

Despite Edwin Hubble's groundbreaking discovery of the expanding universe, many skeptics still regarded the theory as a fringe idea, perhaps even worthy of ridicule. In fact, the term "Big Bang" was coined in 1949 by the British astronomer Fred Hoyle during a BBC radio broadcast where he, yes, mocked it. Yes, the name Big Bang was intended as a sarcastic put-down of the theory.

Over time, however, more and more observations began to support the Big Bang theory. A crucial breakthrough came from two radio astrono-mers named Arno Penzias and Robert Wilson. They worked at Bell Labo-ratories in the 1960s, and their mission was to search for faint radio signals or microwaves reflected from satellites orbiting Earth. The task was excit-ing but also frustrating – such reflections were notoriously fleeting.

But one day, their instruments picked up something strange. Not an echo, but something faint and constant that filled the entire antenna. It was an electromagnetic signal, and depending on how you tuned the instru-ments, it would appear either akin to the background noise on an old TV, or a hum, or even a visual glow. But in all cases, it was a bit eerie because it wasn't coming from satellites. *It was coming from all directions.*

How could a signal from space come from all directions? They checked everything – pigeon droppings on the dish? Nope. Faulty wiring? Nope. Instrument malfunction? No, again.

Time passed, and slowly a crazy idea emerged. Could this be an echo from the Big Bang itself billions of years ago? Proponents of the strange Big Bang theory had actually predicted such a cosmic echo from the initial explosion. They had also predicted that since, according to the Big Bang theory, the universe shouldn't have a ground zero, the cosmic static would come equally from all directions. But few people had actually hoped to detect this signal.

Penzias and Wilson became increasingly excited and analyzed the data, finding that this hum in every way matched the predicted signature of the Big Bang's afterglow. It was then they realized they were actually listening to the roar from the very moment of the universe's creation.

This discovery, published in 1965 and later called the Cosmic Microwave Background (CMB) Radiation, shook the world. It once again confirmed the Big Bang theory, and it would later earn the two scientists a shared Nobel Prize.

Mysteries About Expansion

It's incredible that we humans can listen to the very explosion that created our world and, later, ourselves. But we can. And with the James Webb Space Telescope, we can even see back to a time just 300–400 million years after the Big Bang, 13.4 billion years ago. This is possible because the light from the most distant objects has taken billions of years to reach us.

However, even with the most powerful telescopes we could ever build, there will be distant galaxies we'll never be able to see. After the Big Bang, the universe's expansion slowed down but later began to accelerate again – now it's expanding faster than the speed of light!

This means that the light from the most distant galaxies will never reach us. The distance between us and these galaxies is simply growing too quickly. In fact, scientists estimate that 97% of the universe is beyond our reach, hidden behind the "cosmic horizon." However, we can still observe the light that was emitted before it passed this horizon – a glimpse of the past.

Einstein's theory of relativity only forbids travel "through" space faster than light, but space itself can expand freely. This expansion explains the universe's enormous size (94 billion light-years across!) despite its "young" age of 13.8 billion years.

Apart from this, one of the most perplexing observations for astronomers has been that no matter which way they look, the distribution of galaxies in space is more uniform than expected. Considering gravity's tendency to form enormous clusters interrupted by vast empty areas, this relatively even distribution is surprising. However, the initial dramatic inflation can explain this.

But there are plenty of things scientists are grappling with. For example, one theory says that so-called dark matter holds galaxies together, while dark energy drives the universe's accelerating expansion. But these explanations rely on our current understanding of physics, which might be incomplete. For example, 150 years ago, people believed heat was a substance. We now know it's just energy expressed by how fast atoms move. Similarly, dark matter and dark energy may not be separate things, but hidden properties of space, time, or gravity. For instance, so-called Modified Newtonian Dynamics (MOND) suggests that the laws of gravity change at large distances, eliminating the need for dark matter. Likewise, some theories propose that dark energy is a fictitious stand-in for the so-called quantum vacuum, a fundamental property of space itself.

Mysteries Upon Mysteries

So the universe is filled with fascinating and perplexing puzzles. Among the most baffling questions are surely these three: First, what triggered the Big Bang? Second, what existed before the Big Bang? And third, where do the laws of physics come from?

Many religions answer the first two questions by assuming that God created the universe. However, this leads to a philosophical dead end known as the infinite regress problem, which can be incredibly frustrating. "If God created the universe, who or what created God?" This line of thinking leads to an endless chain of creators, leaving the ultimate origin unanswered.

Some religions address this by postulating that God exists outside of spacetime, making him or her eternal and uncreated. Of course, it can be difficult to grasp how something can exist but be uncreated. Not to mention how it can exist outside of spacetime yet still be able to act within it.

No, it's not easy. Outside of religion, a thought-provoking hypothesis has emerged in recent decades. The idea is that our reality is a sophisticated computer simulation. This notion could explain some of the universe's perplexing peculiarities, as simulations can be programmed with any conceivable parameters. For example, if a simulation doesn't need to make sense, the universe can come from nothing and things can be infinitely weird. In other words, a simulation can include nonsense.

But the simulation hypothesis raises a host of new questions. To begin with, consider the sheer absurdity of constructing such a colossal machine capable of simulating every atom, quark, and particle in our universe. The computational resources required would be staggering, with circuits spanning unimaginable distances. And if we exist in a simulation, who created it? Another entity, perhaps also in another simulation? This again leads us down a rabbit hole of infinite regress, where the origin of reality remains elusive.

Many Universes?

In more scientific circles, one explanation is based on the so-called Cyclic Universe model. Imagine that our universe at some point reaches a turning point where gravity takes over and starts pulling everything back inwards, eventually leading to a "Big Crunch." Then we get a new Big Bang, and so on, ad infinitum. It sounds enticing, but we have no evidence for it. In fact, the universe's expansion is now accelerating instead of slowing down. It's a bit annoying when something does the opposite of what a theory predicts.

There's a prominent variation of the cyclic model that addresses the question of how we can simultaneously have accelerating expansion and still end up with a new Big Bang. In Roger Penrose's so-called Conformal Cyclic Cosmology, all matter eventually decays into radiation, so that the late universe will only contain energy, but no stars or planets, for example. According to Penrose, this allows for a so-called conformal rescaling of spacetime, where the size of the universe eventually becomes irrelevant, enabling a smooth transition from the end of one cycle to the beginning of the next.

Other scientists lean towards the Multiverse theory, painting a picture of cosmic abundance. Imagine our universe as one bubble in a cosmic sea of countless others, each with its own set of physical laws. These universes may be separated by invisible membranes or exist in entirely different dimensions. Some versions of this theory propose infinitely many universes, others a large but finite collection. But none of these cyclic or multiverse theories escape the problem of infinite regression: What started all of this?

Fine-tuned Universe Theory

Something appealing about multiverse theories is their potential to explain the fine-tuning of the universe's physical constants. This fine-tuning is a perplexing phenomenon, as even slight variations in some constants would have made the universe impossible for life as we know it. Take gravity as an example. If the gravitational force of stars were just 5% stronger, they would collapse under their own weight and become dense fireballs before they could form the heavier elements – the foundation of life. Conversely, if gravity were 5% weaker, stars would never have had enough force to ignite hydrogen, leaving the universe in perpetual icy darkness.

Or consider the electromagnetic force. If its strength deviated by just 0.01%, atoms wouldn't be able to bond by sharing electrons, making the formation of life's building blocks – molecules – impossible. Imagine galaxies filled with unbound hydrogen, eternally lonely and sterile.

And so on. The strong nuclear force, the mass of the electron and proton, and even the proton-to-electron mass ratio are spot-on for life. Even a small change would have made life impossible.

Isn't it strange that these rules are so finely tuned to enable life? The multiverse theory addresses this by suggesting that if countless universes exist, each with randomly different physical laws, at least one will end up with the necessary conditions for life. And that happens to be ours.

But we still haven't figured out how it all began. What if spacetime itself – the fabric of reality – didn't even exist before the Big Bang? Instead of a complete void, there could have been a strange quantum world with no space, no time – just a restless ocean of energy shifting unpredictably. In this chaotic state, energy might have briefly transformed into tiny fragments of spacetime before vanishing again, like quantum "popcorn" popping in and out of existence.

Now, imagine that at some point, this flickering chaos was suddenly influenced by a shift in the rules – perhaps the laws of physics as we know them didn't always apply. If these laws changed, they could have triggered a colossal release of energy, forcing spacetime to stabilize and expand – creating the Big Bang. In this view, the Big Bang wasn't the true beginning but more like a dramatic phase transition, similar to water turning into steam when heated.

The Universe's Spin: Could Black Holes Hold the Key?

A variation of the theory suggests that there are elements of physics that only play out under extreme conditions of critical density. This, of course, turns the attention to black holes. Could they create new universes?

At first, this sounds highly counterintuitive, because we assume that black holes are balls of massively compressed material, which is pretty much the opposite of an expanding and mostly empty spacetime.

However, physicist Nikodem Popławski and others suggest that the critical density of energy and matter within black holes may facilitate the formation of new spacetime. This theory doesn't necessarily require fundamental changes in the laws of physics but could suggest that such critical density could activate aspects of them that manifest only under these extreme conditions.

This concept leads to an intriguing question: could a universe born by a black hole inherit properties from its black hole origins? Its spin, for instance, is a prime candidate, given that most black holes are assumed to spin, often at extremely high velocities. If a universe emerges from a rotating black hole, it is not implausible that this rotational motion is imparted to the nascent universe.

To investigate this, scientists have turned to observations from the James Webb Space Telescope to study the rotation of galaxies as seen from our vantage point. The analysis, published in 2025, provided rotation direction annotations for 263 galaxies. Of these, 158 galaxies exhibit clockwise rotation from our vantage point, while 105 galaxies rotate counterclockwise. If galactic rotation directions were random, we'd expect roughly equal numbers spinning in each direction. However, the observations showed a clear imbalance, a result that would be expected to happen by chance only about 0.07% of the time. This suggests that the observed pattern is unlikely to be due to chance alone.

While this is by no means proof that black holes create universes, it can be interpreted as lending support to that hypothesis.

Stars: The Cosmic Alchemists

Let's return to what we know with great certainty. Fast forward millions of years after the Big Bang. The universe, still expanding, has cooled considerably from its original fiery state. Now, large, empty spaces are interrupted by clouds of gas. The clouds consist almost entirely of hydrogen and helium.

During this era, the first stars begin to appear. The birth of a star begins as a massive, slowly rotating cloud of gas and dust. This cloud stretches over thousands of light-years. Over time, it evolves into a protostar, denser and hotter, as the atoms get closer and closer together due to gravity. Eventually, the center of the cloud becomes so compact and hot that it begins to radiate heat and light. The outer layers of the cloud, however, remain cooler and hide the glowing core from outside observers.

The crucial moment in a star's birth occurs when the core's temperature and pressure become so intense that hydrogen atoms fuse into helium. This nuclear fusion is typically ignited under pressure 100 billion times greater than the atmosphere at the Earth's surface. At such pressure, an amount of energy is released that is millions of times more powerful than any atomic bomb. And although this energy is continuous, it bubbles like lava in a volcanic eruption, sending enormous shock waves through the star's mass. Meanwhile, intense light and heat radiate from the core, but due to the star's enormous size, it can take hundreds of thousands of years for this energy to reach the surface.

Stars are cosmic alchemists that transform lighter elements into heavier elements through nuclear fusion. They primarily fuse hydrogen into helium, then helium into beryllium, then into carbon and oxygen and so on, creating ever heavier elements up to iron. This process, along with something called reionization, shaped the early universe. Ionization occurred when the first stars began to shine. Their strong light blew electrons away from hydrogen atoms. Without electrons, the hydrogen

Protostar. *This image, taken by the NASA/ESA/CSA James Webb Space Telescope, shows the protostar L1527, which is at the center of a cloud of material being pulled towards it. Over time, this will evolve into a regular star like the sun.*

atoms became protons. This ionization of the gas made the universe more transparent.

The time it takes for a star to ignite depends on its mass. Smaller stars like our sun take 10–20 million years to evolve and can then shine for billions of years. Heavy stars form faster, live wilder and die young. They create elements up to iron and then explode in a supernova, a monumental event that forges the heavier elements like gold and uranium. Elements created by stars are then scattered throughout space and provide the building blocks for future stars and planets.

Interestingly, much of the matter in our bodies comes from the burning cores of stars: the hydrogen in our bodies was created in the first minutes of the universe. The rest is literally made of stardust. And if we have a gold watch or wear gold jewelry, we are carrying around the remains of exploding stars.

COMPLEXITY CASCADE #3

- **What?** Formation of heavier atoms
- **When?** 200–300 million years after the start of the Big Bang
- **Why?** Cooling of the universe within the first fraction of a second

Supernova. *This Hubble image shows the enormous Crab Nebula, the remnants of a star that exploded around 5500 BCE, although it was not observed on Earth until 1054 CE due to the time it took for the light from the explosion to reach us.*

About 13 billion years ago, a vast cloud of gas and dust began to contract, forming our galaxy, the Milky Way. In one of the Milky Way's spiral arms, a portion of this cloud collapsed and gave birth to our sun about 4.6 billion years ago. In the rotating disk of gas and dust that surrounded the young sun, particles coalesced to form the planets, including our own. This is how our wonderful Earth came into being. From almost nothing.

2.
HYDRO'S HOT DATE

Believe it or not, the universe's complexity is built on simple building blocks. In this chapter, we trace tokens of information from the Big Bang's particles to the formation of atoms and molecules. We delve into self-organization, fractals, and chaos theory, revealing the hidden mathematical patterns that shape the cosmos and drive its growing complexity.

Imagine a little atom named Hydro, born about 20 minutes into the Big Bang, feeling a bit lonely. In his search for companionship, the little guy creates a Tinder profile, showcasing his best selfie and an enticing bio:

"Hey, I'm Hydro. I'm a simple guy with just one proton and one electron. I'm incredibly versatile and love connecting with other atoms. I can even crystallize into a solid. I have a valence of 1, which means I have an electron to share, and I'm open to forming both covalent and ionic bonds. I'm especially attracted to oxygen (H_2O, anyone?) and carbon, but I'm also known to get along well with other elements like nitrogen and

halogens. If you're looking for a stable, reliable, and adaptable partner, swipe right! 😉"

Now he sees a profile from Oxina, a lively oxygen atom, with a Tinder profile that reads:

"Hey, I'm Oxina (O), the life of the party! 💃 *I'm a social butterfly always looking to make connections and form lasting bonds, though I'm also open to something more short-term. Whether you're a carbon looking for a long-term commitment (CO_2, anyone?) or a hydrogen seeking a passionate fling, I'm open to exploring new connections.* 😉"

Hydro and Oxina swipe right on each other, and their passionate fling quickly ignites. But there's a twist! Hydro soon discovers that he's not Oxina's only flame – another Hydro is also in the mix. It's a love triangle!

Now imagine Hydro as a hydrogen atom, Oxina as an oxygen atom, and their *ménage à trois* resulting in the well-known compound H_2O – or, as we know it, water.

The Emergence of Tokens

There's a point to this fictional story, and it's about complexity and something called tokens. The word token comes from the Old English word *tācen*, which means "sign" or "symbol." Today, the word is used to describe various identifiable units that represent information or meaning. It may sound academic, but in this book, for example, every word or number is a token.

Hydrogen and oxygen each have some properties that can be described very concretely. These include, for example, mass, magnetic moment, energy levels, isotopes, radioactivity, electron configuration, and so on. Together, these make up 53 tokens for the two atoms, meaning 53 different representations of information or meaning.

We've already seen that the universe arose from a single unified energy field. In the first fractions of a second after the Big Bang, the four fundamental forces separated. This separation significantly increased the complexity of the universe, as each force has its own unique properties and interactions. Within the first three seconds, the fundamental particles and antiparticles also emerged – the building blocks of all matter. Each of these particles has specific properties such as mass, charge, and spin, which further contributed to the complexity of the universe. In fact, the complexity increased by 194 tokens due to these particles. In just three seconds, the universe had gone from a state of extreme homogeneity to a diversity of forces and particles.

The subsequent emergence of the first four elements – hydrogen, helium, lithium, and beryllium – further contributed to the universe's complexity. Each element can have a varying number of neutrons in their nucleus, so they are called "isotopes." That term, by the way, comes from Greek and means "same place" because they occupy the same place in the periodic table. While the fundamental particles together provided a couple of hundred tokens, the description of these first atoms and their isotopes required thousands, bringing the total number to about 5,000–6,000 tokens. So the complexity had now, just 20 minutes after the Big Bang, increased considerably.

Stars are the true architects of atomic diversity. They create the remaining 88 naturally occurring elements through nuclear fusion, giving rise to the vast periodic table with 80 stable elements and about 260 stable isotopes. These elements can combine to form countless molecules. That being said, to date, we have only identified about 250 unique molecules in interstellar and intergalactic space. While unconfirmed discoveries suggest slightly greater molecular diversity, the current estimate for the total number of different atoms and molecules in the lifeless cosmos is around 350. A far higher number was theoretically possible, but the conditions to create it were not present.

In any case, 350 atoms and molecules represent thousands of new tokens. This chemical diversity likely increased the universe's token count to around 15,000–16,000. But with the full periodic table at its disposal, the universe can potentially generate up to 10^{60} unique molecules. It just doesn't happen in the absence of life. And that means that for at least millions of years after the Big Bang, the complexity of the universe remained very stable and, on a chemical level, very simple.

In fact, this marked the beginning of what quantum physicist David Deutsch calls "the Great Monotony." After the first waves of drama and innovation in the Big Bang and the formation of atoms, the universe fell into a state of repetitive events, such as star formation and cometary orbits, making cosmic events predictable over vast timescales. Deutsch attributed this monotony to what he called the "hierarchy rule," where larger celestial bodies like stars remain largely unaffected by smaller objects like comets. For example, if two objects collide, you just end up with one. Thus, there was virtually nothing present to create more complexity.

Self-organization and Self-similarity

So how did we get from this stagnation in complexity to Maria, our woman by the water's edge? Here we must talk about how structure arises. Let's start with the fact that atoms and molecules can create fascinating structures without forming new molecules. Imagine this: On a distant planet, where clouds of water vapor drift across the sky, a small dust particle gets caught in a cold air current. Water molecules cling to the particle and freeze into ice, and slowly a sparkling snowflake grows. In a few minutes, the snowflake grows large enough that gravity begins to pull it down.

The delicate, branched patterns in snowflakes hold something truly amazing, namely that despite being made of exactly the same thing, and all being hexagonal, they are never ever alike. This intricate nature arises from the hexagonal lattice structure that water molecules form when they freeze. The lattice promotes growth at the six corners, forming branches whose tips attract more water molecules, causing further branching. Snowflakes have a slight tendency towards so-called self-similarity, where each small arm to some extent reflects the overall snowflake shape. This repetition of similar patterns at smaller and smaller (or larger and larger) scales is called fractals. So it is a cascade of copies at different scales within the larger structure.

Snowflake. *All snowflakes are hexagonal, but no two are alike. The repetitive process at the molecular level ultimately results in the intricate beauty of snowflakes.*

Snowflakes exhibit amazing diversity. Some researchers estimate that there may be up to a septillion possible snowflake designs. And Kenneth Libbrecht, a snowflake physicist, explains that even though it is theoretically possible, the probability of two snowflakes being identical is almost infinitely small, or about 10^{-24}. So this is an example of how complexity can arise from simplicity.

The Mathematics of Order and Chaos

There is a long way from the complexity of snowflakes to the complexity of Maria, our woman by the water's edge. But there is an important similarity between them: Both are largely built on a combination of something that is ordered and something else that creates randomness within the ordered framework. And then there's another parallel. We can study snowflakes with a microscope, but we can also model them chemically and mathematically. The same goes for Maria, even though she is far more complex. In general, this applies to everything in nature. A well-known example is ripple marks, formed by the interaction between loose sand and a flowing medium such as water or wind. They are found on all planets where there is sand moved around by atmosphere or water, and the ripple size and spacing will be controlled everywhere by flow strength and grain size, which can be accurately modeled. But they can also be described statistically without knowing their causes.

Here we come to the mathematics that can model these kinds of things. Math is not a human invention. Mathematical relationships existed before us; we just discovered them. And they will be recognized by any intelligent life form that may exist anywhere in the universe. Even in hypothetical universes with different physical laws, the underlying principles of logic and mathematics would likely remain consistent.

The same would apply to all the mathematical phenomena around us. Take, for example, a pile of sand: When you add grains, small avalanches are common, but large ones are rare. However, the way these avalanches occur follows a consistent pattern, meaning that if you know how often different small avalanches occur, you can statistically predict when larger avalanches are likely to occur. Such predictability can also be calculated for earthquakes and floods with the concept of hundred-year events. Because we know that large earthquakes occur, and there hasn't been one in 100 years, for example, we can expect them to happen soon. The important thing here is to understand that all these regularities arise spontaneously when the conditions are right. This is called "emergence," and that complexity cannot be directly read from the number of tokens used to describe their basic parts.

The Building Blocks of the Universe Are Made in Giant Forges

Nature thus has a fascinating ability to create complexity. This often happens through emergence processes, where especially compact clusters of matter, energy, or something else entirely, such as information, suddenly trigger the formation of something completely new. We call this triggering factor "critical density," and it plays a crucial role in the development of the universe and its evolving intelligence.

To understand critical density, let's look at the normal distribution. Most things in nature follow a bell-shaped curve. Think of grown people's height, where most are close to average. There is no one who is 10 cm or 10 m tall, which would fall too far outside the norm.

But when self-reinforcing processes come into play, nature can deviate dramatically from this normal distribution. Examples of this are known from e.g. earthquakes, floods, forest fires, and avalanches. Here, the outcomes are distributed much more wildly. This kind of natural phenomenon

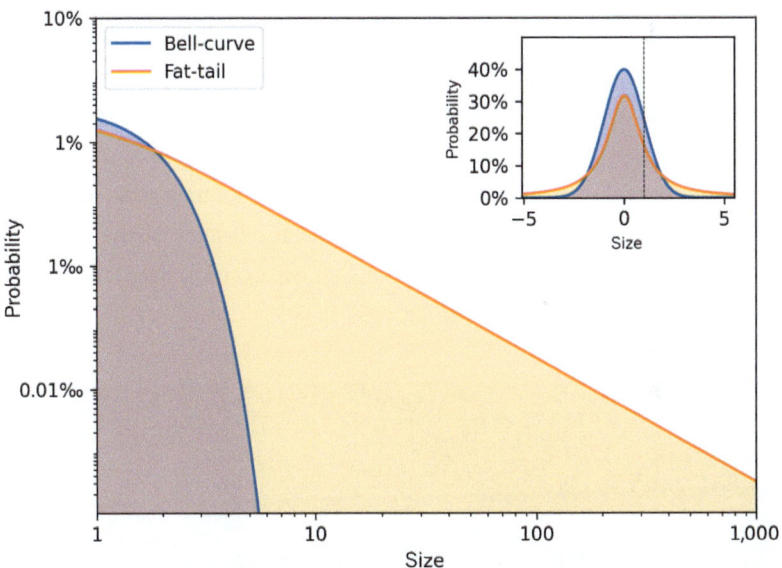

Distributions with and without "fat tails." *In the small inset figure you see two distributions, but one (orange) shows much wilder and more extreme sizes. It's hard to see why they are so different. Therefore, in the large figure, we zoom in on the right "tail" for each of the two bell-shaped distributions. For the normal distribution (blue shade), it is very unlikely to find anything larger than 10, so it has a very, very "thin tail" and quickly dives into the infinite depths. The orange one, on the other hand, has a "fat tail" because it is still realistic to find something that is size 10, 100 and maybe even 1,000.*

is based on a mechanism running wild and reinforcing itself. It can even resemble a statistical bell shape to be confused, but it is very different.

Critical density occurs when the density of something becomes so great that it triggers a whole new dynamic, which can create more complexity. An example is the density in the early universe. Shortly after the Big Bang, matter was evenly distributed. But gravity began to pull matter together. Small differences in density were amplified, and compact areas emerged. After 20–100 million years, these areas formed stars – objects with extremely high density. At the same time, the stars' nuclear fusion raised the temperature to 10–300 million degrees, while the surrounding space remained ice cold. In addition, black holes arose, where the density was even greater. As an example, if the Earth were compressed to the density of a black hole, it would be less than a centimeter in radius! Black holes have critical density if anything, and a speculative theory is that new universes are actually created from here.

Regardless of whether black holes create new universes, the phenomenon of critical density is a frequent turning point where self-reinforcing forces push a system into a new state. It is a rebellious force that breaks with the normal distribution, creates extreme phenomena and creates fertile ground for new complexity. Throughout the history of the universe, critical density has played a crucial role in overcoming barriers of complexity and driving evolution forward.

Section of the Milky Way seen from the James Webb Telescope. *This image shows both a large nebula, as well as groups of protostars and stars of very varying sizes about 25,000 light-years away. The distribution of matter follows a "fat tail" distribution, and you can make a simulation of it, which we will discuss later in the book.*

Deterministic Chaos

Some of nature's methods for creating structure fall under what is known as chaos theory. It is a world of patterns so thought-provoking that it took science until the 1970s to truly understand them. After which it became well known to the general public, as even the simplest systems can create wildly complex and fascinating behavior thanks to something called deterministic chaos. Think of it as the universe's way of keeping us on our toes, where even small changes can lead to unpredictable outcomes. Take, for example, the famous Mandelbrot set. It is a fascinating pattern generated by a super-simple equation:

$$z_n = z_{n-1}^2 + c$$

This creates infinite detail at every zoom level – like a snowflake, but with endless detail.

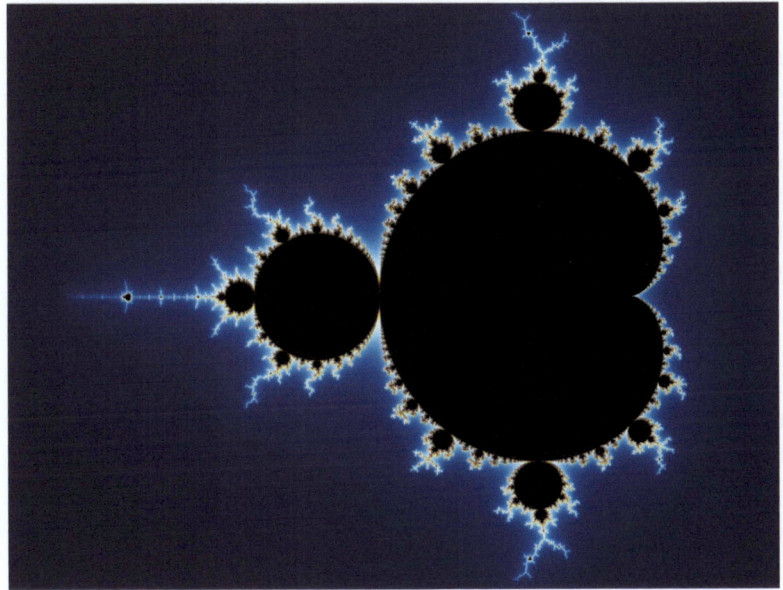

The Mandelbrot set. *This looks very complex, and on top of that it is even more complex than you can see. Because if you zoom in further and further, it will constantly repeat itself! For example, if you look at the marked "tip," you can see the Mandelbrot set sitting right there. Zoom in on it, and it happens again. And again. And again. Forever.*

However, the Mandelbrot set is not made to describe anything real. If you want to see how easily chaos actually arises in something moving, think of something as incredibly boring as a pendulum. It just swings back and forth, so if you look at it for more than 10 seconds, you fall asleep with a bang.

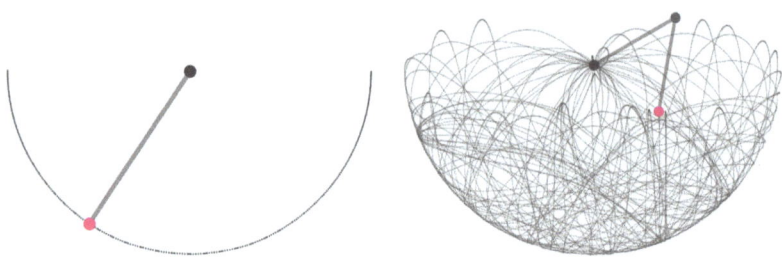

Simple pendulum (left) and double pendulum (right).
The simple pendulum swings regularly and predictably back and forth. The double pendulum, on the other hand, is unpredictable and can suddenly swing in a completely different direction than expected. This is an example of a chaotic system. The arms and legs of mammals can be seen as double pendulums of bones, controlled by muscles and nerves. However, evolution has ensured that the range of motion in elbow and knee joints is limited, preventing chaotic movement and providing precise control over our limbs. Evolution has, in essence, tamed chaos and created order in complex biological systems.

Deterministic chaos means something that is predetermined, but at the same time so complex that you cannot predict its behavior for a very long time to come. Perhaps the most famous chaotic system is the so-called Lorenz attractor. In 1963, physicist Edward Lorenz sat and simulated the weather so that better weather forecasts could be made. He tried again and again, but the weather kept being unpredictable and moving on a mysterious, hidden quantity we call an attractor. The problem is that in the long term, very small uncertainties in the initial conditions can lead to very large changes in the weather in a given location in, for example, two weeks.

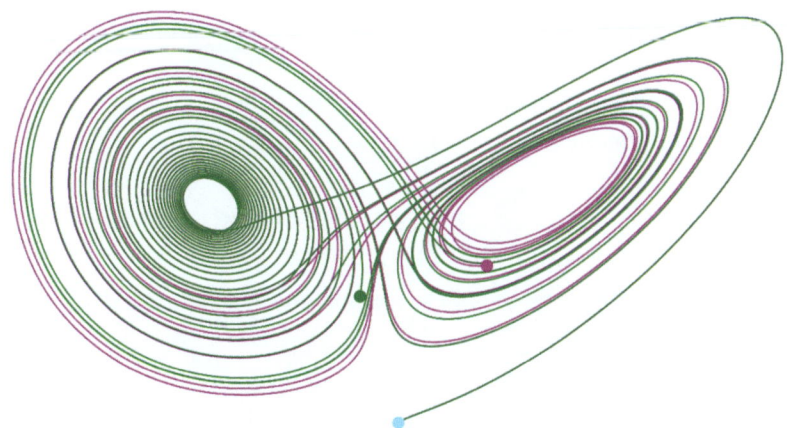

Lorenz attractor. *The figure shows how you can start the weather almost in the same place (blue dot), but after some time you separate. In the picture, the weather starts at the light blue dot on two different days, where the weather is almost the same. The green weather curve covers a purple curve. The weather is pretty much the same for a while. Suddenly, however, one sees the weather in one week stand out on the purple curve and forever follow its own path. In principle, the difference in the beginning is as little as a butterfly flapping its wings, or an ant pushing the air in a different direction.*

So nature follows processes that can be described by mathematical rules that sometimes create wildly strange outcomes. For example, we can also think of the so-called Barnsley fern; a virtual fern created by repeating four simple mathematical routines. It looks like a real fern, but it's pure math. In fact, it is named after the British mathematician Michael Barnsley, who introduced it in his 1988 book "Fractals Everywhere."

Nature 'loves' such patterns. Have you ever noticed the fascinating spirals on a pinecone or the intricate patterns on a Romanesco broccoli? It's like nature's own work of art, and it turns out there's a simple mathematical code behind it: the Fibonacci spiral.

This beautiful spiral is built from the Fibonacci sequence, where each number is the sum of the two before it. It starts with 0 and 1, then $1 + 1 = 2$, $1 + 2 = 3$ and so on:

$$0, 1, 1, 2, 3, 5, 8, 13, 21, 34, \ldots$$

Image of the Barnsley fern. *Notice that each branch just needs to be rotated and zoomed in on – then you get a fern again. It repeats itself endlessly, just like the Mandelbrot set.*

It's like nature's way of saying: "Keep it simple, keep it optimal, and keep it going!" Here's the twist: Plants don't have a built-in calculator to become these perfect shapes. Instead, it simply forces each new shoot away from the previous shoots as the internal meristem grows. That's all.

The same spiral patterns can be observed, for example, in the arrangement of pine cones, sunflower seeds, the chambers of a nautilus shell and even certain proportions in the human body. It seems that nature has an ability to find elegant solutions to complex problems, often converging on the same patterns over and over again.

As we continue our journey through the history of the universe in the next chapters, we will encounter more of these patterns. Nature and other dynamic systems are constantly discovering structures that are either just there and can enchant us like snowflakes. Or that we encounter because

Romanesco broccoli. *You can clearly see that various Fibonacci spirals start at the top and go out from there. Notice that the shoots are each small replicas of the whole head. Yes, in fact, the shoots on them, the sub-shoots, are also small replicas of the head. The plant is therefore also a self-similar fractal, just like the Barnsley fern and the Mandelbrot set.*

they, like the shape of broccoli, bring success. By understanding these patterns, we can model things from the ground up and explain how complexity and intelligence evolve over time and eventually become hyper-intelligence.

3.
FROM LEGO TO LIFE

This chapter dives into the engine that most of all drives the universe's creativity, namely combinatorial complexity. Discover how simple building blocks can create an astonishing number of possibilities. And get ready to explore the 10 great leaps in complexity that have brought us from the Big Bang to the brink of a hyperintelligent future.

When we explore the mathematics behind the natural world, we encounter a fascinating phenomenon: the principle of combinatorial complexity. This principle explains the exponential increase in possibilities that arise when we combine even a small number of elements. Imagine a system with just two components, "a" and "b." Initially, they can be combined into "ab," and we now have three different options: "a," "b" and "ab." But when we add combinations of the three possibilities, the number of possible outcomes doesn't just increase linearly – it increases exponentially. At the next level we already have several options, like "aab" and "bab." This pattern continues, and with each addition of an element or a new interaction between the elements, the number of possible combinations explodes. Instead of a simple increase, each new possibility creates multiple layers of complex relationships that can quickly become almost infinite. This is why complex systems like nature or technological networks can achieve enormous diversity with just a few basic elements.

Combinatorial cascades are inherently exponential, but not only that. When several such phenomena intersect, the result can be hyperexponential – like a kind of growth on steroids, where the growth rate itself increases exponentially.

The Complexity Cascades on the Journey to Hyperintelligence

In reality, the growth of complexity in the universe does not happen smoothly; it tends to unfold in bursts. Imagine that a new element appears in a system, which triggers a cascade of combinations and possibilities. It gives a creative explosion, but only until the system reaches its immediate limits. In the following, we call this world of possibilities in a creative explosion a "design space." In other words, a space of possibilities. The outer edge of the design space is called a "scaling barrier," as previously mentioned. Creativity goes that far, but no further.

Now let's review the history of complexity from that perspective. The first two steps were the creation of subatomic particles and then the creation of the four simplest atoms. The two steps together took a few minutes. But then complexity stagnated for millions of years until stars emerged. These cosmic high-pressure furnaces provided the necessary environment for atoms to fuse. This created a wider range of elements. It was like upgrading from a basic LEGO set to a set with an incredible number of possibilities.

But even stars have their limits. Eventually they had delivered all they could, and the universe fell into a more predictable pattern, where the design space was apparently once again filled. Sure, these atoms could in principle be combined into countless molecules, but there weren't many processes present to create these combinations. Therefore, there was stagnation again.

The most significant leap occurred from step 3 (atoms and molecules) to step 4 (living cells). Starting from step 4 and thus the living cells, the process involves coding not only complexity, but also intelligence. This combination turned the universe into a spontaneous computer that wrote its own software – code that could evolve and adapt in ways never seen before. It's actually a wild thought. After that, it completely took off, and what we can now see is a pattern with the 10 aforementioned phases passed and the 11th just around the corner:

- **Subatomic particles** combined to form . . .
- **Atoms**, after which stars created . . .
- **The entire periodic table**, which led to . . .
- **Living cells**, and finally . . .
- **Organelles and multicellular life**. This gave rise to . . .
- **Biogeochemical transformations** of Earth, followed by . . .
- **Consciousness and exploratory intelligence** and . . .
- **Technologies** that paved the way for . . .
- **Computers and telecommunications**, which then led to . . .
- **AI swarm intelligence**, followed by . . .
- **AI-based hyperintelligence**.

This entire cosmic pattern of expanding, encountering a scaling barrier, and then breaking through to a cascade of even greater complexity has been a constant throughout the history of the universe. But the pace has increased. There were stagnation levels of millions of years between phase 2 and 3, and again between phase 3 and 4. And once again between phase 4 and 5. But then it went from strength to strength, and right now we are witnessing a development with unprecedented speed, as if the world's intelligence is almost exploding. Therefore, we can also predict with considerable certainty even more after the achievement of AI-based hyperintelligence. We will discuss this in Part 4 of the book.

Singularities

This pattern of building complexity, hitting a limit and then breaking through to even greater heights, fits well with what Stuart Kauffman describes in his book *Investigations* (2000). Kauffman explains that at any given time there is a set of all potential new combinations of existing elements – this is the "adjacent possible," as he calls it. Every time a new combination arises, it not only adds to what already exists, it also creates new, adjacent possibilities. For example, hydrogen and helium atoms minutes after the Big Bang were within the then adjacent possible, but snowflakes and proteins were not yet. As the universe cooled and more atoms emerged, the adjacent possible eventually expanded to include more complex structures like snowflakes – and much later also proteins.

When moving from a combinatorial cascade through its scaling barrier and into the next cascade, one can experience this shift as a so-called "singularity." This term means a point in time where the prevailing order breaks down and something fundamentally new and unpredictable arises. At these times, prediction seems impossible, because at any given moment you have too little data and insight to fully understand the consequences of what has just begun to happen.

The start of a larger combinatorial cascade is each time a singularity. And the world has gone through 10 of these so far. The 11th, which is now right in front of our noses, concerns our imminent introduction to hyper-intelligence, where artificial intelligence surpasses human intelligence in all areas.

What is it that Kauffman's formula says that captures all this so well? The formula predicts that even if a small fraction of the new combinations are useful, the number of useful combinatorial tools grows exponentially anyway. In this way, each combinatorial cascade in the universe pushes the boundaries of what is possible, leading to even more breakthroughs.

This process of spontaneously generating complexity and intelligence is not only fascinating, it is downright overwhelming because the way it creates combinatorial cascades is itself a combinatorial cascade. Wild, but true: The creation of complexity thus exhibits self-similarity, and the logic behind intelligence itself becomes more intelligent. For example, it is fundamental innovations that the universe can write code, and that code can then create intelligence, and that intelligence can then create technology.

The Creative Pulse

In practice, the process is not just about adding new combinations, as is evident from Kauffman's equation. Systems often have a back-and-forth rhythm: things unite, separate, and unite again. Think, for example, of atoms that form molecules, which later split again. Or stars that are born from collapsing dust clouds, which then explode and spread their stardust to form new stars and planets.

It's as if the world in many places has a creative pulse. Each cycle provides a chance for new combinations to emerge. These new things are then combined with others, and the cycle repeats itself and accumulates complexity over time. This pattern is not just about stars and atoms; it is everywhere. Species come and go, but extinct species may have left useful traces of their DNA in other species. Civilizations similarly come and go, but leave behind useful information. The creative pulse is also found in national economies. The economist Joseph Schumpeter introduced the concept of "creative destruction" to describe how shifts between economic growth and decline can drive innovation forward. It is a rhythm that drives the development of complexity and ultimately also of intelligence.

Shakespeare and the Infinite Monkeys

Let's just go back to the emergence of the periodic table of atoms to the beginning of life. To truly understand the genius of it, we need to appreciate the unique role that code plays. We can define code as systems that store, transmit, and manipulate information. But its true strength lies in its ability to create action. Sometimes this action involves gathering elements from nature to build things – think, for example, of DNA constructing wild things like a butterfly. In addition, code can also create more code.

A thought experiment captures this idea beautifully, primarily because the experiment, in an instructive way, doesn't make much sense. It's called the Infinite Monkey Theorem. This hypothetical idea postulates that a monkey randomly typing on a typewriter for an infinite amount of time will eventually produce any given text, including, for example, the complete works of Shakespeare. In 2002, a group of students attempted to test its merits by placing a typewriter in a zoo's monkey enclosure with five macaques. After a month and a half, these monkeys had only managed to produce five pages of text, consisting primarily of the letter "s." Meanwhile, the monkeys had also partially destroyed the typewriter and used it as a toilet.

A more theoretical approach was taken by the physicist Manon Bischoff. He calculated that to achieve just a 40% probability of writing the word "banana," a monkey would have to engage in a staggering 10 billion attempts! Another researcher estimated how long it would take a computer program to generate a single sentence from Shakespeare's *Hamlet*. The result: 10^{32} years, which is 100,000 billion billion billion years. The universe is only 13.8 billion years old, so it would most likely take much longer than the universe has existed. Actually much, much, much longer. And just for a single sentence! So yes, it would require an astronomical number of parallel universes, each consisting solely of typing monkeys, typing away over an unimaginable period of time, before one suddenly wrote the entire *Hamlet* play with its 174,379 characters and about 2,000 sentences.

However, there was actually someone named Shakespeare, and throughout his life he wrote 39 wonderful plays, 154 sonnets, and a number of longer poems. Here's the point: There's a crucial difference between creating text and creating code. A text is a result, while code is an instruction, which can create both more code, but also other results. Although Shakespeare's genius may seem almost supernatural, he, like all humans, was essentially a product of code – genetic code. This kind of code underlies all life, and even small variations in the code can lead to large differences in the outcome. For example, the difference between a monkey's random keystrokes and Shakespeare's sonnets lies in a variation of only 6% in their genetic code.

Now imagine our hypothetical monkeys typing on computers instead of typewriters so that they write code instead of text. Can this simple change lead to a different outcome? Absolutely. Code, even in small amounts, can generate remarkable complexity and elegance, especially when it then spontaneously evolves through random mutations and replication. Shakespeare's text cannot write further on itself, but code can further develop itself and become Shakespeare.

It was the emergence of genetic code that transformed our world so radically. This triggered an explosion of complexity and diversity.

Disorder vs. Complexity and Intelligence

However, this whole story raises a fundamental question. It concerns the basic laws of physics that most of us learned about in school. For example, Isaac Newton formulated four laws of mechanics in 1687, which deal with how an apple falls from a tree, among other things. In total, there are 10 basic laws, but they fall into these five groups:

- Laws of mechanics
- Laws of electromagnetism
- Laws of relativity
- Quantum mechanics
- Laws of thermodynamics

In connection with the story of the complexity of the universe, we apparently come into conflict with one of the laws, namely the "second law of thermodynamics," which falls under group 5. The second law of thermodynamics was first formulated in 1850 by the German physicist and mathematician Rudolf Clausius. It introduced the concept of entropy, a measure of disorder or randomness in a system. Simply put, Clausius's law states that the entropy – or disorder in any isolated system – will either remain constant or increase over time. This is unique among the 10 classical laws of physics, as it has a direction. The arrow points towards the future and indicates that disorder inevitably grows.

And that's strange, because complexity created by combinatorial cascades represents order, which is the exact opposite of disorder. How can both disorder and order increase at the same time?

The answer lies in the local nature of both laws. The point is that complexity can flourish in specific regions, even if there is an average trend of increasing disorder. Take humans, for example. Each of us is a marvel of complexity, but after death we return to dust, which has far higher entropy than humans.

In other words: While the universe as a whole tends towards greater disorder, there are local, pinched pockets where complexity spontaneously increases. And such processes can, as we have seen, continue even over billions of years and come a very long way. We live in such a pocket, and the complexity in it is growing exponentially – and on some fronts hyperexponentially.

Measuring Combinatorial Complexity

It's not easy to measure the magnitude of the emergence of complexity and intelligence in a universally accepted way. But throughout this book we will describe its different levels. Our story has already begun with the Big Bang and the formation of atoms, which we will now call alpha-level complexity or alpha-tokens, i.e. level 1. Then came molecules and stars (beta-tokens, level 2). The next levels are life (delta) and technology (gamma), which we describe in Parts 2 and 3. Part 4 examines how artificial intelligence will ignite a fusion of combinatorial cascades and create a maelstrom of co-evolution and creativity that will reshape our world with unprecedented speed. We have done our best to estimate tokens of complexity created by the different combinatorial cascades. The graph we ended up with looks like this:

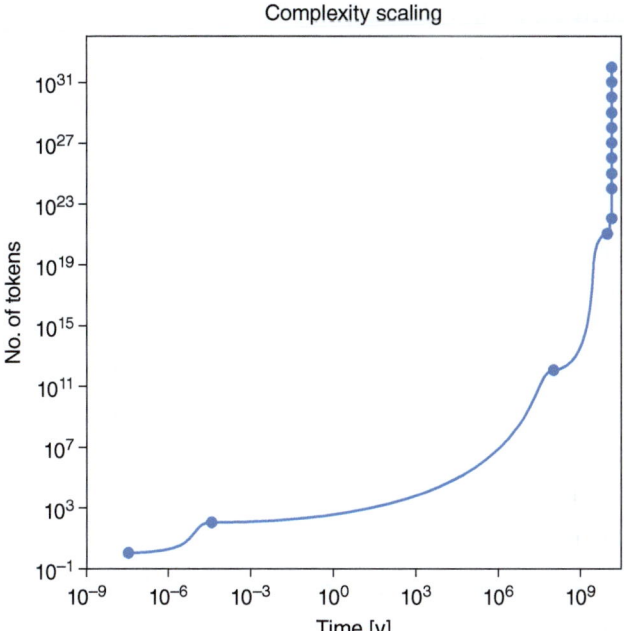

The growth of universal combinatorial complexity.
The graph compiles alpha, beta, gamma, and delta tokens that accumulate over 13.8 billion years. The perspective is only what we know, meaning that gamma and delta tokens only involve Earth, not other planets that potentially have life. While both axes on this graph use a logarithmic scale to represent huge numbers, the main conclusion is striking: The complexity of the universe, measured by the number of different tokens or units of information, is now skyrocketing at a hyperexponential rate.

In fact, as mentioned, we are now heading towards an 11th singularity, where the curve shoots upwards so steeply that predictions become incredibly challenging. This kind of growth is explosive and resembles in its speed the enormous, violent inflation in the early moments of the Big Bang. But unlike the Big Bang, where the expansion quickly slowed down, we now see a constantly accelerating complexity. This growth is almost infinite, because it is driven by code, which creates more and more self-reinforcing complexity. And as we will explore further in Part 4, it involves a fusion of a number of combinatorial cascades.

The Ingenuity Feedback Loop Summarized

Many ideas and concepts have been introduced in this first section of the book, so let's summarize them here at the end:

1. **A natural law of complexity:** A basic principle in nature drives the spontaneous creation of ever-increasing complexity.

2. **Combinatorial cascades as an engine:** The central driving force behind this complexity is the phenomenon of combinatorial cascades.

3. **Exponential and hyperexponential growth:** Combinatorial cascades are inherently exponential, but when multiple processes intersect, the outcome can be hyperexponential.

4. **Periods of long stagnation:** Occur when the system runs into solid scaling barriers – until a triggering event for the next cascade ignites.

5. **The emergence of code:** Some combinatorial explosions generate code, and code-based explosions lead to the formation of intelligence.

6. **The formation of intelligence:** Where tokens are created flexibly instead of just directly from genetic code. Consciousness and exploratory knowledge that can ask new questions, think creatively, and generate new hypotheses that ultimately lead to . . .

7. **Technologies:** Where we amplify our effect by transforming the environment. This paves the way for . . .

8. **Computers and telecommunications:** These then lead to . . .

9. **Computer-based hyperintelligence.**

It was this remarkable transformation, the birth of a spontaneous biological computer, that along the way made possible our chemophysical marvel Maria, who enjoyed her Croatian vacation, surrounded by other chemophysical marvels such as birds, butterflies, pine trees, wildflowers, and fish.

It is the story of these wonders that we will explore in more depth in the next part of this book, as we delve into the intricate workings of the biosphere – the living, breathing testament to what a spontaneous computer can create.

PART 2.

BIOSPHERE

The biosphere is the global ecological system that integrates all living beings and their relationships. It encompasses all forms of life, such as plants, animals, fungi, bacteria, and other microorganisms.

- **Beginnings:** Let's Say "Slimy"
- **Age of Earth's biosphere:** A respectable 3.5 to 4.2 billion years (plus or minus a few hundred million years)
- **Genetic code produced:** Perhaps 20,000 trillion DNA base pairs. Yep, that's 20,000,000,000,000,000 base pairs.
- **Weight:** A whopping 1841 gigatons (that's a lot of biomass!)
- **Energy production:** Surprisingly efficient – 100–200 terawatts (powered by sunshine!)
- **Number of species (excluding bacteria):** An astounding 8.7 million (and still counting. . .)
- **Number of living bacteria now:** An incomprehensible 10^{30} (they're everywhere!)
- **Happy with Earth?** Yes, the biosphere is content after moving in and changing pretty much everything.
- **Greatest moment:** It's the human brain. Its capacity is 10 trillion operations per second.

4.
THE CREATION OF MARIA

Imagine a primeval time with steaming seas and volcanoes spewing fire. Deep down in the dark ocean, where boiling water gushes up from the seabed, a secret hides: the first code of life. In this "primordial soup" of molecules, cooked in nature's own pressure cookers, which also happens to be a battery, a miracle occurred.

Journey back to a time when simple molecules randomly formed the building blocks of life. Experience how these building blocks learned to copy themselves and create even more complex structures. This is the story of the spark that ignited the flame of life on Earth – and created the foundation for all life, including Maria.

As Maria stands with her feet in the water on the quiet summer morning in Croatia, her mind filled with peace and gratitude, she is almost motionless. However, looks can be deceiving. Even in this peaceful moment, her body is a flurry of activity. In just one minute, she takes about 16 breaths, where her lungs exchange billions of oxygen molecules for carbon dioxide with every breath. These vital oxygen molecules are carried into her bloodstream, where they are transported around to every single cell in her body. At the same time, her eyelids move synchronously, while her heart beats at a steady rate of 70 beats per minute, pumping 5 liters of oxygenated blood through her system.

In the muscles that keep her stable while her toes move slightly in the sand, her body makes thousands of small adjustments so as not to fall. This harmonious balance, orchestrated by her muscles, is fueled by sugars stored in her body, which are broken down using the oxygen she breathes. While some of this activity can be consciously controlled by her brain, most of it happens automatically.

Zooming in at the microscopic level, the activity becomes downright hectic. Maria's body contains about 37 trillion cells, and every minute approximately 300 million of them are replaced as part of the body's constant renewal process. At the same time, Maria's brain sends more than 50 trillion signals through neurons out to the body every minute. And so on.

Her body is thus a whirlwind of activity at all levels. Some cells, such as those in the intestinal lining, are replaced within a few days, while others have an even shorter lifespan. The mitochondria, the cells' energy factories, renew half of their stock in a month. Microtubules, which are crucial for the structure of the nervous system, only last a few days. NMDA receptors, which play a central role in learning and memory, are replaced in a matter of hours. Synapses in the brain are formed and broken down on average every 90 minutes. Maria's memories, even her short-term memory, depend on synapses constantly feeling their way, sticking together and sending signals.

So while a poet can describe Maria in this moment with words of beauty and serenity, and philosophers can ponder the depths of her consciousness, a natural scientist would see her as an incredibly complex entity operating with the accelerator fully depressed, driven by a complex calculation system. But how did Earth create Maria? Let's go back in time and look at that.

Maria's Many Ancestors

Imagine a line of Maria's ancestors standing in a long line. Start with Maria herself. Then imagine her mother, grandmother, great-grandmother and so on, standing next to each other and stretching back countless generations. Each mother is a stepping stone further back in time. The line continues as far as the eye can see.

Now try to imagine that you are walking down this incredible line. At a leisurely pace of 4 km per hour, you stroll past the latest relatives. In an hour you have walked 4,000 m and passed approximately 4,000 generations. In the beginning, you see ancestors who look a lot like Maria. But as you move further down the line and thus back in time, subtle changes begin to appear. After two hours you have passed about 8,000 ancestors, and now it becomes clear that their brains – or skulls – look a little smaller, and their bodies may be a little hairier.

As you continue your walk, the changes become even more profound and striking. When you reach Maria's ancestors who lived about one million years ago, you encounter ancestors that resemble *Homo erectus*. *Homo erectus* had a more robust build than Maria, with a larger face, prominent brow ridges, and an even smaller braincase. But they walked upright and had body proportions similar to Maria's.

You continue on, and after many months of walking you see ancestors from about two million years back in time. Here you see *Homo habilis*, one of the earliest members of the genus *Homo*, or man. These ancestors were smaller and more ape-like in appearance, with brains about half the size of modern humans. Despite their more primitive appearance, *Homo habilis* showed significant advances in toolmaking and used simple stone tools to hunt and gather food.

Going back to around six million years ago, you encounter ancestors who are smaller in stature, with bodies covered in fur, and hands that resemble those of apes, well-suited for knuckle-walking. These fascinating creatures, our common ancestors with chimpanzees, are known as the Chimpanzee-Human Last Common Ancestor (CHLCA).

More Than 10 Million Years Ago

You need a car now, because the line with Maria's ancestors apparently goes on and on. As you continue your journey, now with the help of an engine, you reach 10–12 million years back. Here you will find ancestors such as *Proconsul*, an early primate with a mixture of both ape-like and human-like features. Proconsul lived in the trees and had a more flexible spine, which gave them greater freedom of movement.

You have now come a really long way back in time, but continue your journey. About 20 million years ago you meet ancestors like *Aegyptopithecus*. These early primates had brains the size of walnuts and were fully adapted to life in the trees. And yes, Maria is also descended from them.

At some point you reach the time 200 million years ago, where you meet early mammalian ancestors such as *Morganucodon*. These small, nocturnal creatures were among the first mammals and stood out with their differentiated teeth and larger brains compared to their reptilian predecessors. The existence of *Morganucodon* marks a crucial phase in the evolution of mammals and shows the transition from reptile-like creatures to true mammals.

You may now be quite excited about what Maria's ultimate ancestors looked like, but there is still a long way to go. About 300 million years back you meet the early amniotes, including creatures like *Hylonomus*. These small, lizard-like animals were among the first vertebrates to lay eggs on land, a significant evolutionary step that allowed greater independence from aquatic environments. It's almost unbelievable to think that Maria is descended from these creatures, but she is.

About 400 million years back you meet early vertebrates like *Tiktaalik*, a fish-like creature with characteristics that mark the transition from water to land. *Tiktaalik* had both gills and primitive lungs, as well as limb-like fins that allowed it to move in shallow water and perhaps even venture onto land. Maria can breathe today because *Tiktaalik* learned to do it millions of years ago.

Even further back, about 500 million years ago, you meet early chor-dates like *Pikaia*, small worm-like creatures. These chordates are some of the very first ancestors of all vertebrates. Incredibly, Maria is descended from a worm!

It is not until about 3.5–4 billion years ago that you meet LUCA, our very first common ancestor – also Maria's. This single-celled pioneer, who swam the primeval ocean, carried the seed of subsequent life. In LUCA, which stands for Last Universal Common Ancestor, we find the funda-mental processes that bind all life on Earth together. So have we now found Maria's ultimate origin?

No, the story begins even earlier. Before LUCA, there were simple, primitive structures that can barely be called alive. These first burgeoning life forms could grow, react to their surroundings, maintain an internal balance and even reproduce. They were the first branches on the tree of life, from which all life, including Maria, has evolved.

And yet not. Because in reality Maria is descended from a soup from the dark depths.

The Real Beginning

Unraveling the mystery of the origin of life on Earth is a quest that has fas-cinated scientists for centuries. If the first spark of life were to be ignited on Earth shortly after the planet's formation, it would be in an inferno of heat and chaos. Earth was then a glowing sphere, where the average tempera-ture on land was between 60 and 90 degrees Celsius. It was an era rightly called the Hadean, after the god of the Greek underworld. The air was thick with steam, and the entire planet could be described as a gigantic, steaming sauna. Even at the poles it was unbearably hot (by human stand-ards), as there was no ice sheet yet to reflect the sun's rays. This extreme heat was due to a cocktail of greenhouse gases, radioactive heat from the Earth's interior, residual heat from the planet's formation and countless volcanic eruptions.

In the oceans, temperatures ranged from 50°C to 70°C. Let's assume that you are now diving deep into the ocean, far beyond the reach of sunlight, wearing a suit that protects against extreme heat. In the absolute darkness, lit only by your diving light, you encounter a crack in the seabed where superheated water flows out, a hydrothermal vent. The spring towers in front of you, perhaps 10 m high, while clouds of minerals swirl out and form a "chemical soup."

What you can't see is that this spring is an amazing bioreactor. Here, simple molecules such as hydrogen, methane, and ammonia are found in abundance, and the clay around the spring is filled with iron and nickel sulphides. But most importantly: The spring is a natural battery. The difference in acidity between the hot spring water and the colder seawater creates a proton flow, an energy source that can drive complex processes.

The first primitive organisms harness this energy. By allowing the protons to flow through their membranes, they can convert raw materials into building blocks and copy themselves. The spring is the catalyst that enables the leap from chemistry to biology – the very source of life. Along the way, ribozymes evolve into RNA. RNA is primarily an information carrier involved in genetic expression and regulation, while ribozymes are a specialized subset of RNA that can catalyze chemical reactions like protein enzymes. And now something really fascinating happens: The heat drives the chemical reactions, while the cooler periods give the RNA strands time to repair damage.

"Repair?" you might ask. "As in self-repair?" Yes exactly! RNA molecules possess a remarkable ability to heal themselves, a property that surpasses their seemingly simple structure. They are nature's little miracle workers, constantly adapting and overcoming the challenges they encounter in this dynamic environment.

RNA is magic. First of all, these chemical strands are like code. Imagine a computer that randomly generates code. That's kind of what happens when RNA is created. The phenomenon is overwhelming in itself. But in addition, RNA can do something that the universe had previously only managed in crystals: make copies of itself. This ability to replicate is a key ingredient for life as we know it. And it is precisely because RNA can copy itself that it can also repair itself.

Third, RNA can create proteins. These are chains of amino acids, but unlike RNA, they can fold into an almost infinite variety of shapes and do amazing things like act as little chemophysical robots. We will return to them.

Finally, some of the proteins that RNA creates can make DNA – a molecule that carries the genetic instructions for life. DNA is a perfect storage unit for the code of life because it is far more stable than RNA. It has a double-sided backup where each side can repair the other if it gets damaged.

So now we have replicators that can do both a kind of backup memory trick and little robots all on their own. This is a very early step on the way to what ultimately created Maria.

COMPLEXITY CASCADE #4

- **What?** Formation of living cells
- **When?** We don't know, but they are first seen on Earth 3.5 to 3.8 billion years ago
- **Why?** Hydrothermal vents created a critical density of all necessary ingredients

---

Proteins Are Wild

Approximately 15–20% of Maria is made of protein. But this is not just filler, almost everything in her body that is smart is made or regulated by proteins. Think of protein molecules as tiny nanomachines with superpowers that do everything from building Maria's muscles to fighting her infections or pumping her heart.

Some proteins are like delivery drivers, transporting essential molecules through her cells. These kinesin proteins have small feet and a head, and they literally walk along cellular highways carrying their cargo inside Maria. Others are like master chefs in a kitchen, speeding up the countless chemical reactions that keep her alive. These enzymes chop, slice, and rearrange molecules with incredible speed and precision.

Each type of protein folds into a unique 3D structure, a bit like spaghetti Bolognese on a plate. The shape of the "spaghetti" plays a crucial role. For example, some proteins fold to create pockets that fit precisely to specific molecules, allowing them to interact and trigger reactions with precisely those. Other proteins form long fibers that give the body structure and help it move.

But proteins cannot make themselves completely on their own – they need a plan. That plan is found in DNA, which contains the recipe for the protein and transfers it to RNA, which then ensures that the protein is produced.

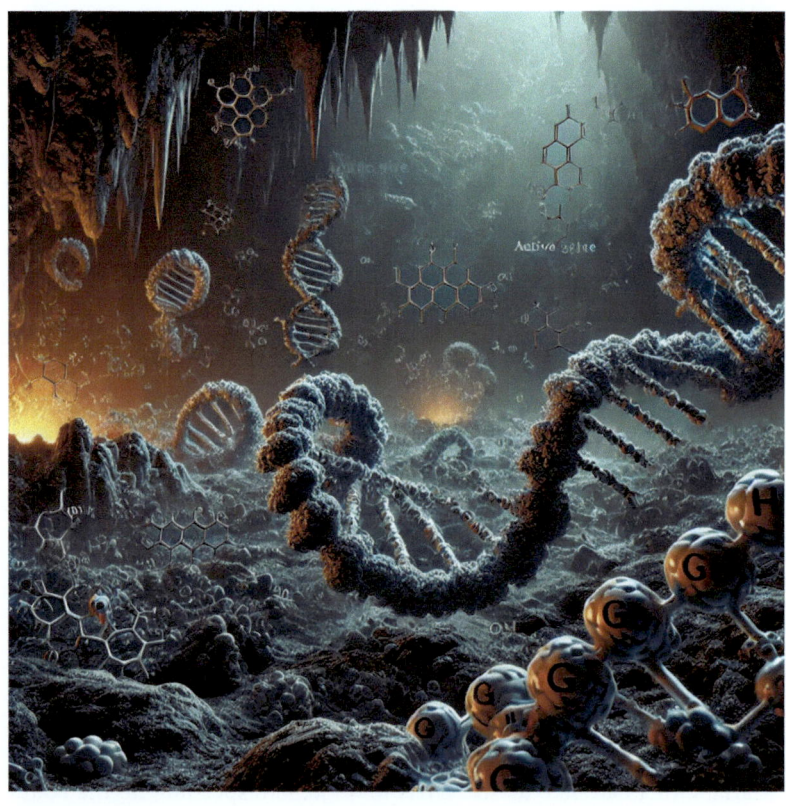

Ribozymes in an underwater hydrothermal vent. *These could replicate each other. The illustration is a rendering.*

Although the combination of RNA, DNA, and proteins is essential for life as we know it, Marie's very first ancestor was not one of these. It was something even more fundamental: a primordial soup. In this soup, something called ribozymes played a central role.

Ribozymes are like a Swiss Army knife in the molecular world, a key player in the story of the origin of life. Imagine ribozymes in this early chemical soup forming a self-sustaining network – a microscopic ecosystem where one ribozyme creates another, which in turn helps create a third, and so on in a continuous loop of collective self-replication. This primitive system can grow, reproduce, and maintain an internal balance – three of life's four essential properties – all without the need for DNA or a cell membrane. Such a self-replicating soup is not quite "alive" yet, but it is very close.

Hydrothermal vents can make such soups, which can simmer in porous pockets in clay and rock. This interconnected network, where different ribozymes catalyzed each other's formation, is called an autocatalytic set. That's what Maria comes from.

5.
ARE *WE* THE ALIENS?

Explore an exciting theory that suggests that life may have originated elsewhere and hitchhiked to Earth on comets or asteroids. Recent discoveries of amino acids in space suggest a universe teeming with the building blocks of life. This theory may explain the complexity of Earth's early life forms. Are we all descendants of cosmic travelers?

Among the countless structures that molecules can create, bubbles stand out as some of the most fascinating. We may ignore them in our everyday lives, but just consider the following: While, for example, rock crystals can take millions of years to form, and snowflakes require several minutes, bubbles form in a few milliseconds. In a minimal moment, trillions of water molecules organize themselves into a thin film. And although bubbles are fleeting, they show surprising strength and resilience. They can withstand gentle breezes, bounce playfully on surfaces, and even merge or split into fascinating patterns.

How is that possible? Imagine molecules as small creatures with two body parts: heads and tails. The tail, a supple chain of carbon atoms bonded to hydrogen, behaves like oil and avoids water, preferring to stay dry. The head, on the other hand, is like a water-loving magnet, thanks to a special phosphorus atom that eagerly dives into the liquid around it. This is how soap bubbles work. The tails simply like fats, but not least each other, and the heads like water, but also most of all each other. In this way, the bubble arises because tails lie next to tails, and heads next to heads.

We normally see bubbles at interfaces between air and liquid, but you can also have bubbles underwater. These can gather in small spherical clusters called micelles, where their tails hide inside and their heads face outward, creating a stable emulsion.

This phenomenon is one of the reasons why life arose. In the turbulent currents near a hydrothermal vent, these micelles often collide. Some merge and transform into double-layered bubbles like miniature water balloons, each encapsulating a small drop of water. These bilayers, the precursors of cell membranes, can randomly trap some of our genetic soup of self-replicating molecules, providing a safe haven for life's earliest chemical

A protocell. *This has formed by a soup of self-replicating ribosomes being randomly encapsulated in a micelle. The illustration is a rendering.*

reactions. Within this protective enclosure, the seeds of cellular life can begin to sprout. We are looking at the birth of the protocell, a crucial step on the road to life as we know it. All created in a bubble.

From Protocells to Life

Some atoms and molecules can pass through the membrane in this proto-cell, while others cannot. Over time, the membranes evolve and differenti-ate; their lipid layers become more complex, and their internal chemistry more sophisticated. The result is cells with a fairly complex, self-replicating content.

It's starting to sound a bit like living cells, isn't it? And sooner or later some of these bubbles will contain RNA, DNA, and proteins. But life as we know it is much more than a bubble with some biochemical replica-tors, nanorobots, and memory sticks thrown together. Life, as we define it, must encompass the abilities to (1) grow, to (2) react to the environ-ment, (3) to maintain internal balance and (4) to replicate. What does that require? First and foremost, DNA contains the code of life, but this code must be useful. DNA, which acts as the memory chip in every cell, uses a sequence of four different types of molecules to write the recipe for life. Each group of three molecules forms a "word" called a codon. A series of codons, which together have the recipe for making a protein, is called a gene, and the sum of all our genes is our genome. Your cells know how to read these recipes and, so to speak, prepare the proteins from them.

How simple can a single living cell be? To create a living cell with a prim-itive genome and a cell wall, but without DNA, you need ribozymes. Here are the basic functions – with the estimated number of ribozymes – needed to achieve the function of a living cell:

• Self-replication: 1–2	• Response to environmental stimuli: 1–2
• Replication: 1–2	• Lipid synthesis: 1–2
• Repair: 1–2	• Lipid transport: 1–2
• Recombination: 1–2	• Lipid assembly: 1–2
• Metabolism: 2–3	• Membrane maintenance: 1–2
• Homeostasis: 1–2	

This suggests that a surprisingly small number of basic functions – perhaps as low as 11 to 23 – are necessary for the simplest possible cell-based life. Each of these functions will likely trigger a cascade of derived responses involving about 10 ribozyme "workers" each, based on our understanding of typical cellular regulation. This would then require a total of approximately 120–230 genes.

How many different kinds of atoms will this super-simple life require? Actually, only hydrogen, carbon, nitrogen, phosphorus, oxygen, and sulfur – all the same fairly simple atoms. Hydrogen already existed, and the others were quickly created by the first stars. The heavier an element, the more fusion steps are required for its formation.

Of course, that number is just an estimate. Interestingly, in 2016, researchers at the J. Craig Venter Institute achieved a remarkable feat: They created a synthetic bacterium with only 473 genes, the smallest known genome seen in any living organism. Although this is still more than twice our hypothetical minimum, it supports the idea that early life forms could have been remarkably simple.

Remember Maria's very old ancestor LUCA, who lived 3.5 to 4 billion years ago? We have no physical trace of LUCA, but by comparing DNA, scientists have found that all life forms share some basic genes and molecular structures. This means that LUCA probably had the same essential parts. When all these are added together, a recent and widely cited 2024 study suggests that LUCA likely had a genome of at least 2.5 million base pairs encoding about 2,600 proteins.

The Timing Problem

This story, however, has a challenge. When we look at the complexity of life's genetic code, from worms to fish and on to mammals like us humans, we see a doubling of the information content in the genome approximately every 350 million years. But if we rewind time at this doubling rate – where genome size halves every 350 million years – we encounter a problem: Earth's history simply seems far too short to trace back to LUCA's original, simplest ancestor, which emerged as a self-replicating ribozyme soup with 120–230 genes.

To reach the beginning of life with this calculation, it appears that we would need approximately 9.5 billion years. But Earth is less than half that old. How can we explain this discrepancy?

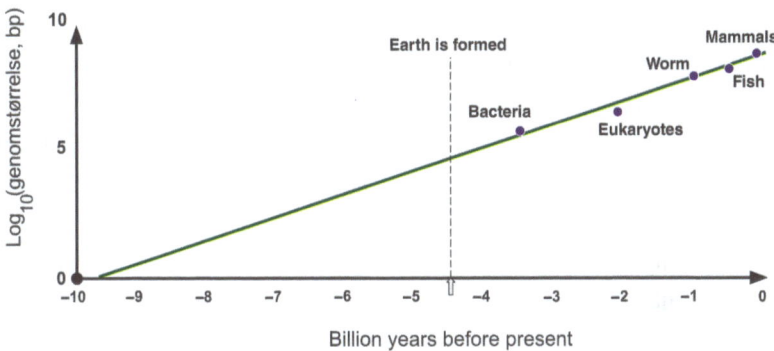

Estimate of the origin of life. *This graph shows the logarithm of genome sizes on the vertical axis and the logarithm of time on the horizontal scale. The graph suggests that it has been approximately 9.5 billion years since our form of life originated. This is about twice as long as Earth has existed.*

The Panspermia Theory

You may have heard of the Goldilocks zone, the perfect area around a star where conditions are just right for liquid water – and potentially life – to exist. Earth, luckily for us, is smack-dab in the middle of the sun's Goldilocks zone. This is crucial, because if a planet strays too close to a star, its water boils away. Conversely, if it is too far away, the water freezes into ice. In fact, temperatures in the depths of space far away from a star hover near absolute zero, where a human would freeze into an icicle.

Interestingly, many scientists now believe that the entire universe itself may have gone through a similar "Goldilocks" period, where conditions everywhere were just right for complexity to arise. Why? As we have seen previously, the universe just after the Big Bang was an extremely hot furnace before it rapidly expanded and cooled. In this cooling phase, a period arose where temperatures throughout the universe were low enough to allow liquid water. This favorable condition, often called the "Goldilocks Era," lasted from about 10 million to 30 million years after the Big Bang. However, it may well have lasted considerably longer in pockets of the universe where there were higher gas concentrations.

Recent observations from the James Webb Space Telescope have revealed that massive galaxies, such as "Red Monsters," existed just a billion years after the Big Bang. The telescope has also shown us the earliest known galaxy to date, JADES-GS-z14-0, which was formed just 290 million years after the Big Bang. This indicates a rapid formation of stars and planets, as these come before the galaxies they are part of. All of this could mean that life arose quite early and, due to cosmic pockets with Goldilocks conditions, had good opportunities to spread. This possibility is one of several so-called *panspermia* theories.

The interesting thing about this theory concerns not only planets with water, but also smaller celestial bodies. In this early and denser universe, planets, moons, comets, meteors, asteroids, and smaller rocks would collide with each other far more often than now. This means that if life arose in one or more places, the relatively mild temperatures in the early universe could have allowed these simple life forms to hitchhike on these wanderers, spreading far and wide throughout the young cosmos. Likewise, they could also be blown around in space by cosmic wind from the stars.

This is the essence of the so-called *panspermia* theories. The term comes from the Greek words *pan*, meaning "all," and *sperma*, meaning "seed." The common thread among these theories is that they explore various mechanisms by which life or its building blocks could spread across the universe. These include *lithopanspermia* (transport via meteoroids), *radiopanspermia* (carried by radiation pressure), and *directed panspermia* (intentional seeding by advanced civilizations). Other ideas, like *cosmopanspermia*, propose that life's precursors formed in space, while *necropanspermia* suggests that only remnants of life were dispersed.

The theories are not mutually exclusive and may collectively explain how life or its precursors could have been distributed across planets and star systems. A common interpretation suggests that life may have been widespread in the universe very early – perhaps for over 13 billion years – but only flourishes when it arrives in a Goldilocks zone, where conditions are just right for reproduction.

So . . . is life very widespread? There are some indications of this. In 2020, scientists announced the detection of phosphine gas in Venus's atmosphere, a potential biosignature, although this finding is still under debate. On Mars, the Perseverance rover is exploring a former riverbed in Jezero Crater and has found sedimentary rocks and organic molecules that may indicate the past presence of living organisms. Scientists also believe they may have discovered tryptophan – an essential amino acid and one of the building blocks of life – in a nebula just 100 light-years away. Recently, samples from two asteroids in our solar system also found amino acids and even uracil, one of the bases from RNA. It is unlikely the asteroids came from Earth since most asteroids that have hit Earth will fall towards the Sun and not persist in orbits further out for millions of years. These discoveries, along with previous finds of other organic molecules in nebulae, suggests that the universe may be filled with the chemical precursors to life, and perhaps even dormant life forms just waiting to be activated. More recently, in January 2025, scientists reported the discovery of essential organic compounds in samples from the asteroid Bennu, collected by NASA's OSIRIS-REx mission. These samples contained 14 of the 20 amino acids used by life on Earth to make proteins, as well as all five nucleobases that form DNA and RNA.

Just a note about amino acids. In 1952, before the theory of hydrothermal vents as bioreactors became widely accepted, chemist Stanley Miller and his mentor, Nobel laureate Harold Urey, conducted a groundbreaking experiment. They constructed a sealed glass container and filled it with what they believed represented Earth's original atmosphere: methane, ammonia, hydrogen, and water vapor. To simulate lightning strikes, they added electrical discharges. After a few days, they noticed a brownish substance in the container. What was in it? Amino acids, the building blocks of proteins! This was revolutionary because it demonstrated that the basic ingredients of life could be formed from simple chemicals under conditions similar to those on early Earth. And it all happened in just a week!

Further observations supporting the Panspermia theory are the discovery of simple so-called "extremophiles," which, for example, may survive extreme radiation environments in nuclear reactors and the dryness of outer space. These extremophiles live in the wildest places. The deep biosphere, which is a hidden ecosystem beneath the Earth's surface, 4 km deep and twice the size of all the oceans combined, is packed with extremophiles. Such a deep biosphere may not be unique to Earth, and similar ecosystems may exist on other planets and moons, expanding the possibilities for life.

Such life forms would have plenty of time to emerge within the presumed 20–100 million year Goldilocks period after the Big Bang. They may then have clung to asteroids or comets and eventually – much later – found their way to Earth. And yes, this may explain why LUCA, the Last Universal Common Ancestor, looks so complex and robust for its time. We don't know if the panspermia theory is true, but if it is, then we are all aliens.

6.
EVOLUTION'S BRUSHSTROKES

This chapter explores how DNA, the code of life, not only shaped the various creatures on Earth, but also dramatically transformed the planet itself. From changing the atmosphere and creating continents to coloring the landscapes and much more, DNA's influence is seen everywhere. We look at how this remarkable molecule shaped the very world we inhabit, leaving its artistic influence on everything from the sky above our heads to the sand beneath our feet.

Maria's brain is that gray, soft thing she has in her head; we all know that. But in a way, there's also a kind of brain inside every living cell in her body. A different kind of brain for sure, but still a form of intelligence in each of her cells.

The same goes for single-celled life. Take ordinary baker's yeast, for example. It is a single-celled fungus that has delighted people for millennia by helping us make bread, beer, and wine. But how does it do it? It turns out that it is incredibly complex. Just take a look at the diagrams below of what's going on inside it. Each dot represents a protein, and the

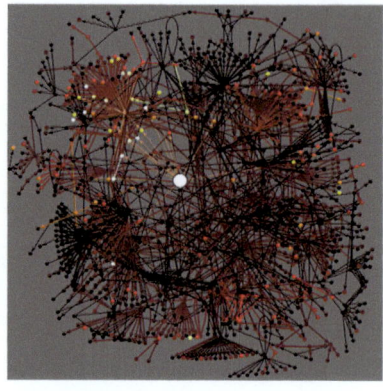

The regulatory network of the yeast. *Saccharomyces cerevisiae colored by functions (left). The darker version (right) is colored by the activity that occurs when the cell is exposed to heat shock, and the appropriate emergency system is activated (lighter colors indicate activity). Note the "fan" motifs at each function, which represent isolated cascades of effects.*

lines show how these proteins interact and regulate each other. Information flows through this network and causes tons of action all the time.

The complexity enables yeast cells to react intelligently to their environment. First of all, they have special proteins on their surface called receptors. The receptors pick up signals from the outside and send them to a network of genes. The genes then figure out what the signals mean and what to do with them. For example, what happens is that when they sense sugar, they activate their "eating mode." If it gets too hot, they turn on a "heat protection mode." And so on.

The whole system is organized as a smart hierarchy. There are central "control genes" at the top that make the big decisions. They then instruct "commander genes," which in turn direct the "worker enzymes" to carry out the tasks. So each cell makes decisions and takes action to stay alive and healthy. So yes, we are definitely talking about cellular intelligence – created spontaneously by the universe.

Solving Bureaucratic Collapse

For nearly three billion years, all these small, clever cells were loners, and they had a problem: bureaucratic collapse. There is simply an upper limit to how much complexity a single cell can contain without it all drowning in internal coordination problems. This bureaucracy problem meant that while different types of single-celled organisms constantly appeared and disappeared, new records in single-cell complexity were no longer set. In other words, they had hit our fourth scaling barrier.

The early *eukaryotes* – organisms with cell nuclei and organelles – found a solution to the challenges of cooperation by separating their internal functions into small, delimited units or organelles. This internal organization managed the complexity of each cell and made it possible to combine several different functions in a more efficient way. It was a crucial development that spurred a new evolution, where specialized cells began to work together as parts of a larger organism.

Then, about 900 million years ago, bacteria randomly became sticky so that their offspring would remain attached to them. This evolved into protective biofilms. Such biofilms provided "critical density" of bacteria, where those at the outer layers began specializing in different tasks than the ones further towards the center.

COMPLEXITY CASCADE #5

- **What?** Formation of organelles and multicellular life
- **When?** Organelles emerged within single-cell organisms about 1.5 to 2 billion years ago. And the first multicell organisms evolved around 900 million years ago
- **Why?** To solve bureaucratic collapse problems

This critical density paved the way for specialization. Some bacteria focused on absorbing nutrients, while others, for example, removed waste products. This collaboration was an early form of proto-multicellular dynamics, where different cell types worked together for common survival. A fascinating example of this hybrid between single-celled and multicellular life is seen in *Bacillus subtilis*, a soil bacterium. Under stress, such as lack of nutrients, thousands of the cells form "fruiting bodies." Inside the fruiting body, the cells specialize: Some form a stalk that lifts the fruiting body up, while others become spores that can survive extreme conditions. The fruiting body gives us a glimpse of the evolutionary processes that may have led to multicellular life. But the bacteria stopped here. So they remained trapped in either single-celled life or this intermediate state for billions of years. It was the eukaryotes who took the decisive step to true multicellular life.

If we compare with the universe's first concentrations of mass, we can say that the transition to multicellular life is in its own way a transition to greater complexity and order – like stars in a kind of biological cosmos. The critical density of bacteria created new possibilities, just as mass concentrations in the universe created new nuclear fusion and thus new atoms. In both cases, the concentration of resources and energy formed the basis for achieving a new and more complex form of existence.

DNA then constantly changed to optimize for these new trading opportunities. In fact, the cells often adapted so much to cooperation that they could no longer survive on their own. Cells even stole genetic recipes from each other through a process called horizontal gene transfer. It was like sharing DNA directly through contact or even having it delivered by a virus.

Another way cells combined things was by randomly making – and keeping – extra copies of their genes, so the duplicates could develop new functions. This, which is equivalent to opening a research and development laboratory in a factory, happened across all types of organisms, from simple bacteria to more complex creatures.

Approximately 1.5 to 2 billion years ago, a pivotal event occurred: certain cells merged with others, incorporating specialized structures called mitochondria. These mitochondria efficiently extracted energy, enabling these new life forms to grow and evolve into more complex organisms. This energy surplus allowed organisms to develop specialized structures and functions, enhancing their ability to interact with their environment purposefully.

Sophisticated Agentic Life

Consider the evolution of the eye. The skin of many animals contains melanin, a pigment that absorbs harmful ultraviolet (UV) radiation, protecting skin cells from damage. This protective mechanism operates within the skin cells themselves and doesn't involve neurons. Additionally, skin neurons respond to stimuli like touch, pressure, heat, and movement. This combination made the skin ready to develop light-sensing organs. Here's a plausible sequence for how eyes evolved, with each stage still observable in some of today's animals:

1. **Simple Light Detection:** A small indentation on an animal's surface could detect light and shadow. You can mimic this by creating a pinhole camera with a shoebox; light entering through a tiny hole projects an image inside.

2. **Improved Imaging:** As the indentation deepened and its opening narrowed, it could produce clearer, though still blurry, images.

3. **Lens Formation:** The opening filled with a transparent substance, like a primitive lens. This likely originated from proteins secreted for other purposes, such as those involved in heat responses.

4. **Iris Development:** Muscles, similar to those causing goosebumps, evolved to control the opening's size, forming a basic iris.

Through these steps, a simple eye emerged from existing skin structures. Evolution could shape these indentations and repurpose genes because neurons were already present in the skin. Thus, skin and neurons preceded the development of eyes. The emergence of eyes transformed organisms into what we can call "agents" – capable of perceiving and responding to visual information, enhancing their ability to navigate and survive in their environment. An agent, in this context, refers to an entity that can perceive its surroundings and take actions to influence its own state or that of its environment. This development marked a significant shift toward what we can describe as "agentic life," where organisms actively engage with and adapt to their surroundings.

Another example of the emergence of sophisticated agentic life is how single organisms became mobile entities. Consider the bacterial flagellum, a tail-like propeller. A motor embedded in the cell membrane rotates this propeller, allowing the bacterium to move. The bacterium senses when it's approaching food and moves toward it. If it moves away from food, it reverses the motor, causing it to tumble and seek a new direction toward food. The flagellum's motor resembles protein complexes that bacteria already use to pump ions across their membranes. The filament, acting as the propeller, is made of proteins similar to those in other hair-like structures that help bacteria attach to surfaces. Even the hook, a flexible joint connecting the motor and filament, seems adapted from proteins involved in building other cellular structures. This efficient reuse of existing parts allowed bacteria to develop effective swimming mechanisms. The development of the flagellum enabled bacteria to act as agents, actively seeking out favorable environments and resources, thereby increasing their chances of survival.

About 1.2 billion years ago, an interesting cellular specialization happened among plants. At that time, cyanobacteria had learned to harness sunlight through photosynthesis, essentially creating biological "solar panels." This innovation enabled them to convert sunlight into chemical energy and produce their own food. The plants then absorbed these cyanobacteria, and this synergistic collaboration enabled plants to carry out photosynthesis and harness the sun's energy to produce food and oxygen. This development transformed plants into agents capable of producing their own energy, fundamentally altering their role in the ecosystem and supporting more complex life forms.

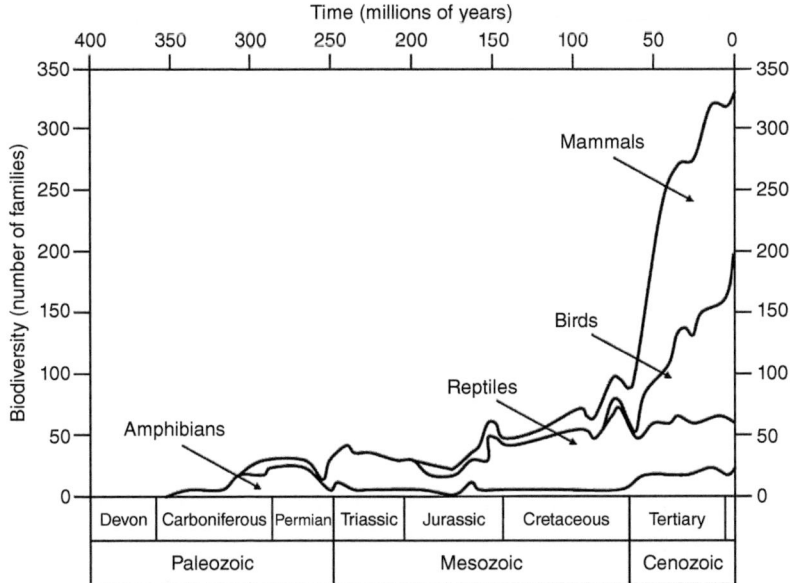

The development of life's diversity through Earth's history. *Despite repeated mass extinctions caused by natural disasters, life has not only survived but has flourished in ever-increasing diversity over billions of years.*

How DNA Cooled the Earth

The emergence of DNA had a dramatic impact on Earth's climate. Photosynthesis, the process by which plants convert carbon dioxide (CO_2) into glucose, reduced the CO_2 concentration in the atmosphere by as much as 99.8%. This reduction of CO_2, an important greenhouse gas, led to a significant cooling of the planet.

During the Great Oxidation Event, which began about 2.4 billion years ago, photosynthesizing cyanobacteria also released large amounts of oxygen into the atmosphere. This oxygen reacted with methane, a potent greenhouse gas with a warming effect 84–87 times greater than CO_2. Before the release of oxygen, methane made up about 78% of the atmosphere. The reaction between oxygen and methane significantly reduced methane levels, causing a further and dramatic cooling of the Earth. This massive shift in atmospheric composition is evident in Table 6.1.

Table 6.1 **How photosynthesis changed the composition of Earth's atmosphere**

Gas	% before photosynthesis	% today (with photosynthesis)
Methane	78%	0.03%
Carbon dioxide	20%	0.04%
Nitrogen	2%	78%
Oxygen	Minimal	21%

It took over 2.5 billion years for single-celled bacteria to evolve into multicellular organisms. This is probably due to several things: The cells had to learn to cooperate and specialize. They needed stable energy sources and more oxygen in the atmosphere. All of this required complicated genetic and biochemical changes. When the first multicellular organisms appeared about one billion years ago, Earth's average temperature had dropped to less than 50°C. Since then, life and climate have continued to influence each other, resulting in the relatively stable and dynamic climate we experience today. While Earth's average temperature has fluctuated by about 15 degrees over the past five million years and 10 degrees over the past 500,000 years, these changes pale in comparison to the dramatic shift caused by DNA's early innovation.

Genetic Landscaping

DNA's influence extended far beyond the creation of life and the alteration of our climate; it played an indirect role in shaping Earth's landscapes. For example, it created soil. This happened when microorganisms and plant roots slowly dissolved rocks and stones into smaller fragments. This process, combined with the accumulation of broken down plant and animal material, enriched the soil and created a fertile foundation for various ecosystems to thrive. This is why Earth now contains rich, life-sustaining soil, unlike, for example, the barren landscapes of the Moon or Mars.

In the oceans, our wonderful coral reefs stand as another testament to DNA's transformative power. These amazing underwater ecosystems can be towering, sometimes over a kilometer from the seabed to the surface of the water. But coral reefs exist because of coral polyps, which in turn are possible because of DNA. Thus, DNA's fingerprints are etched across the very landscape of our planet.

DNA's genetic code did even more. Before it appeared, and life took hold, our planet probably looked pretty boring. Think of a hazy, orange sky filled with methane and murky green oceans. But thanks to oxygen-producing organisms, the sky transformed into a vibrant blue, and the oceans and lakes followed suit. Then the plants burst onto the scene with a kaleidoscope of colors. Forests and grasslands, painted in shades of bright emerald green and olive green, were all created thanks to DNA's code.

And the magic didn't stop there. The sharp white grains of sand on many beaches come from limestone, formed from the skeletal remains of countless marine animals. Other coasts boast vibrant pink and red hues, a testament to the crushed shells of tiny snails and molluscs. So these beautiful grains of sand are all created by animals, which are coded by DNA.

But perhaps DNA's most breathtaking work of art is the amazing visual diversity of life itself around us. From the delicate pink of cherry blossoms to the peacock's flamboyant plumage, from the intense blue of a forget-me-not to the iridescent wings of butterflies, every living organism is a testament to the beauty of life.

Together, DNA created all of this, but it also tied it together in a gigantic global ecosystem, where all life became connected to everything else and to the Earth itself. James Lovelock's *Gaia* hypothesis, developed in collaboration with microbiologist Lynn Margulis in the 1970s, proposed that living organisms interact with their inorganic surroundings on Earth to form a synergistic and self-regulating complex system that helps maintain and perpetuate the conditions for life on the planet.

A fascinating example of this interaction is Saharan dust, which is blown across the Atlantic and enriches the Amazon rainforest with essential minerals such as phosphorus, which acts as a fertilizer for the forest's vegetation. In addition, algae in the Pacific Ocean produce gases that contribute to cloud formation, which increases rainfall over the Andes Mountains. This rainfall leads to leaching of nutrients, which in turn are essential for algal growth, illustrating a complex feedback mechanism in nature.

All of this means that when Maria basks in the morning sun on the Croatian beach, she can not only marvel at how DNA has shaped the various living things around her, but also at how it enabled the gentle climate and shaped the landscape she is currently enjoying. The azure blue color of the sky and sea, even the white sand between her toes, all came about through DNA's tireless work over billions of years. In other words, Earth was completely and utterly transformed by code. In fact, the globe had become a giant computer that was transforming itself.

COMPLEXITY CASCADE #6

- **What?** Formation of biogeochemical cycles, which terraformed Earth
- **When?** Gradually over the last 4–5 million years
- **Why?** Hydrothermal vents brought all the necessary ingredients together

7.
THE GLOBAL COMPUTER

The emergence of multicellular life and the collaboration between cells accelerated evolution, leading to the incredible diversity we see today. In this chapter, we explore the extent of Earth's genetic code, which contains trillions of useful units of information, and how it has shaped life. And raise a toast to your drinking buddy T-Rex!

Here's a question: Since Earth became a spontaneous computer that wrote genetic code, how much of this code has it written? If we want to find an answer, we should not focus on the amount of DNA, but instead on the amount of meaning inscribed in DNA. In other words, on tokens.

How do we do that? This is complex, but let's just get a basic sense of it, where we can take the human genome as an example. The human genome consists of approximately three billion base pairs that form about 20,000 to 25,000 protein-coding genes. These genes are regulated by promoter regions (approximately 20,000 to 25,000), enhancers (estimated between 200,000 and 1 million), as well as silencers and insulators (around 50,000 in total). In addition, the genome contains non-coding RNAs, including approximately 2,600 microRNAs and over 16,000 long non-coding RNAs, as well as exons (approximately 160,000 to 250,000) and introns (approximately 140,000 to 225,000), all of which play important roles in gene expression.

We can reasonably think of all these genetic elements as represented by tokens. If we add estimates of their number, we reach between 600,000 and 1.6 million tokens in the human genome. To keep things simple, let's just pick a number in between, i.e. 1.1 million tokens. With this estimate, there are an average of 2,700 base pairs on the DNA for each unit that represents information or meaning. In other words; there are 2,700 base pairs for each token.

Exploding Complexity

But that inventory was only about the human genome. However, there are plenty of other species. Scientists estimate that there are approximately 8.7 million eukaryotic species – animals, plants, fungi, and protists such as algae and amoebas. Despite the undeniable negative impacts humans have had on biodiversity since the end of the last ice age, this number still represents almost a peak in the diversity of life forms throughout history. This is because speciation is directional: Any single species can split into many new ones, but two species can never merge into one.

How much DNA do these 8.7 million species contain in total? We will probably get a good answer soon, because scientists are in the process of mapping the complete genetic code of Earth's living beings. Projects such as the Earth BioGenome Project (EBP), Darwin Tree of Life Project, Genome 10K Project (G10K), and i5K Initiative are all working towards this ambitious goal. For example, EBP aims to have sequenced the DNA of all animals, plants, fungi, etc. by about 2028. This will give us a whole new level of understanding of biology, how life evolved, and how to protect endangered species.

In the meantime, we can guess that extant eukaryotic species have about 14 trillion base pairs in their combined genomes. Add to that all the species that have ever lived, and we get closer to a staggering 20,000 trillion base pairs. That's a lot. If we were to take 20,000 trillion DNA base pairs and convert them to digital data, it would take up five petabytes of storage space. To put that in perspective, a petabyte is a million gigabytes and looks like this when written out:

5,000,000,000,000,000 bytes, or

40,000,000,000,000,000 bits

Now let's bring this down to something more familiar: books. A typical book can be digitized to about a megabyte of data (assuming it's plain text). This means that five petabytes equals about five billion books. If we place these books on a giant bookshelf that is 2 m high, with 8 shelves, its total length would span roughly halfway around the Earth at the equator, or about 20,000 km.

These rough estimates give an idea of the approximate size of all genetic material describing all extant species ever, except bacteria. Of course, it's huge. And we can probably add somewhere around 20 trillion base pairs for all bacterial strains that have ever lived – especially since they had a very long head start.

The Sign Language of Life

Let's translate this into tokens. As we argued earlier, a token in this context typically represents a sequence of about 2,700 base pairs in DNA. Based on the previous estimates, life has thus created 7.4 trillion of these tokens since the beginning. Although only 7.4 billion of these are currently represented in living species, it is still an astonishing number.

Again, these are extremely loose estimates, but they give a sense of an interesting phenomenon. Think of it this way: As we have discussed, the universe generated 5,000–6,000 tokens within the first 20 minutes. But then not much happened for millions of years until the stars appeared. The stars forged the rest of the naturally occurring elements, bringing the total number of tokens to around 15,000–16,000.

Then very little happened until life arose in hydrothermal vents and subsequently exploded in diversity. It gave us the biosphere, which has a complexity that is many orders of magnitude greater than anything that happened before. In fact, a single bacterium like *E. coli* can boast more complexity than the entire inanimate universe. Today, life on Earth contains an estimated 100,000 times more signs of complexity than the cosmos without life.

And that's even a big understatement. So far, we have only reviewed the species of life as such. Homo sapiens is one species, but there are actually more than eight billion of us and we are not the same. Across all current species except bacteria, the current population of living organisms on Earth is an astounding five nonillion.

And when we consider the vast, hidden world of microbes, especially bacteria, the actual number could be far greater, reaching into the decillions – 10^{33} – or even more.

In other words, life on Earth, after its uncertain beginnings, has not only endured but has flourished into an astonishing diversity of forms. Its resilience is so profound that it seems very likely that before the Sun makes Earth uninhabitable in 1–1.5 billion years, life will have inadvertently spread throughout the solar system and beyond, whether through asteroid impacts or accidental contamination from human space exploration. It may even have already happened.

Have a Drink with T-Rex!

This abundance of life is not just a random collection of individuals; it is a vast, interconnected web, woven together through billions of years of evolution. The cycle of life stretches even further, as the resources that sustain us today are the same ones that nourished the dinosaurs millions of years ago.

Consider this astonishing fact: The water you drink today almost certainly contains billions of water molecules that have previously been drunk by T-Rexes. There have been many of these giants. It has been estimated in a study that combined body mass, population density, geographic distribution, and the duration of the species' existence. Researchers used Damuth's law, which relates body mass to population density, and calculated that about 20,000 adult T-Rexes lived at any given time. Over approximately 127,000 generations and about 2.5 million years, this equates to a total population of about 2.5 billion T-Rex individuals throughout history. As Earth's water cycle constantly recycles, the same molecules have quenched the thirst of these ancient giants. So every sip you take connects you with some T-Rexes, which are also ancestors of the birds around us.

And it may give the thought that when our planet became a computer, it created an infinitely complex system that was basically totally connected across time as well as space.

8.
THE DNA OF CULTURE

In this chapter, we delve into how the human neo-cortex, with its remarkable ability to generate and process information, has become a powerful meme-making machine. Discover how the evolution of memes, from simple gestures to complex ideologies, has shaped human societies and continues to drive our progress, leading us to the brink of a new era of intelligence.

The brain of a fruit fly is incredibly small – about the size of a poppy seed, or about 0.5 mm in diameter. But despite its diminutive size, it houses a surprisingly complex network of 139,255 neurons that control everything the fly does, from navigating the air to finding food, avoiding danger, mating, and much more.

How do we know that it contains precisely 139,255 neurons? We only know the exact number from a single fruit fly brain, which has been measured accurately in three dimensions. It is not easy to achieve such a detailed neural map, and the measurement represented the culmination of decades of research, with several teams contributing to the effort since the 1970s. The culmination came in 2024, when researchers published a detailed 3D visualization of the fruit fly brain. This model not only revealed the 139,255 neurons, but also mapped approximately 54.5 million synaptic connections – the junctions where neurons communicate.

The work along the way had involved cutting the fruit fly brain into incredibly thin sections and then using AI software to painstakingly trace the complex paths of neurons through each slice, finally reassembling them into a comprehensive map. The slicing was performed with diamond knives and beams of gallium atoms. Each slice revealed a new layer, which was then recorded with electron microscopes. These millions of images were carefully assembled with the help of 622 researchers from 146 laboratories around the world and AI software. The result looked as shown in Figure 8.1.

The enormous complexity of the tiny fruit fly brain is the result of billions of years of evolution. Before brains existed, life on Earth was limited to a world of simple stimuli and reactions. But over 600 million years ago, the first nerve cells emerged and opened the door to a world of sensation and complexity. Organisms could now not only react, but also interpret and learn from their surroundings. It was like a silent movie suddenly getting sound.

Figure 8.1 The 50 largest neurons of a fruit fly brain.
Fruit fly brains contain approximately 140,000 nerve cells, which are connected at around 55 million points.

About 520 million years ago, a crucial leap occurred: The first primitive brains emerged. These early brains were simple clusters of nerve cells that functioned as our critical density, where the increased density of nerve cells enabled a whole new kind of information processing and coordination of bodily functions.

Brains were a revolutionary innovation that allowed organisms to react more effectively to their surroundings and develop more complex behavior. Life crawled onto land, and the first four-legged creatures faced new challenges in a far more complex environment. They had to navigate, find food, and avoid danger. The brain had to keep up. Memory became crucial for survival, and reptiles developed an ability to remember and adapt.

But it was with the mammalian neocortex that the brain really took a tiger leap. This new brain structure opened up abstract thinking, planning, and problem-solving on a whole new level. The neocortex, which our friend the fruit fly, for example, must do without, became the true game changer that paved the way for human consciousness and our ability to create and explore.

But what does the neocortex actually do? Here are three of its most notable features:

- **Identifies correlations:** The neocortex can see connections between different ideas and phenomena. This is how we understand metaphors, such as "he is a lion on the field" without believing that he actually transforms into a lion. This is also how we associate the feeling of warmth with happiness.

- **Spreads ideas:** Unlike other parts of the brain, the neocortex can send signals far and wide. This means that it can mix and match information from the entire brain, helping us to create new ideas. We can combine the memory of a song with a picture of our best friend and create a unique emotional experience. That is why memories are often a mixture of different sensory impressions and information.

- **Multitasks:** The neocortex can handle millions of patterns at once, all interacting in complex ways. This is what allows us to imagine new scenarios, think about abstract ideas and solve complex problems.

These three superpowers make the neocortex the engine of creativity. Unlike the cerebellum at the back of the head, which learns extremely slowly over generations through evolution, the neocortex allows for lightning-fast learning within your lifetime and even the next 10 seconds.

COMPLEXITY CASCADE #7

- **What?** Formation of consciousness and exploratory intelligence
- **When?** Gradually over the last 520 million years
- **Why?** There was a critical density of nerve cells in brains

Runaway Human Intelligence

The neocortex became a crucial evolutionary advantage for humans. Our brain size more than doubled between 800,000 and 200,000 years ago, mainly due to growth in the neocortex. But what was the driving force behind this dramatic brain growth?

Imagine our early ancestors navigating the changing African landscape, where climate fluctuations created recurring shifts between dry savanna and lush forest. These changing conditions created a creative pulse in evolution. How? During periods of drought and savanna, populations shrank and became isolated. This isolation increased inbreeding, which concentrated both bad and beneficial mutations within smaller groups. When the climate changed, and the jungles spread, the tribes grew again and came into contact with each other. The groups that had developed the most advantageous traits, including larger brains and increased cognitive capacity, thrived and reproduced, while other groups were outcompeted.

This creative pulse honed our ancestors' brains over millions of years and ultimately shaped us into the intelligent beings we are today.

The fluctuating climate also had another effect. Some of our distant ancestors stayed in the trees, but others adapted to life on the open savanna and learned to walk upright. This freed the hands of the savanna people, which were previously used to swing through trees. Now they could use their hands for tools. And they were good at it – thanks to their opposable thumbs, which were actually developed for tree climbing. The best tool users survived, leading to the co-evolution of brains and tools. From then on, human evolution was inseparable from the development of ever better tools. A rather unique feature of human development.

More happened to early humans. During periods of savanna, it was also difficult for males to guard several females at the same time. Due to the open landscape, one was more exposed, and one had to move further away to find enough food. This led to pair bonding, where the males focused on protecting a single female and her children. This social shift created a capacity for personal devotion and laid the foundation for more collaboration. Children could now identify both parents, leading to less violence and more cooperation within groups. This recognition led to a decline in arbitrary violence within the tribe and an increase in cooperation, because one was less likely to attack a tribe if one was directly related to it. It reflects a pattern seen in recent human history, where royal families in neighboring states would marry their children to each other to counteract internecine warfare. So humans became smarter, more devoted, and better at cooperating.

Along the way in this story, the human species branched into many subspecies. One of them was later named the "thinking" people. Or "Homo sapiens" as it is called in Latin. That's us.

Maria's Brain

Now let's think back to our friend Maria, who is enjoying the morning with her feet in the water in Croatia. Inside her brain it's buzzing between billions of neurons, neatly organized in columns. There are over a million of these columns in the brain.

The real magic happens within the different levels of these columns. Here, specialized cells called place cells and grid cells act as Maria's brain's built-in GPS. Imagine Maria walking back from the water's edge to the sun lounger. The place cells in her memory center are now sending signals like small location markers that fire specifically when she is in certain places. This creates a mental map that helps her recognize and navigate familiar places. Grid cells, located nearby, operate on a more abstract level. They create a mental pattern that forms a hexagonal grid over Maria's surroundings, like an invisible coordinate system. This internal GPS calculates her position and how far she has moved, regardless of the specific details of her location. Together, place cells and grid cells give Maria a complete picture of her surroundings, helping her remember specific places and understand her position in them. But this system is not just for physical spaces; it also helps her navigate memories and ideas. When Maria thinks back to an event in her childhood, her brain uses similar mapping strategies to travel through the "mental space" of the past. That is why mnemonic techniques of assigning words and subjects to a specific place work so well.

The columns in Maria's cortex are connected by six levels, five of which control the flow of information, while the sixth acts as a communication network, ensuring that all parts of the brain are constantly in conversation with the other parts. With trillions of synapses firing up to ten times per second each, Maria's brain has an estimated computing power of somewhere between 10^{14} (100 trillion) and 10^{17} (100 quadrillion) operations per second. This enormous complexity allows for thought, memory, imagination, and the countless other abilities that make her human.

Two Main Systems

Maria's brain is not just one big thinking machine. In his book *Thinking, Fast and Slow* (2011), Daniel Kahneman describes the two different ways our brains work: His "System 1" is the fast, intuitive and automatic mode, and "System 2" the slower, conscious, and analytical mode.

System 1 is always on and makes quick judgments based on gut feelings and past experiences. It's the part that makes Maria react instinctively to a sudden sound or speak effortlessly on a daily basis.

System 2 is the slow and thoughtful part of her brain. It kicks in when she needs to focus, solve problems or make careful decisions. It's the part that helps Maria figure out a math problem or plan her weekend. These two systems always interact. System 1 constantly bombards Maria with suggestions and quick solutions, while System 2 is there to check these ideas and sometimes step in with a more logical solution.

This shift in thinking explains why Maria sometimes makes impulsive choices that she later regrets – like ordering the evening's seventh espresso martini. Or conversely, overthinking what clothes to wear to go to the cinema. The distinction may also explain why people with autism, who may be more reliant on System 2, tend to be more introverted and deliberate in their actions.

Here's a fun fact, by the way: A majority of people experience some form of inner speech or inner monologue. This often manifests as a verbal stream of consciousness, where they talk to their minds, recount events, ponder thoughts, or plan actions. Research suggests that 5–10% of people do not experience this inner voice. Their thoughts may instead manifest as visual images, abstract concepts, or feelings without accompanying verbal narration. Some studies suggest that they may lean more towards introversion, mindfulness, and present moment awareness. People who experience inner speech often have stronger verbal skills, but not necessarily higher intelligence.

Adjustment, Pruning, and Prediction

Although Maria's brain only weighs about 2% of her body weight, it is also a true energy guzzler. It consumes about 20% of all the energy her body needs. For newborns, that number is even wilder – they use almost 90% of their energy to power the small, growing brain. And without mitochondria, the ingenious power plants in our cells, it wouldn't be possible at all.

How can it be that the brain uses so much energy when it doesn't physically move in the same way as muscles? The reason lies in the trillions of chemical reactions that constantly occur in brain cells. Partly, the brain constantly transmits signals, which requires energy, and partly it is in a perpetual state of restructuring. Millions of new connections between neurons are formed every day, especially in young individuals who learn and adapt quickly.

Let's look at the restructuring. Imagine Maria's brain as a gardener tending a rose bush. The brain continuously prunes weak or unused connections – sometimes within minutes – to make way for new and stronger ones. This pruning process is the reason why some memories are anchored and skills are learned, while other information disappears. Remarkably, some connections only last about 90 minutes before they are pruned.

The more Maria uses a neural connection, the stronger and more robust it becomes. This principle explains why practicing a skill improves it. Conversely, rarely used connections are gradually weakened and can disappear altogether. This adaptability, known as neuroplasticity, allows the brain to learn a wide range of skills, from math to language to music.

When groups of connected neurons send signals in parallel, their connections are strengthened. These strong connections play an essential role in the brain's decision-making processes. Think of it as a voting system: Each signaling neuron casts votes, and those with stronger connections have more "voting rights." This tuning process helps Maria's brain integrate sensory input from sight, sound, smell, and touch into a coherent and flexible understanding of the world.

Predictions and Perceptions

One of Maria's brain's most fascinating abilities is to create "invariant representations" – consistent core concepts derived from ever-changing input. Take her favorite song, for example. She recognizes it immediately, even if it's played on a piano instead of the usual band arrangement. This recognition occurs because her brain discerns the deeper patterns in the song, such as melody, rhythm, and structure, which remain constant regardless of the instrument.

Maria's brain also continuously predicts the events around her. When she listens to a familiar song, her brain anticipates every note. Even with new music, her brain begins to predict the rhythm almost immediately. This predictive ability contributes to the enjoyment of music, as it creates a dynamic interplay between expectation and surprise.

Her brain's prediction system shapes how she sees the world. For example, if John tells her one evening in Croatia that the wine they are about to drink is expensive, her brain may predict that it will therefore taste better. This prediction can change her actual perception of its taste for the better.

Each part of the cortex functions as a mini prediction machine, gathering information from different brain regions to make educated guesses about when to activate. This flexibility allows her to learn new skills. As she navigates the world, her brain constantly generates and interprets hundreds, possibly thousands, of tokens every minute. Her brain thereby produces more complexity in a single minute than existed in the entire early universe.

Predictions are at the heart of how Maria perceives the world. What she sees is a mixture of incoming sensory data and her brain's best guess as to what happens then. These predictions are so ingrained in her System 1 brain that she mostly reacts automatically without conscious thought. Only when something unexpected happens does System 2 kick in. Now she becomes truly aware and learns from the surprise.

The ability to predict unconsciously is greatly enhanced with practice. A child learning to read goes from recognizing individual letters to understanding whole words at a glance. And that's why most people can read this jumble: "According to a rsceearch at an Elingsh uinervtisy, it deosn't mttaer in waht oredr the ltteers in a wrod are, the olny iprmoatnt tihng is taht the frist and lsat ltteer is at the rghit pclae. The rset can be a toatl mses and you can sitll raed it wouthit a porbelm. Tihs is bcuseae we do not raed ervey lteter by it slef but the wrod as a wlohe."

If you could read that, it was with your System 1 brain.

Memes – The Genes of Culture

Now let's discuss the so-called memes. The term "meme" was coined by Richard Dawkins, a famous evolutionary biologist. His world-renowned book *The Selfish Gene* (1976) is primarily about genetic evolution under competition – about the genetic principles behind Charles Darwin's famous "Survival of the Fittest" concept. Here Dawkins describes genes as "selfish replicators" that exploit organisms to spread and copy themselves. This view ultimately sees life as a competition between snippets of genetic code – a kind of spontaneous mathematical competition.

Later in the book, however, he introduces the concept of memes and describes them as the cultural equivalents of genes. Memes are patterns of behavior and beliefs that spread – sometimes like wildfire – and constantly evolve in societies. They function as tokens of social meaning, and they can relate to concepts, behaviors, and beliefs that spread through communication and imitation. Like genes, memes typically create action. In that sense, they can be seen as code.

The analogy between genes and memes is obvious and important. Cultures are like patchworks of competing memes, composed of different ideas and traditions, some as simple as a gesture, others as complex as a religion. The use of paper money is an example of a strong meme. A dollar bill is just a piece of paper, but the idea – or meme – that such is valid as a store of value allows us to use it for trade.

Both genes and memes can be described as tokens, and just as genes fight to survive in the ruthless game of evolution, memes also fight to be remembered and passed on. The most successful memes are those that win the battle and become part of the culture of the future.

So there is a memetic ecosystem with survival of the fittest. Memes therefore also play a major role in the long-term evolution of complexity and intelligence. The point is that genes are human machines – genes make humans. But we humans are then meme machines – humans make memes.

In this way, a combinatorial cascade – the genetic one – has created a new one that broke through the previous tentative scaling barrier. This new cascade, the memetic one, is born out of our neocortex and has set humanity on a course towards unknown horizons of cultural and intellectual evolution.

In the next chapter, we delve deeper into the mechanisms in brains that created the new cascade.

9.
MINDS IN
THE MAKING

This chapter examines the evolution of consciousness and intelligence, from the first nerve cells to the complex human brain. Discover the fascinating development of emotions and moral instincts, and explore how the neocortex changed the way we perceive and interact with the world.

Let's look at consciousness. Consciousness is your remarkable ability to be aware of yourself, your thoughts, feelings, and the world around you. It is more than just knowing that you exist; it is the living experience of existence in all its fascinating forms, including the emotional depth it brings.

For something to truly be said to be conscious, several key elements must be present. First, self-awareness is crucial. This is the understanding that you are a separate individual, separate from everything else. Second, the conscious mind experiences a wide range of emotions, from joy and sadness to pain and excitement. This emotional spectrum is a crucial aspect of consciousness. In addition, subjectivity plays an essential role. Your unique perspective shapes how you perceive the world, making your experiences your own. Finally, perception through your senses – sight, hearing, smell, taste, and touch – helps you build a rich understanding of your surroundings.

Consciousness is the bridge between merely existing and living fully. It is the difference between seeing a sunset and experiencing it – losing oneself in the symphony of colors, feeling the awe in one's chest and feeling a deep gratitude for witnessing the beauty of nature. Consciousness gives us the ability to reflect on our existence, to feel, understand, and marvel at the world around us.

The Dimmer Switch of Consciousness

The emergence of consciousness and the search for exploratory knowledge led the world's complexity to pass its seventh "complexity cascade." Of the ten breakthroughs on the universe's journey towards hyperintelligence, this is perhaps the most fascinating. Think about it: a collection of atoms and molecules becomes aware of its own existence and begins to reflect on the world. So how did life develop this totally bizarre ability?

The emergence of consciousness in the living world was a slow and complex process, similar to a light gradually illuminating a room. It is believed to have started small in simple organisms like bacteria, which developed basic senses over 540 million years ago.

As life evolved, the need for consciousness also evolved. Amphibians, venturing onto land about 443–419 million years ago, needed better attention spans to navigate their new surroundings. Insects that flew about 359–299 million years ago needed even more precise focus. Birds and early dinosaurs, which appeared between 240–145 million years ago, may have developed early forms of simple consciousness. Mammals and their complex social groups, which arose 66 million years ago, likely developed consciousness further. A big leap clearly happened around seven million years ago with the emergence of our early ancestors.

This gradual emergence of consciousness over millions of years is beautifully reflected in the development of each individual human being. A fetus starts as a single cell without a nervous system. Around week 25 of pregnancy, the brain begins to take shape and the foundation for consciousness is laid. Newborns come into the world with a basic consciousness that reacts to the environment, but they need time to learn to integrate different sensory impressions. Recognizing mother's face takes weeks to months after birth, and it is not until around 18–24 months that the child begins to understand themselves as a separate individual.

Although we do not fully understand how consciousness works in the brain, we know that it is not just in one place. Some children who have had parts of their brains removed to counteract severe epileptic seizures develop fairly normal personalities. Others, who have a severed connection between the two hemispheres of the brain, still show full consciousness and remarkable adaptability.

The difference between conscious and unconscious beings is evident in various mental aspects, as shown in Table 9.1.

Which animals have consciousness, and how much? It is not easy to determine, but in 2024 a group of scientists, including zoologists, signed the New York Declaration on Animal Consciousness, which points to the growing indications that a wide range of animals, including insects such as bees, are to some extent conscious and capable of subjective experiences.

Table 9.1 **How the presence of conscience impacts mental characteristics**

Feature	Beings without conscience	Conscious beings
Instincts and intelligence	Only instincts	Possesses instincts, but also experiences subjective intelligence
Moral instincts and ethical standards/ moral agency	Basic moral instincts	Possesses moral instincts, conscious ethical standards, and moral agency subject to free will
Emotions and feelings	Only emotions	Possesses both feelings and emotions

However, a fly shows little sign of consciousness. It will instinctively dodge a fly swatter, but can then immediately land back in the same dangerous place, suggesting an absence of the fear we would feel. And while flies avoid dead companions because of the potential danger they represent, there is no evidence that they experience empathy for their deceased comrades.

However, bees seem to feel optimism, frustration, playfulness, and fear – traits we otherwise relate more to mammals. Experiments have shown that bees can experience posttraumatic stress disorder (PTSD)-like symptoms, recognize different human faces, process long-term memories while sleeping, and perhaps even dream.

Elephants, with their much larger brains, show signs of very advanced consciousness. For example, they have been observed covering the bodies of dead elephants with leaves, branches, and soil. They have also been seen standing guard over the bodies and showing signs of grief, such as touching the deceased's bones and tusks with their trunks.

Consciousness has a profound effect on the way instincts and intelligence work. Living beings without consciousness rely on instinct – the automatic behavior they are born with. However, conscious beings use both instincts and subjectively felt intelligence, which allows them to learn, plan, and adapt based on experience, but also, for example, enjoy feelings of flow during intellectual pursuits.

Moral Instincts, Ethics, and Freedom of Action

As brains evolve, a multitude of instincts arise, and some of them can be called moral. Moral instincts are the innate tendencies that govern our perception of right and wrong, and they are not unique to humans. Animals, from wolves and lions to ants and fish, rely on such instincts for social cohesion and survival. This behavior, which is often encoded in their genes, increases their chances of thriving individually and collectively. Even our beloved pets such as parrots, cats, and dog also exhibit moral instincts.

While morality in less complex animals is largely genetic, human moral instincts are strongly influenced by our individual DNA. Studies of identical twins reveal striking similarities in their moral reasoning, suggesting a strong genetic basis.

Social psychologist Jonathan Haidt identifies six core human moral instincts: care versus harm, justice versus cheating, loyalty versus betrayal, authority versus subversion, respect versus degradation, and freedom versus oppression. Haidt argues that these are deeply embedded in our nature, shaped through millennia of selection pressure.

But as humans, we have a unique advantage: advanced consciousness. This therefore gives us the ability to make ethical choices and take responsibility for our actions. Our upbringing, social circles, and personal experiences all contribute to shaping these standards and our moral compass.

Interestingly, it seems that the number of moral instincts an animal possesses is related to the size of its brain. In fact, we can derive a scaling law for the relationship between brain mass and moral instincts, which we show in Figure 9.1.

Animals with a more developed consciousness often also have more complex social behavior. Take monkeys, for example. They show clear signs of empathy and cooperation, suggesting a link between consciousness and a form of moral understanding. The more conscious the animals are, the better they are at understanding and responding to the needs of others. This ability to cooperate and show care for each other has certainly played an important role in evolution, as it makes it easier for groups of animals to survive.

It should be added that social systems can add a twist to this. For example, social models can either make individuals behave better than they otherwise would – for example, towards the environment. Or worse – for example, in the contemplation of fundamentalist ideologies.

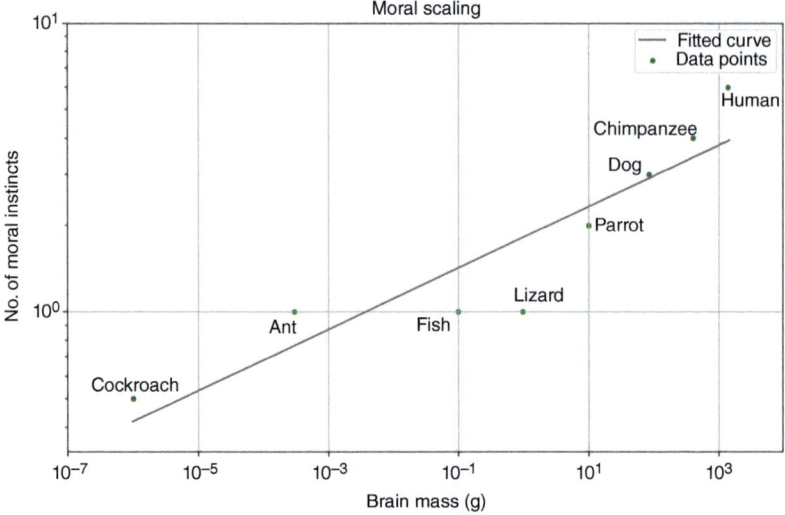

Figure 9.1 **The relationship between brain mass and the presence of moral instincts.** *As shown, moral complexity approximately correlates with brain size.*

Brain Mass, Sensations, and Emotions

Let's move on to sensations and emotions. Whether an animal has consciousness or not, it will always have sensations. These involve chemical reactions that ripple through the body. Incidentally, often very quickly and powerfully. Even simple organisms like bacteria have basic reactions to their environment and can therefore be said to have sensations.

However, sensations are not the same as emotions. Emotions arise when we become aware of these sensations and begin to process them consciously. Emotions color our lives and relationships and make us who we are. Imagine friends who never showed any emotion – they would be as lifeless as robots!

Our pets, like dogs and cats, exhibit emotions that we can recognize and relate to. And yes, even parrots, distant relatives of dinosaurs like T-Rex, exhibit a wide range of emotions, from playful joy to jealous outbursts. Some even claim that parrots have a good sense of humor, which may lead one to consider whether the ancient dinosaurs also had a funny side. Imagine T-Rexes pranking each other!

All emotions have chemical aspects.

These chemicals trigger physical reactions. For instance, a surge of adrenaline can make your heart race and your palms sweat, while oxytocin can give you a warm and comfortable feeling. Your brain then picks up these bodily signals, which reinforces the associated emotion and creates a fascinating mind-body loop. It's like a conversation between your brain and your body, each influencing the other.

Scientists have identified 54 different human emotions that each of us likely experiences throughout our lives, all of which involve bodily reactions, emotions, and feelings (Table 9.2).

Table 9.2 List of human emotions

Positive emotions	Negative emotions	Complex emotions
Joy	Pain	Awe
Playfulness	Fear	Expectation
Empathy	Stress/anxiety	Envy
Love	Anger	Jealousy
Optimism	Sadness	Pride
Satisfaction	Guilt	Passion
Curiosity	Surprise	Anger
Sympathy	Disgust	Empowerment
Gratitude	Boredom	Confidence
Hope	Frustration	Confusion
Inspiration	Despair	Loneliness
Excitement	Humiliation	Shame
Acceptance	Embarrassment	
Peace of mind	Uncertainty	

(Continued)

Table 9.2 **(Continued)**

Positive emotions	Negative emotions	Complex emotions
Ecstasy	Angst	
Wonder	Alienation	
Confidence	Meaninglessness	
Self-esteem		
Desire		
Preference		
Devotion		
Intimacy		
Affiliation		
Admiration		

How Many Emotions Do Animals Have?

Parrots exhibit quite a few, and science speaks here of approximately 20 different emotions. Dogs seem to have more, and chimpanzees surpass dogs in this respect. Table 9.3 gives an estimate of the total known emotional diversity of different species, including humans.

Table 9.3 Correlation between brain sizes and number of sensations/emotions among different species

Species	Brain size (grams)	Number of sensations/emotions
Cockroach	0.000001	~5
Ant	0.0003	~8
Bee	0.003	10

Species	Brain size (grams)	Number of sensations/emotions
Fish	0.1	13
Octopus	0.5	17
Lizard	1	15
Parrot	10	17
Dog	85	28
Wolf	120	19
Macaque	100	15
Chimpanzee	400	28
Dolphin	1,500	17
Human	1,600	55
Elephant	5,000	31

If we plot brain weight against the number of sensations and emotions in different species, we can see that the spectrum of emotions grows slowly as the brain gets larger. However, this trend doesn't always hold true. For example, dogs exhibit a remarkably wide range of emotions compared to their brain sizes. This is likely due to their long history of domestication. By selectively breeding for traits like friendliness and sociability, humans have inadvertently fostered a greater emotional repertoire in dogs compared to their wolf ancestors. In essence, domestication has enriched their emotional lives.

Similarly, humans exhibit a far richer emotional spectrum than predicted by the scaling law. This can be attributed to a form of "self-domestication." As our culture evolved, individuals who excelled in cooperation, empathy, and altruistic behavior – traits often associated with

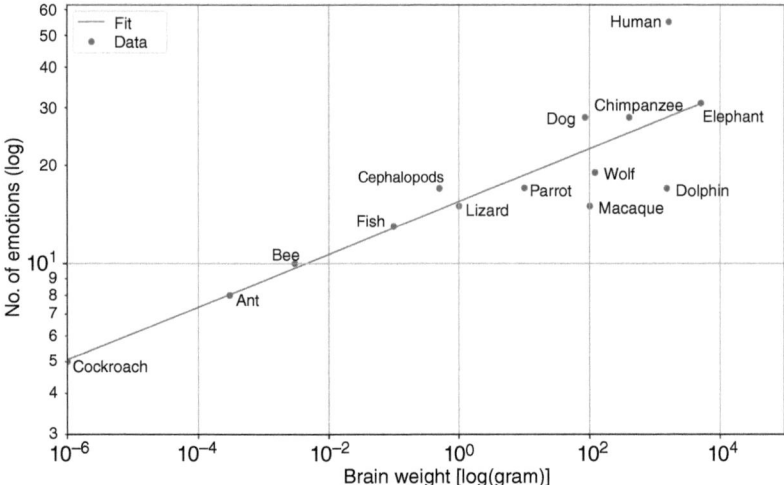

Correlation between brain size and the number of emotions. *The graph shows how emotional richness scales brain size relative to humans.*

positive emotional experiences – were more likely to survive and reproduce. This selection pressure has led to the development of a complex emotional landscape in humans, characterized by a wide range of social and moral emotions.

PART 3.

THE TECHNOSPHERE

From humble stone tools to towering skyscrapers, the technosphere is humanity's vast playground for innovation. It is the sum of our creations, our eternal pursuit of progress and our insatiable curiosity. But let's be honest, it wasn't always that impressive. We started small with sticks and stones, and it took us a while to figure out this whole thing we call "civilization." So let's take a look at the technosphere's profile:

- **Age:** Relatively youthful (compared to the universe), and seen from where it really took off, about 12,000 years.

- **What started the party?:** Mostly mastering fire and inventing trade. As well as the development of complex language.

- **Turbochargers kick in:** We've had our bursts of genius, but things really took off around 1450–1500 (Gutenberg and the Renaissance).

- **Weight:** A staggering 30 trillion tons (that's about 50 kilos of technology for every square meter on Earth).

- **Energy production:** A whopping 163,000 TWh annually (we're firing up).

- **Number of products:** Around a billion different things (from paper clips to book titles to spaceships – that's how creative we are).

10.
CODE, SYNERGY, AND ENERGY

In this chapter, discover how man's control of fire and the transformative power of trade created a new era of innovation and collaboration. We explore the fascinating interplay between fire, trade, human ingenuity, and the development of intelligence.

The word technology descends from the Greek terms for "craft" and "knowledge," i.e. using skills or knowledge to create or achieve something. An axe, a fishing net, or a wheel is technology. A building can be considered a result of technology, as its design, construction, and materials involve technical skills and knowledge.

Interestingly, the first technological inventors were not humans. One can argue that it was termites, since they already started making simple caves for collective habitation around 350 million years ago. Over time, their architectural skills evolved to create complex mounds and nests that not only protected them from predators, but also demonstrated remarkable engineering skills. About 200 million years ago, ants followed suit with their own architectural innovation. Their early nests were probably simple, but as they evolved, their constructions became increasingly advanced.

Over time – and here we are looking across many millions of years – more and more species began to use tools and apply technology in a broad sense. For example, about 250 million years ago, spiders began to spin webs, and these gradually became more sophisticated. Meanwhile, the termites had moved on, and about 150 million years ago, using combinations of soil, saliva, and manure, they began to build high-rise buildings for thousands of individuals. These high-rises weren't just bigger; they were smarter and incorporated features like ventilation and temperature control.

Leafcutter ants began a symbiotic relationship with fungi about 15–20 million years ago. They cut leaves from plants, not to eat them directly, but to use them as fertilizer for fungi, which they then ate. They became farmers!

Primates, including our early ancestors, began using simple tools about seven million years ago. This included chimpanzees, who used sticks for termite fishing. Two million years ago, capuchin monkeys in South America used stones as hammers and anvils. Similarly, sea otters used stones to break open shellfish. About 500,000 years ago, birds and mammals used natural materials such as feathers, fur, and hair for nest lining, while birds also used mud and clay to build nests. Table 10.1 shows some of the first examples of technology on our planet.

Interestingly, humans appear three times in this table of technological milestones. The first entry marks their use of stone tools about 3.3 million years ago. But it pales in comparison to termites, spiders, and ants, which had made far more advanced tools, constructions, and even agriculture millions of years earlier.

However, the second entry marks a truly revolutionary moment: Humans gain control of fire. Before we delve into how wild it was, it must be said that this incredible leap would not have been possible without a specific factor: the availability of suitable concentrations of oxygen. Fire cannot sustain itself if there is less than 15% oxygen, as was likely the norm until about 400 million years ago. Conversely, if we get above 30%, even small flames easily become uncontrollable.

But over the past few million years, oxygen levels have stabilized at around 22%, what we might call the "Goldilocks zone" for fire. At that concentration, fire burns steadily and typically remains fairly manageable. This stable environment provided a unique opportunity to harness the power of fire – an opportunity that only humans, with their growing cognitive

Table 10.1 Ancient technological milestones

Years	Animal	Innovation	Significance
350 million years ago	Termites	Building complex nests	Early example of architecture and social structure
250 million years ago	Spiders	Using webs to catch prey	New hunting strategy and habitat creation
40 million years ago	Dolphins	Using sponges for protection while foraging	Using tools for protection and resource acquisition
20 million years ago	Herons	Using objects for bait fishing	Strategic use of tools for hunting
15 million years ago	Leafcutter ants	Growing fungus with leaves	Early agriculture and resource management
3.3 million years ago	Humans (australopithecines)	Using stone tools	Practical for tasks such as scraping and hammering
2.6 million years ago	Chimpanzees	Using sticks for termite fishing	Early use of tools for food extraction
2 million years ago	Capuchin monkeys	Using stones to crack nuts	Complex tool use and understanding of function
1.8 million years ago	Sea otters	Using stones to crush shellfish	Use of tools for food processing
1.4 million years ago	Humans	Control of fire	Provides a highly scalable energy source
700,000 years ago	Humans	Earliest known cooking in fireplaces	Increase the nutritional value of their diet and make food easier to digest
10,000 years ago	Woodpeckers	Advanced tool use for extracting insects	Specialized tool use and adaptation
100,000 years ago	Fish	Use of cleaning stations to remove parasites	Cooperative use of tools and symbiosis

abilities, were able to seize. We don't know exactly when it started, but findings from Kenya suggest it happened as early as 1.42 million years ago. Another trail, also from Kenya, goes back about 1.5 million years in time. But the strongest actual evidence of controlled fire use comes from around 1 million years ago.

So what were these early humans who could control fire like? One and a half million years ago they had about half the brain size that we have today, but they were still the smartest beings on the planet. Also, because of their hands with opposable thumbs, they could manipulate things in sophisticated ways. And then it helped that they lived on land, where fire is possible, and not in the sea like the otherwise quite intelligent dolphins.

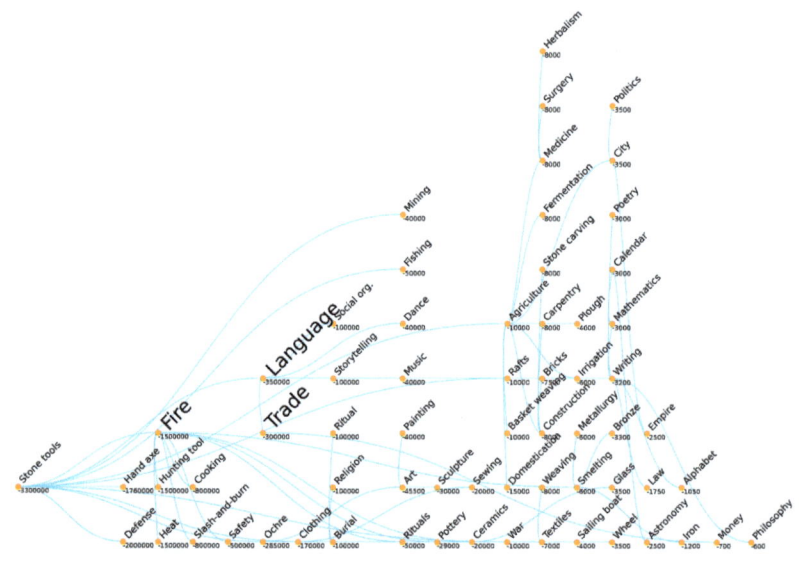

Combinatorial cascades in early human innovation.
The Supertrends model maps 16,000 human innovations and approximately 160,000 interdependencies among them, tracing back over 3 million years. Among early key innovations, control over fire likely emerged around 1.5 million years ago; complex language may have developed approximately 350,000 years ago; and trade is thought to have begun around 300,000 years ago. Notably, innovations were most prevalent during interglacial periods, when warmer climates provided favorable conditions for human creativity and progress.

Strengthening Progress

For humans, control of fire was probably the crucial trait that ultimately came to completely separate them from all other animals. Just think about it: Fire provides extremely concentrated energy, and it is very scalable. Control of fire triggered technological advances. No other species had ever gained access to a powerful external energy resource in this way.

The impact of fire extended far beyond warmth and protection. It shaped basic human cognition and social interaction. It extended waking hours, fostered a new social dynamic centered on the hearth, where stories were shared, knowledge was passed on, and community ties were strengthened.

Furthermore, mastery of fire triggered a cascade of co-evolution. It enabled the development of new technologies, which in turn favored individuals with larger brains who were better equipped to take advantage of these innovations. Cooking with fire made food easier to digest and freed up energy that could be redirected to brain development. Basically, fire not only nourished our physical needs, but also our intellectual growth.

An interesting question, by the way, is: Why do we enjoy cooked food such as grilled chicken? We think grilled food is juicy, flavorful, and often irresistible, so it may seem like a strange question. But the explanation lies deeper. Our preference for roasted meat probably stems from early humans and their ancestors who ate animals whose bodies had been "cooked" by natural forest fires. These prehistoric individuals, who enjoyed the more easily digestible and bacteria-free meat, had a survival advantage.

But overall, control of fire is about energy supply. Let's put the consequences into perspective. Various studies have estimated the development of human energy consumption per capita over time. Originally, early human species such as Australopithecines used about 2,000 kilocalories per day, solely from the food they ate. After humans gained control of fire, this number nearly doubled as they began cooking and using fire for warmth and protection.

The advent of agriculture about 10,000–12,000 years ago dramatically increased human energy consumption, six times that of pre-agricultural times. But it was the Industrial Revolution, powered by fossil fuels, that really accelerated per capita energy consumption, increasing it to about 30 times that of early humans who did not yet have control of fire. Today, in the wealthiest societies, energy consumption has risen to about 130 times this baseline, and by the end of this century it could reach 500 times or even thousands of times higher. The development of civilization is inextricably linked to our growing energy needs, and our early ability to control fire marked the beginning of this expansive journey.

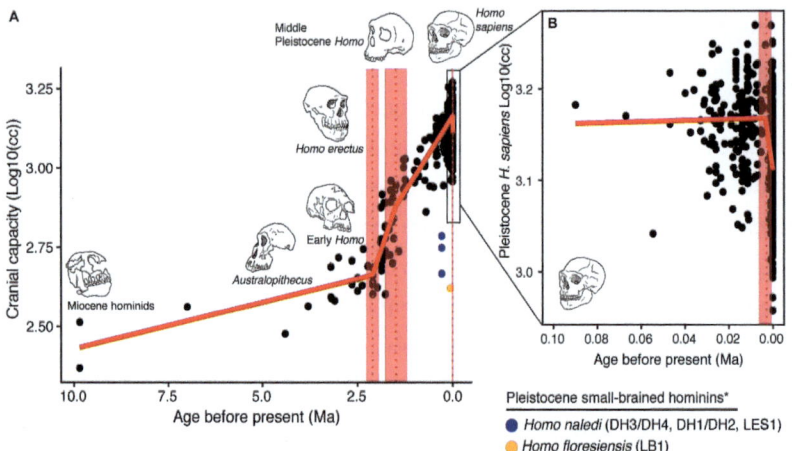

Growth in human cranial capacity over the last 10 million years. *This graph illustrates the significant increase in human cranial capacity over the past 10 million years. Notably, cranial size expanded substantially following the advent of stone tool use and later with the control of fire.*

From Grunts to Grammarians

One of the most important outcomes of human intellectual development is our complex language. Many animals have the ability to communicate in various ways, and in some cases their communication is quite sophisticated. For example, African gray parrots have been observed to use over 1,000 different words, and they can even combine these to form relatively complex sentences. However, human language capacity is far more advanced. A typical adult native English speaker is estimated to have a vocabulary of between 20,000 and 35,000 words. Literate and multilingual people can have a vocabulary of over 100,000 words.

Although we will never be able to pinpoint the exact moment when complex human language arose, a confluence of evidence from anatomy, genetics, archaeology, and comparative studies suggests that it probably occurred around 350,000 years ago. Of course not all at once, but gradually over a long period. Regardless of the exact time frame, the development of complex spoken and written language has separated humans from other species by our unique ability to convey detailed and abstract concepts.

Trade Is the Trigger for Combinatorial Cascades

So now humanity had gained control of energy supply through fire and communication through language. These were two big steps on the road to greatness, but a third was missing before the road was truly paved: Getting the combinatorial cascades started. The solution to that was trade. The archaeological indications of when tribal societies began to trade are tentative, but many archaeologists assume that people began to trade in pigment as early as 300,000 years ago.

The effect cannot be overestimated, because the idea of exchanging objects with strangers is magnificent. Early societies were heavily dependent on the resources that were immediately available to them. Trade, however, allowed them to evolve into "combiners," as the Swedish economist Johan Norberg calls it. Trade acted as a powerful engine that transformed basic resources into complex goods. Anything could be exchanged for something else or combined with a third thing to create a fourth. This triggered combinatorial cascades.

There is something fascinating about how combinatorial cascades work in interaction with trade. Take copper, for example, which was mined in the Alps 5,000 years ago. Then think of tin, which was mined in Cornwall,

England, during the same period. Through trade, these two metals could be combined to create bronze, an alloy with superior properties compared to the individual metals. Bronze could then be traded to distant lands, where it might be combined with wood from local forests to create new and more efficient tools and weapons.

With trade, one could continuously move through Stuart Kauffman's sequences of combinations, each leading to new possible combinations. It also means that many can recognize the new possible at roughly the same time. Historical examples include the telephone, where Alexander Graham Bell and Elisha Gray filed patents on the same day, and the light bulb, which was developed independently but almost simultaneously by Thomas Edison and Joseph Swan. Similar parallel developments were seen in the zipper, invented by Gideon Sundback and Whitcomb Judson, and the airplane, which was developed by the Wright brothers and Alberto Santos-Dumont.

Because trade brought people together, it also led to increased exchange of ideas, which is why something similar happened here. For example, the theory of evolution was formulated roughly in parallel by both Charles Darwin and Alfred Russel Wallace. A main basis for physics' use of mathematics, differential calculus, was similarly developed almost simultaneously by Newton and Leibniz. The economic cobweb theorem was independently developed by Nicholas Kaldor, John Maynard Keynes, and Eugen Slutsky, and two of them, Kaldor and Keynes, even published their results in the same issue of the *Review of Economic Studies*. And so on.

Trade revolutionized human interaction, paved the way for collaboration beyond close circles and created fertile ground for large social networks, where personal relationships were no longer a prerequisite. This development was a crucial driving force behind man's unique sociality, and later hypersociality, which is the ability to form complex societies and cooperate on a large scale.

Just as gravity gathers atoms into stars and creates new complexity, trade acted as a social gravity. It brought people closer together and increased the density of societies. This critical density was a catalyst for further complexity, innovation and cultural development.

COMPLEXITY CASCADE #8

- **What?** Formation of technologies and civilization

- **When?** Control of fire probably around 1.5 million years ago, mastery of language and trade probably 300–350,000 years ago. Civilization mostly took hold about 10,000 years ago.

- **Why?** A co-evolution between technology, genetics, and social patterns of behavior drove increasing complexity in all three.

II.
FROM WARRIOR KINGS TO OFFICE MICE

This chapter explores the development of human organizational structures, from the power-driven chiefdoms to the hierarchical bureaucracies of ancient empires. We will delve into the management styles of the Han Dynasty and the Roman Empire, and how they promoted innovation and stability. Also discover the impressive technological advances in these ancient civilizations, but also why they ultimately failed to trigger an industrial revolution.

With humanity's access to energy, communication, and trade, the way was paved for accelerating innovation and development of civilizations. The emergence of agriculture between 12,000 and 10,000 years ago marked a crucial transition from mere survival to the establishment of permanent settlements, and this turbocharged development. In areas such as the Fertile Crescent of the Middle East, humans now began to domesticate animals and cultivate plants, leading to a local surplus in food production. This enabled the growth of larger populations and promoted job specialization in crafts, trade, and administration. This created a new case of critical density. Previously we have described this with atoms in stars, cells in bacterial films, or nerves in brains, but here it happened with people in cities.

What effect did this critical density have? We can start by saying that the need for efficient resource management, when so many people lived together, led to the development of irrigation systems, which significantly increased agricultural productivity. Stable food supplies then allowed populations to grow, and villages expanded into cities. In 3000 BCE, the first urban centers arose in Mesopotamia and Egypt, such as Uruk and cities along the Nile. Uruk had grown to approximately 50,000 inhabitants at this time. At about the same time, the Harappan civilization also arose in the Indus Valley and the Yangshao and Longshan civilizations along the Yellow River in China. In these hubs of trade, culture, and political power, writing systems emerged around 3200 BCE, preserving knowledge across generations.

The Bronze Age (in the Mediterranean area from around 3300 BCE) marked a technological leap with the smelting of copper and tin to produce bronze. After this, civilizations such as the Sumerians, Egyptians, Mycenaeans, and Minoans arose with populations in the tens of thousands. Trade networks were expanded, and goods and ideas were disseminated.

Around 1200 BCE, the Iron Age began in the Middle East, introducing more durable iron tools and weapons, leading to the rise of empires such as the Hittites, Assyrians, and Persians. Iron tools revolutionized agriculture and supported larger populations and complex societies.

From Chiefdoms to Empires

Along the way, people had to develop new forms of organization. Frederic Laloux describes in his 2014 book *Reinventing Organizations* a spectrum of leadership styles that have evolved over time.

The first forms of complex organizational life arose with the emergence of chiefdoms. Think of early hunter-gatherer societies led by powerful individuals. This stage of organization was, as Laloux describes it, dependent on the exercise of overwhelming personal power to maintain order. A single leader had absolute authority, often through fear, charisma, or a combination of both. These small, tightly controlled groups were very reactive, focusing on meeting immediate needs and survival. Interestingly, this form of organization is also common among many mammalian species. Lions, for example, have a clear hierarchy with a dominant male leading the pride. This leader maintains order through the display of power and strength.

With the advent of agricultural societies, the need for a more complex organization grew. Laloux explains how this gave rise to the first examples of political states, social institutions and established religions. A fun fact is that the animals that come closest to this are insects such as ants rather than the more intelligent mammals.

About 2,000 years ago, two great empires, the Han Dynasty in China and the Roman Empire, flourished at either end of the Eurasian continent. Despite frequent conflicts at the borders, both empires maintained unusual degrees of internal peace, facilitating investment and trade.

Both empires introduced varying degrees of leadership characterized by hierarchical structures, strict control mechanisms, and a focus on stability, order, and compliance with established rules and procedures. As they grew larger, power shifted from a single dominant person to a ruling elite. Military leaders, senators, and administrators each had authority based on their position in the hierarchy, not just on personal power. Every ruler in this system was subject to limits, and civilizations enabled large projects such as aqueducts, roads, canals, and postal services across the empires, while engaging in long-term planning. This approach involved giving managers budgets and evaluating their performance against those goals. Because these organizations were more decentralized, they could grow very large while still functioning efficiently.

Imperial Ingenuity from Silk to Suspension Bridges

These empires gave the world an impressive array of inventions: paper, concrete, gunpowder, compasses, silk, crossbows, watermills, sanitation systems, glass, paper money, printing press, suspension bridges, central heating, and underground drilling, to name just a few examples. In addition, they both excelled in shipping and trade.

Mass production was also well developed in both empires. For example, Roman pottery such as terra sigillata was produced on a large scale. The largest kilns could fire up to 40,000 pieces at a time, and the extensive distribution of these goods throughout the empire testifies to advanced organization. Weapons and military equipment were also produced on a large scale to supply the Roman legions. This led to extensive mining for metals such as gold, silver, lead, and iron, where the Romans used advanced techniques such as hydraulic mining. In addition, they used watermills for a variety of purposes, including grinding grain, sawing wood, and crushing ore.

The Han Dynasty also experienced efficient mass production. A prominent example is silk production, where specialized workshops used advanced weaving techniques to produce large quantities of high-quality silk fabric, both for domestic use and international trade. The dynasty even established imperial workshops dedicated to the mass production of textiles, ceramics, and iron tools, often using standardized parts and processes reminiscent of assembly line work.

But the question arises: Did these empires have the necessary building blocks for an industrial revolution? Did their innovative spirit manage to translate into the kind of massive production and social upheaval that characterizes an industrial era?

They at least came close. The Chinese exploited fossil fuels such as natural gas as early as 900 BCE and even drilled for gas in deep wells. The Romans discovered coal in Britain and used it for both heating and iron processing.

However, what both civilizations lacked was a steam engine that could convert the energy from fire into kinetic movement. Interestingly, the Romans actually had an early form of steam engine, they just didn't understand its full potential. Around 100 AD in Alexandria, an early version of a steam engine was invented. It is known today as Hero's engine, named after the Greek-Egyptian engineer Hero who described it. This simple engine had no moving turbine blades, but it rotated when the water in the middle was heated. Although this could have been a key component in an industrial revolution, its use remained limited to entertainment and demonstrations, and its full potential was never understood. So the industrial revolution had to wait.

Combinatorial Disasters

The story rarely ends well for empires. Historian Carroll Quigley gave a sharp explanation of the typical cause of this phenomenon: "Over-institutionalization," he called it. Over-institutionalization occurs when civilization's systems become too complex and inflexible. So they hit a scaling barrier that hinders further growth and often leads to collapse.

We find parallels to this problem in single-celled organisms, which, as mentioned earlier, risk a "bureaucratic collapse" when their complexity becomes too great. Remember that our eukaryotic cells separated the functions into "pockets" so that there would be no confusion. But most civilizations eventually fail at this, after which they do the same thing we see everywhere in nature: their elements separate and later reunite in a different form.

12.
THE GREAT ACCELERATION

Get ready to be blown away as we journey through the dizzying acceleration of human progress, from the printing press to supercomputers. We examine how innovations in communication, transportation, and data processing have driven an unprecedented explosion of collective intelligence and reshaped our world in ways that were unthinkable just a few centuries ago.

In the year 406, a shiver of fear struck the Roman Empire when Germanic barbarians, those unruly outsiders, boldly crossed the Rhine. Just four years later, they stormed Rome itself, leaving a trail of plunder in their wake. Although they eventually retreated, the magical aura surrounding Rome was broken. The once mighty empire began to crumble. Within a short period of 15 years, Rome withdrew from Britain and then lost large territories in Spain, France, and North Africa. Just 50 years later, the proud capital had been reduced to a shadow of its former self, with a population that had shrunk to a quarter of its former size. It was an astonishing collapse – a fall from 500 years of greatness took just 71 years.

The aftermath of the Western Roman collapse left a fragmented Western Europe. In the 14th century, the continent was divided into thousands of competing ministates, all vying for power and influence. A loose alliance, the Holy Roman Empire, attempted to unite some of these territories between 962 and 1806, but it remained largely symbolic, and in reality it was a chaotic jumble of autonomous entities. The former empire consisted to a large extent of up to thousands of small city-states, reminiscent of today's Liechtenstein, Luxembourg, Andorra, San Marino, Malta, Monaco, and the Vatican, all of which are remnants of that time.

A Boom in Innovation

However, this era was far from as stagnant as one might think. In fact, it was a time of significant innovation and transformation. For example, agriculture saw significant advances during this period. Horses replaced oxen as draft animals, the heavy iron plow was introduced, and crop rotation techniques were developed to alternate crops, all of which led to a significant increase in agricultural productivity. Gravity pipes also revolutionized irrigation and water management, improving the utilization of water resources.

As former slaves flocked to the cities and got paid work, it sparked a lot of new inventions and ideas. Double-entry bookkeeping, new lending opportunities, joint-stock companies, commercial laws, and stock trading began to take shape and laid the foundation for modern finance and trade.

Meanwhile, open markets, where farmers could sell their products, became increasingly widespread. This created an incentive for farmers to improve the quality and competitiveness of their goods, stimulating further innovation and productivity.

Between 1000 and 1450, Europe experienced a rapid flow of new ideas and inventions. Europeans found a number of practical inventions such as wheelbarrows, four-wheeled horse-drawn carriages, boat oars, paper, spinning wheels, magnetic compasses, spectacles and new techniques for glass-blowing. Hard work, previously performed by thousands of slaves, was now performed with treadmill cranes, stationary harbor cranes, jib cranes, and slewing cranes. At the same time, several useful inventions such as wine presses and buttons for clothes appeared, while advances in medical knowledge were symbolized by the use of illustrated anatomy atlases by local doctors.

The lifestyles of the wealthy were simultaneously transformed with the introduction of pianos, fountains, underfloor heating, and beautiful oil paintings, while architectural innovations included rib vaults in ceilings and fireplaces with chimneys. The ships became larger and more robust, and they went from labor-intensive galleys to more profitable sailing boats, tailored for long-distance transport. Military innovations also played a significant role with the introduction of stirrups, spurs, and saddles, which strengthened cavalry attacks, as well as the development of crossbows, longbows, catapults, gunpowder, cannons, and early machine guns.

In the middle of the 15th century, Europe was therefore far more advanced in technological and economic terms than the Roman Empire had ever been. But it was only a prelude that set the stage for one of the most remarkable developments in human history. One of the triggering factors was book production.

The Printing Revolution

Until 1439, European books were handwritten by monks or scribes, and it could take up to a year to produce a single copy. These early books were made of specially prepared animal skins, where a Bible, for example, required the skins of over 200 sheep. This labor-intensive process made books extremely expensive – a handwritten Bible could cost around 300 florins, which is equivalent to about 100,000 dollars in present value. For a single book!

The introduction of paper reduced costs somewhat, but the real breakthrough occurred in 1439, when Gutenberg introduced printing with movable type. His first printing press, incidentally a modified wine press, made it possible to produce pages about 200 times faster than by handwriting. This drastically reduced costs. In 1454, Gutenberg could sell printed Bibles for 30 florins each – a tenth of the price of a handwritten Bible.

However, printing technology was constantly being improved, and in 1483 the Ripoli publishing house was able to produce books 500 times cheaper than traditional writing. This rapid efficiency increase meant that the cost of book production from 1439 to 1483 was halved approximately every five–six years.

By 1500, Europe was home to 220 printing houses producing eight million books, from specialized texts to popular pocket-sized editions. This surge in book production democratized information, enabling individuals to access knowledge independently, without relying on the church or state. In marketing terms, this effectively removed the middleman, granting direct access to knowledge. Intellectually, it sparked combinatorial cascades, transforming societies into parallel data-processing organisms capable of evolving insights at an accelerated pace.

Books created a new kind of community – a spiritual community where thoughts and ideas could meet and be exchanged across cultural patterns and geographical boundaries. This intellectual critical density helped pave the way for the Enlightenment a couple of hundred years later – a movement that placed reason, science, and individualism at the forefront. The Enlightenment challenged superstition, dogma, and groupthink and instead emphasized rationality, cosmopolitanism, and systematic doubt. Thinkers such as Montesquieu, John Locke, Thomas Hobbes, Adam Smith, and Edward Gibbon were among the Enlightenment's standard bearers. Their influence was reinforced by a network of underground printing houses and pamphlets that spread both legal and banned books – an early form of intellectual trade that fueled the flame of the Enlightenment.

The Enlightenment also replaced fatalism with ingenuity, encouraging people to seek practical solutions to problems rather than viewing them as divine punishment. This shift in thinking paved the way for scientific progress. The movement was also characterized by a strong optimism, where many Enlightenment thinkers believed in humanity's potential for significant progress through science and technology. This belief laid the foundation for futurology, the systematic study of potential futures based on emerging trends, and some Enlightenment figures can be seen as early pioneers of the field.

One of the earliest was Francis Bacon, whose *New Atlantis* (1627) envisioned a society governed by scientific inquiry, where scholars worked in state-supported research institutions – foreshadowing the modern scientific method and national research institutes. René Descartes, in his *Discourse on the Method* (1637), suggested that science would one day allow humanity to master nature, predicting advances in medicine that could extend human life indefinitely. Gottfried Wilhelm Leibniz imagined a future where universal knowledge would be systematized and logic could be mechanized – an idea that later inspired the development of computers and artificial intelligence. Similarly, Bernard de Fontenelle, in his *Conversations on the Plurality of Worlds* (1686), popularized the idea of extraterrestrial life and speculated about human expansion into space, centuries before the Space Age. Later, Marie-Jean-Antoine-Nicolas de Condorcet, in *Sketch for a Historical Picture of the Progress of the Human Spirit* (1795), boldly predicted that scientific and technological progress would lead to social equality, the eradication of disease, and even the indefinite extension of human lifespan.

European book production, meanwhile, increased from 2.8 million copies in the 15th century to one billion in the 18th century – 360 times as many. This transformation later led to the emergence of daily newspapers, which gave people new content every day – basically like reading a new little book every morning.

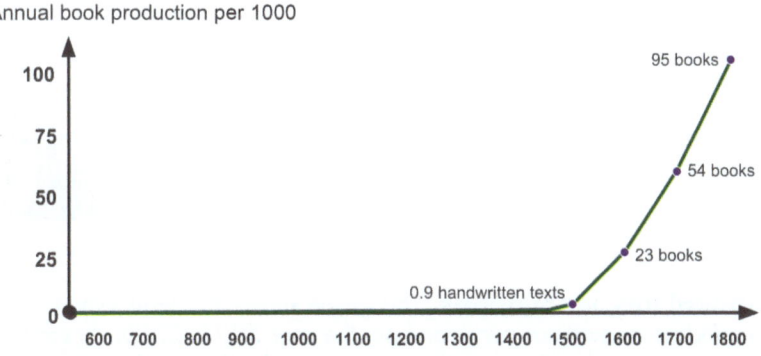

Annual book production per 1000

Europe's book production per capita from the year 500 to 1800. *Production exploded after Gutenberg's invention.*

Reinventing the Steam Engine

And then, in 1765, something truly remarkable happened. A young man named James Watt began experimenting with the construction of a steam engine. His crucial breakthrough came in 1769, when he discovered the importance of diverting the steam away from the driving cylinder and into a condenser, which significantly improved the machine's efficiency. As the potential of the steam engine became apparent, its uses spread rapidly. In textile mills, ironworks, and shipyards, steam power thus began to replace traditional methods, leading to increased production and transforming industries.

Steam power, this incredibly clever conversion of heat to movement, did not remain confined to factories; it also began to move people and goods at unprecedented speeds. The first steam-powered railway locomotive was invented in 1804. Later versions, such as George Stephenson's "Rocket," could travel at speeds that significantly exceeded horse-drawn carriages. In the same period, the first ocean-going ship with a steam turbine engine was launched, and the revolution in transport was thus truly underway.

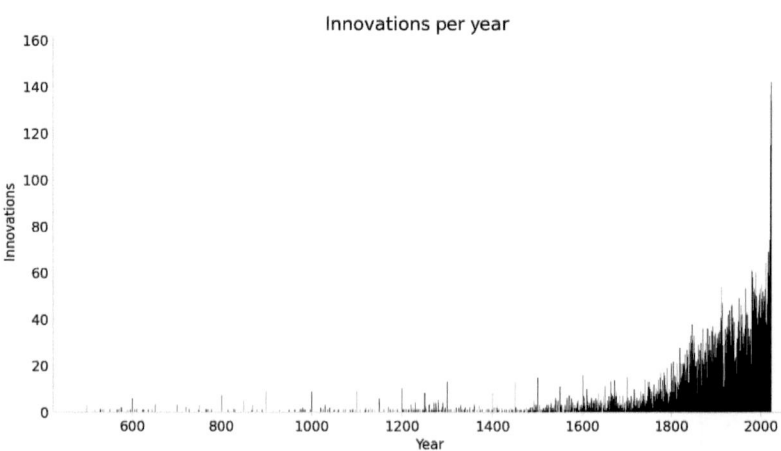

Annual key innovations. *This graph shows the development of significant innovations per year from the year 500 to 2025. As seen, the innovation density is accelerating massively. These data are from the Supertrends database which maps approximately 20,000 historical and predicted innovations and 200,000 dependencies between them.*

Take-off Speed

So the world really started to pick up speed, while the industrial revolution spread from country to country. But let's fast-forward to a day in 1953, where an exciting meeting took place at NASA. Here, a planning team looked at a graph illustrating the dramatic increase in transport speeds over the centuries. Starting with the modest pace of the Pony Express in 1750, it moved through the steady development of steam-powered and then diesel-powered trains, the rapid acceleration of cars, the soaring speeds of airplanes and finally rockets. Germany's V-2 ballistic missile from 1944 had achieved a top speed of 5,400 km/h on descent, which in itself showed the technological acceleration over the centuries.

The graph had an ambitious perspective, as its extrapolated progress in top speeds indicated that humanity was only four years away from reaching so-called escape velocity, i.e. the escape velocity needed to send a rocket into orbit around Earth. It was about 28,000 km/h.

Four years? This prediction puzzled the team, as NASA had no such plans. The Russians, however, did, and four years later the Soviet Union set a global speed record by sending a rocket into orbit. Then the Americans joined the space race. In 1969, Apollo 10 zoomed back to Earth from the Moon, barely touching 40,000 km/h. In 1976, Helios 2, a probe designed to almost touch the sun, flirted with absurd speeds of around 252,792 km/h. Then came the Parker Solar Probe in 2018, which is destined to pass the Sun at up to 700,000 km/h. Just to make it concrete: At 700,000 km/h (200 km/s) you will travel around the Earth in just 3 minutes and 26 seconds.

Let's think about the perspective of these varying speeds. The first single-celled organisms on Earth were almost immobile wanderers. Fast-forward to the dinosaur era 76–66 million years ago, where predators such as velociraptor and ornithomimus could probably reach speeds of around 60 km/h. Nature's current speed record is held by the cheetah, which can sprint with bursts of up to 120 km/h. It took the biosphere an astonishing 3.7 billion years to reach this speed level.

In stark contrast, the technosphere's Parker Solar Probe reached a speed of around 700,000 km/h in just 1.5 million years from the time humans presumably gained control of fire. This means that the technosphere was five billion times faster than the biosphere in achieving speed records. And it is just an early example of how extreme the technosphere can be.

From Smoke to Mirrors

There is another story of acceleration that is even more remarkable. Imagine you were in China 3,200 years ago. You stood on a mountain and saw small puffs of smoke rising in the distance. With these smoke signals, the Chinese led the way in communication speed worldwide.

If you considered each puff of smoke as a binary digit – a "1" for smoke and a "0" for no smoke – you could get an idea of how the communication worked. Visual signals, such as the sight of smoke, moved at the speed of light, but that didn't help much if the bandwidth was low. Assuming the sender of the message could turn the smoke on and off three times per minute, this corresponded to a bandwidth of 0.05 bits per second. Despite this painfully low bandwidth, the ability to distinguish these messages over a distance of 10 km was a major advance.

But about 3,000 years later, the industrial revolution brought inventions such as the telegraph, then the radio, and finally computers, revolutionizing communication speeds and bandwidth in ways that far exceeded imagination. In 1837, the first commercial electric telegraph was launched in England.

Let's talk about computers. Computers are fundamentally different from all previous technologies because they are universal machines that can be programmed to perform any kind of data manipulation. Previous technologies were typically designed for one specific task, e.g. a hammer to drive nails or a loom to make cloth. Computers, on the other hand, are capable of performing an infinite number of tasks, depending on the program they are running. This universal property makes computers fundamentally different from all previous technologies and has paved the way for the digital revolution we are experiencing today.

Originally, the term computer did not mean a machine, but a person who performed calculations. If we go far back in history, people would have used pebbles as aids to count – or their fingers. A traditional finger-based counting method used the thumb to touch each of the 12 knuckles on the 4 fingers (except the thumb itself) on one hand. This method made it possible to count up to 12 on a single hand. By using both hands, one could count to 24, which is why a day is still divided into 24 hours. Alternatively, people counted with their 10 fingers, which led to the decimal system.

As far as we know, the first real calculator was the abacus, invented around 2700 BCE in Mesopotamia. Fast-forward a couple of millennia, and we see quirky mechanical calculators in the 17th century. These machines, although different from clocks, used gears and levers similar to clockwork mechanisms. They could perform calculations 10 to 100 times faster than the abacus.

At the end of the 19th century, analog computers played a role. These machines used physical things like electricity or motion to solve problems. They were good at calculating things that were constantly changing, like predicting tides. Although they were not as versatile as today's computers, they were fast and important for developing technology and science.

World War II led to the creation of the first electronic computers: giant machines filled with vacuum tubes.

ENIAC, completed in 1945, was the world's first electronic, programmable computer. It could perform up to 5,000 additions or subtractions per second, which was many thousands of times faster than manual calculation with an abacus.

The next major breakthrough was seen in the 1950s with integrated circuits, or so-called microchips. In 1964, the CDC 6600 became the first supercomputer, which was about 30–300 billion times faster than could be done with an abacus.

Development continued exponentially. In 1993, Thinking Machines CM-5 1 GFLOPS could do in one second what would take a person with an abacus more than 3,000 years. And we repeat that it was in 1993.

Just four years later, ASCI Red became the first supercomputer to break the teraflop barrier (1,000 gigaFLOPS), boasting performance a million times faster than recent supercomputers. In 2023, the world's fastest supercomputer, Frontier, dominated with an astonishing 1.19 exa-FLOPS (1.19 quintillion calculations per second).

So the acceleration has been massive, and while computer performance has doubled roughly every 16 months, the fastest period of human brain growth, which as previously mentioned occurred between 800,000 and 200,000 years ago, saw a doubling in size over a much longer time frame of about 600,000 years. This corresponds to a difference in doubling time between human brains and electronic computer capacity of about 275 million times! And it means that the annual production of tokens after the development of computers also has increased millions of times faster than before.

The explosive advances in computer performance did not stand alone. Similar developments were seen in areas such as data storage and bit rate in telecommunications. In 2025, the fastest commercially deployed bit rate in telecommunications is around 400 gigabits per second. To put that in perspective, that's a whopping 8 trillion times faster than the 0.05 bits per second that ancient Chinese smoke signals could deliver 3,200 years earlier.

The continuous acceleration in the performance of these technologies has also been driven by innovations in so-called heterogeneous computing, where entire ecosystems of different and specialized chips work together to solve complex tasks at lightning speed. This approach is reminiscent of the way the brain works, where different areas specialize in different tasks, but work harmoniously together to achieve impressive results.

COMPLEXITY CASCADE #9

- **What?** Launching computers and telecommunications
- **When?** Telegraph in 1837 and programmable electronic computer in 1945
- **Why?** Scientific understanding of electricity and electromagnetism

Common Denominators in the Development of Complexity

In general, there are many phenomena in our journey from nothing to hyperintelligence that resemble each other. Yakov Zeldovich described a simple mechanism, known as the Zeldovich pancake, to explain the formation of large-scale structures in the universe, reminiscent of what civilization has done for humans. But to start with the universe, galaxies consist of voids, dust, nebulae, stars with planets, giant stars, and black holes. The larger the objects, the rarer they become. If you run a Zeldovich model for extreme values through a computer, it creates a simulated universe/galaxy (see Figure 12.1).

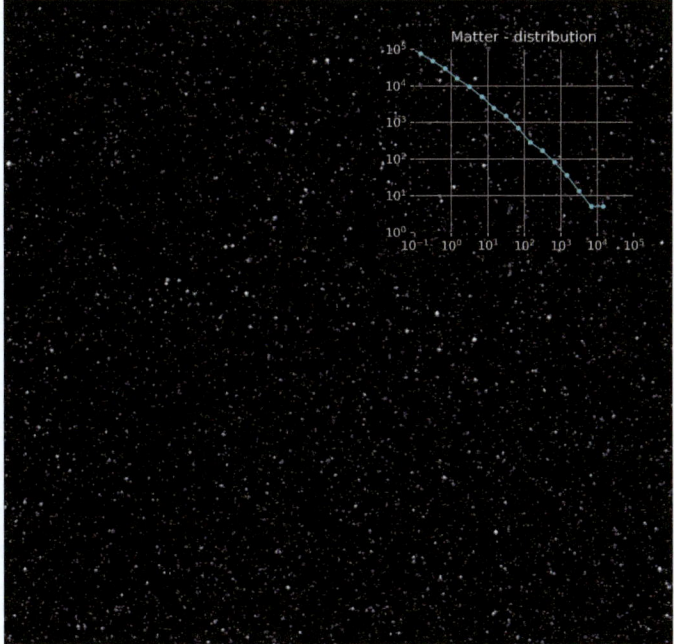

Figure 12.1 Simulated Milky Way. *The mathematical Zeldovich-model manages to both spread and compress matter, which is why it describes both the early and current galaxy evolution of the universe well. The inserted graph shows the occurrence of matter by size in the simulation, and one sees the extreme distribution.*

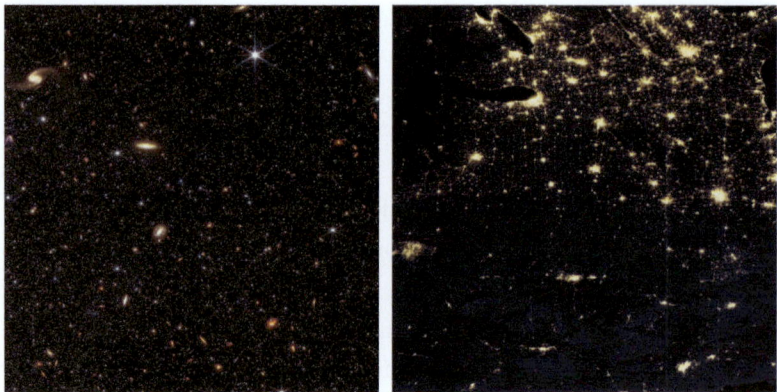

Figure 12.2 Examples of extremes in practice. *The left image shows the distribution of cosmic objects in a galaxy (you see other galaxies in the background) and the right image shows the distribution of human urbanization on a land area, seen as a satellite image of cities at night. The two phenomena in the real world are mathematically the same. Both images illustrate critical density. You could almost say that the innovation of the stars is due to gravity and the innovation of humans is due to cohesion.*

In practice, the consequences of his formula may look like the two images in Figure 12.2.

Overall, we see how 10 key dynamics for dynamic systems play out again and again in, for example, ecosystems and the digital economy:

- **Combinatorial Explosions:** This is our principle of a creative outburst, where new ideas arise by combining existing elements. The Cambrian explosion, a period of rapid speciation 541 million years ago, is an example. Here, a wealth of complex species arose, often by combining existing genetic information and establishing cooperative ecosystems. But something similar happened much later in technology, when, for example, the steam engine or the internet was introduced.

- **Standardized Interoperability:** Just as genetic codes are universal among organisms, digital systems rely on standardized protocols for seamless communication. USB sticks that fit all computers are an example of a standard that promotes innovation and collaboration.

- **Evolutionary Platforms and Coevolution:** App stores and cloud platforms provide space for continuous development, promoting innovation and diversity in the digital ecosystem. These platforms act as "digital rainforests" that support a wealth of apps and services. Hardware and software companies adapt to each other's innovations, just as species evolve in response to each other.

- **Critical Density:** Stars, rainforests, and cities are examples of critical density that creates innovation. Perhaps also black holes. Server parks and computer chips do the same by increasing data density as much as possible.

- **First-mover Advantages and Evolutionary Inertia:** Being first in a new niche gives an evolutionary advantage. Just like owning a prime piece of land, it is difficult to displace the first occupant. Early events can also have long-lasting consequences – "frozen accidents" – that shape evolution. Examples include the mapping of DNA codons to amino acids and the number of limbs in different animal groups. Similarly, early technology innovators such as Microsoft and Apple established dominant positions that were difficult to break. These "first movers" can set standards, build brand loyalty, and create network effects that give them a significant advantage in the market.

- **Cascade Progress:** Ecosystems are constantly changing. Small changes can trigger massive shifts, where species become extinct and new ones arise. This adaptation is a biological arms race. This is so-called "self-organized criticality," where sudden shifts occur naturally in complex systems. Similarly, the first growth on the internet led to exponential growth in online services and e-commerce platforms.

- **Increasing Returns:** The diversity of an ecosystem benefits each species. However, increasing returns is also a key concept within information technology in particular. The more people who use a social network, the more attractive it becomes for others to join. This can lead to a winner-takes-all dynamic, where large platforms dominate the market.

- **Hyper-sociality and Network Effects:** Social networks thrive on connectivity, and the value increases as more users sign up. This leads to platforms like Facebook and LinkedIn dominating the market. Something similar happens in many aspects of biological life where the success of a species or ecosystem depends on the number and strength of its connections, such as mycorrhizal networks in forests or social structures in animal groups, which enhance survival and resource sharing.

- **Freebies and Freemium Models:** Many software companies offer basic services for free while charging for premium features, reflecting how ecosystems provide resources. Think of Spotify, which offers free music with ads, while a premium subscription provides ad-free music and offline listening. But flowers do the same for bees.

- **Disintermediation:** Online shopping allows customers to buy products directly from manufacturers or sellers, without having to go through physical stores. This reduces costs and gives consumers a greater choice. In ecosystems, direct interactions between predators and prey bypass intermediary species, optimizing energy transfer; just as in traditional markets, farmers selling directly to consumers eliminate the need for wholesalers.

All this and more has meant that since the advent of coal-powered steam engines, global real GDP has increased by an astonishing 45,000%, leading to an unprecedented explosion in collective intelligence – and strides on the journey towards hyperintelligence.

13.
THE BIG BANG OF INTELLIGENCE

This chapter explores the emergence of artificial intelligence (AI) and follows its development from early language models to the potential breakthrough towards artificial general intelligence (AGI). We will delve into AI's unique capabilities, such as unlimited memory, instant knowledge sharing, creativity, and fast learning abilities. In addition, we will examine the challenges and controversies surrounding the development of AI, as well as discuss its potential impact on the intelligence and society of the future.

In 2019, the world was introduced to OpenAI's GPT-2, but let's be honest – it went a little under the radar. Although GPT-2 could spit out text, it was often like listening to a confused friend trying to explain quantum mechanics after a long night out: semi-coherent and with a tendency to lose the thread, especially when it came to basic math. So yes, the techies were a bit curious, but most ordinary people never heard of it.

But the following year GPT-3 appeared on the scene, and it was on a completely different level. With its impressive 175 billion parameters, GPT-3 could suddenly create text that could often fool people into thinking it was written by a human. It could write entire essays, summarize complex texts, and answer questions with an accuracy that made many jaws drop. But even though the techies cheered, GPT-3 still remained a bit of a hidden treasure for the general public.

Then in 2022 GPT-3.5 appeared, and suddenly AI became hot. This updated version made people open their eyes and ask: Is this really a machine? The product got 100 million users in just two months! Never before in human history had a new product gained so many users so quickly. It was like watching a rock star shoot to the top of the charts. Suddenly everyone was talking about AI, and it was no longer just for nerds – now it was something everyone could play with.

AI impressively demonstrates how critical density drives innovation. In this case, it is not atoms, nerve cells, or humans that are condensed, but rather global information. Imagine AI as a giant magnet that attracts and gathers data from all over the world into one central point – the data center. Here, an almost unfathomable high data density is achieved: petabyte after exabyte of information, packed into servers and stacked in racks side by side to maximize internal communication, storage space, and access speed.

This digital supermass behaves like a gravitational force, relentlessly pulling in new information and forging novel connections between disparate datasets. AI data centers, in this sense, are not just repositories but engines of continuous learning and synthesis. While search engine data parks also cluster vast amounts of information, they primarily function as reference systems, mapping existing knowledge and indexing content. AI, however, operates on an entirely different level. Here, it is not merely the links between data that hold critical density – but the data itself. Each new piece of information feeds into an ever-evolving intelligence, where raw knowledge is not just stored but actively transformed, refined, and leveraged to generate new insights.

From Dream to Reality

The dream of artificial intelligence has existed in humanity for a long time. In fact, it was discussed in antiquity, where philosophers such as Aristotle considered automated machines and logical reasoning. However, the actual conceptual basis for AI was laid in the 1940s and 1950s. One of the pioneers in AI was the British mathematician Alan Turing. In 1950 he published a groundbreaking article entitled "Computing Machinery and Intelligence." In this article he introduced what we know today as the Turing test. This test is designed to assess whether a machine can act as intelligently as a human in a conversation, by seeing if it can fool a person into thinking they are communicating with another human.

The official birth of AI as a scientific field is often traced back to a conference in 1956 at Dartmouth College, where the term "artificial intelligence" was launched. The mood at the time was characterized by enthusiasm and optimism, and pioneers such as John McCarthy, Marvin Minsky, Allen Newell, and Herbert Simon developed early AI programs. But the AI field soon ran into a dead end, and in the 1970s it almost came to a standstill. This period, known as the "first AI winter," was characterized by low funding and declining interest.

The 1980s offered a revival with the advent of so-called expert systems – programs designed to mimic the decision-making abilities of human experts. However, the joy was short-lived due to a lack of data and computing power, which led to the second "AI winter" in the late 1980s and early 1990s. So it was a bit of a wet blanket, and when a number of international AI experts were asked for the first time in 1999 when an AI would pass the Turing test, about 20% thought it would never happen, while the consensus among the rest was that it would be achieved around the year 2100.

But in the late 1990s and early 2000s, things started to move faster with the advent of so-called machine learning. Driven by increased computing power and data availability, machine learning actually led to decent progress in areas such as natural language processing, computer vision, and robotics. And there were outright triumphs. In 1992, for example, an AI was developed that could beat the best human players in backgammon, and chess grandmaster Garry Kasparov was defeated by IBM's Deep Blue in 1997.

Despite these achievements, however, AI had not yet begun to revolutionize society as a whole. A major breakthrough that paved the way for this revolution came with the development of a technology called deep learning. This involved the use of neural networks with many deep layers (hence the term deep), which were able to learn from huge amounts of data.

In 2016, DeepMind's AlphaGo amazed the entire Go world. Go is the most complex board game in the world, but AlphaGo was trained with data on millions of human games, after which it wildly defeated Lee Sedol, a legendary Go master. It was a victory that many thought was impossible, or at least a long way off in the future. But what really shocked the world was not only AlphaGo's victory, but also the speed with which it had been trained. By playing millions of games against itself over just six weeks, AlphaGo had developed unparalleled skills.

However, the story did not end there. The following year, Google launched the program's successor, which they called AlphaGo Zero. The reason they added "zero" to its name was that this new program literally had zero initial knowledge about how to play the game, apart from the rules. It nevertheless surpassed the pre-trained AlphaGo after just nine hours of training through self-play. AlphaGo Zero's self-learning was astonishingly fast compared to human games. While a typical game between humans can take an hour or two, AlphaGo Zero played 4.9 million games against itself in just three days. It could play over 15–20 games with itself in one second!

Imagine you receive an untrained version of AlphaGo Zero one Saturday morning. You play Go against it before breakfast, and it acts like a complete amateur. The computer is stupid as a door, you think arrogantly, while you munch on your breakfast. After the meal you go out for a run, but meanwhile the computer plays 100,000 games against itself. This dataset is then used to train a new and improved version of the program. This new version learns to predict which side will win from a given position, and which moves that winning version will prefer. Then the new version plays about 100 games against the original version. It takes about five seconds. If the new version wins at least 55% of the matches, the previous version is replaced. If not, the process is repeated, accumulating more data and further refining skills.

You don't know anything about all that, but when you get back from your run and have had a shower and a cup of coffee, you try to play against the computer again. To your astonishment, you lose this time.

Later in the day, while you are out shopping, AlphaGo Zero continues to go through cycles of play, training new versions and replacing older ones. To improve its strategy, the computer uses a method called Monte Carlo Tree Search (MCTS). After about 17 or 18 iterations, it has become able to beat a world champion. You don't know that either, when you get home from shopping at 6 p.m. and take the third game of the day, in which AlphaGo Zero wiped the floor with you.

The Big Breakthrough

With the launch of AlphaGo Zero, optimism among AI experts naturally increased significantly, and many began to believe that the so-called artificial general intelligence (AGI) could be within reach. AGI refers to a hypothetical AI that possesses human-level intelligence across a broad spectrum of cognitive abilities, not just the ability to conduct human-like conversations as measured by the Turing test.

In a 2019 survey conducted by the Lifeboat Foundation, the median prediction estimated that AGI would be achieved around 2075. This was 25 years earlier than the original predictions for passing the Turing test, which was set for 2100. In 2021, the organization Meticulous conducted a new survey, where the consensus prediction for passing the Turing test was moved forward to 2042. The following year, in 2022, the consensus on when AGI would be achieved changed significantly with a new estimate set for 2030. In just three years, the consensus on AGI's achievement thus moved a full 45 years forward!

Meanwhile, the cost of AI processing fell massively. In 2023 alone, the cost per token used for training for GPT-3.5 fell by 96.7%. In this context, it should be said that in the AI community, a token is defined as a word, part of a long word, a grammatical sign, or symbol or a number. So this is a bit more detailed than the way we otherwise describe tokens in this book, where we talk about it as a representation of an overarching meaning.

In 2024, some new models had trained with about a billion times more computing power, or compute, as it is usually called, than DeepMind AI, which excelled in Atari games in 2013. This exponential growth also applied to model size, which with billions of parameters was now the norm.

GPT was a pioneer among so-called large language models (LLMs), and it was an example of what is called generative AI. The fact that AI is generative means that it can create new content, such as text, code, or even images, instead of just classifying or analyzing existing data. So it has creative computer imagination.

One aspect of the new LLMs that surprised many was precisely their enormous creativity. If someone after their launch questioned the importance of AI with statements such as "Yes, but it will never be as creative as humans," you could be sure that they had not experimented much with generative AI. These models could write original stories, poems, songs, and even computer code with a creativity that many previously thought was reserved for humans. And they could make pictures, videos, music, and paintings. In fact, they often surpassed humans in creative tasks.

Training a large LLM like ChatGPT requires enormous computing power, where thousands of specialized processors (graphics processing units [GPUs] or tensor processing units [TPUs]) work together for weeks or months to fine-tune the model's understanding of language, typically using the latest and greatest hardware. Once the model is trained, the same hardware can be used to perform so-called inferences, which is the model's application phase, where it answers questions from many simultaneous users. Because the model's inferences each require far less computing power than its initial training, the system used for training can now handle hundreds of thousands or millions of simultaneous inferences, often through distributed networks. Inference efficiency can be optimized through post-training and inference scaling, where the model can be adapted to handle specific tasks faster and more accurately, for example. These processes can also involve the model learning from user feedback or being optimized to perform better on expected types of queries. It can also on its own initiative constantly search for new patterns in data that no human has ever found or at least uploaded to an online source. In some cases, it can also practice answering questions that it has not yet been asked. Just like an intelligent and curious human learns constantly, so does an LLM.

From Text to Context

Large AI projects often use transformers, a technology that was first introduced in the landmark article "Attention Is All You Need" by Google researchers in 2017. This technology allows models to focus on important words in a sentence, regardless of where they are located, giving them a strong ability to understand the context.

Imagine how this improves machine translation: If an English sentence like "He kicked the bucket" is directly translated to other languages, we lose the meaning. Transformers, however, are context-aware and should therefore know that the expression "kicked the bucket". But they may also understand that the specific text uses slang, which is why "han tog billetten" instead of "han døde" is the best translation of this particular text. At the same time, transformers understand that *The Washington Post* should not have a headline on the front page that says "England's queen has kicked the bucket."

It's kind of the same way we humans use the context of a conversation to understand the meaning behind what is said. A sentence like "That's just fantastic" can mean something completely different depending on whether the tone is sarcastic, genuine, or resigned. Our neocortex understands that.

However, context is not just about a single sentence. When we read news, we link new information to our existing knowledge and experiences. So we draw on a wealth of mental threads all the time. Similarly, a transformer model can draw threads to other texts and ideas. A large language model can link a text with knowledge from millions of books, articles, manuals, and posts on social media, etc. In principle, it therefore has the opportunity to see far more context than any human being. This makes AI transformers a revolutionary technology with endless application possibilities. Inserted into an LLM, they can create a global, omniscient neocortex.

Context is also meaning, and when transformers see the context in, for example, a sentence, they thereby create tokens related to that text. We can therefore view transformers as token machines. These token machines are then placed in AI models, which we can then think of as token factories.

Incidentally, transformers – and thus also the tokens they create – are not just about text. They can also analyze and create other data types such as images, audio, and video, creating so-called multimodal transformers. These can, for example, create connections between text descriptions and visual data or even link audio to visual elements. This has made it possible to develop advanced applications such as DALL-E and CLIP, which can generate or classify images based on text input.

Finally, transformers process data hierarchically. The first steps analyze basic details, while later layers build more complex ideas, creating a form of abstraction. The ability to understand details and see the big picture at the same time gives transformers enormous potential. They can even review their own results to create consistency, just as we humans keep track of a conversation.

Miniature Robot Brains

Now we need to look at AI agents, which are a kind of miniature robot brain that can act independently. Think, for example, of virtual assistants, self-driving cars, and robot systems or AlphaGo Zero. It is largely agents that drive such systems. Agents in a self-driving car use sensors as input. Agents in AlphaGo use simulation and opponents' moves in the Go game as input. Other agents use other input. But all agents process their information and then perform actions based on their programmed goals. This is reminiscent of our brain's sensory and motor systems, where sensory organs collect data, or the imagination creates them, after which the brain processes them, and the body then reacts. When you drive a car while your mind is elsewhere, we can say that it is a number of biological agents in the brain that control the car. Call it biologic agentic driving, if you will.

A crucial aspect of AI agents is their ability to make decisions based on direct rewards, often guided by so-called reinforcement learning. Here they learn through feedback from their actions in the form of rewards or sanctions. For example, losing a Go game or driving a car into a wall can provide negative feedback. This feedback refines the agents' strategies over time, reminiscent of the brain's reward system, where actions that lead to pleasurable outcomes are reinforced by neurotransmitters such as dopamine.

AI agents can also use algorithms to simulate future scenarios and assess potential outcomes. For example, they can analyze the long-term consequences of decisions in a chess game here and now – would it be wise to sacrifice a knight to achieve a better position for a later attack?

This mirrors the function of the brain's prefrontal cortex, which is responsible for planning, decision-making, and predicting consequences. A well-functioning person often makes short-term sacrifices to achieve long-term gains. The brain uses these abilities to navigate complex environments and make informed decisions in dynamic, real-world situations – just as it is mimicked with AI. Furthermore, AI agents can recognize patterns, make decisions, and learn from data. They can thus improve their performance over time. Our brain works in a similar way.

AI Swarms

To understand the difference between AI transformers and AI agents, you can think of it this way: AI transformers are models that are really good at processing and understanding context across text, images, and other inputs, allowing them to write essays, predict the weather, analyze genes, and all sorts of other things. AI agents, on the other hand, are models that can make decisions and perform actions such as driving a car or solving problems in real time. Where transformers focus on data understanding, agents are designed for action and interaction with their environment.

Now, the term agentic workflow enters the picture. It describes clusters of AI agents collaborating seamlessly, often referred to as multi-agent systems (MAS). Think of it as AI evolving its own equivalent of biological complexity – progressing from individual organelles to multicellular organisms, and eventually, self-organizing ecosystems.

There is an important perspective here. Earlier on, we studied the fruit fly brain, with its 139,000 neurons and some 55 million synaptic connexions, or nerve cell connections. This is roughly comparable to an early-generation CPU like the Intel 4004 from 1971, which processed structured tasks with limited power. Like a CPU, the fruit fly brain is optimized for efficiency, enabling flight, sensory processing, and learning within a tiny neural network. However, fruit flies largely function as independent agents, whereas ants, despite having similarly small brains, display remarkable *collective* intelligence.

Now, contrast a fruit fly to a colony of ants. An ant brain has 250,000 to 1 million neurons, but its true power lies in swarm intelligence. Just as modern AI distributes tasks across multiple processors, ants coordinate foraging, nest-building, and defense through local interactions, creating a decentralized superorganism. While fruit flies rely on individual learning, ants function like a distributed computing system, where intelligence emerges from the network itself, which may contain, for instance, 10,000 ants.

This parallels how humans and AI are evolving. The most powerful systems today are not isolated supercomputers but collaborative networks of intelligence, from multi-agent systems to cloud computing. As with ants, true intelligence scales with connectivity, not just individual power.

This is the perspective we have to bear in mind when thinking about AI swarms. In many cases, these systems integrate both AI agents and transformers, forming what we can call a transformer-assisted multi-agent system (TAMAS). A TAMAS functions as a custom-built artificial brain, where the synergy between agents and transformers amplifies intelligence. The more components you integrate, the more emergent and sophisticated the system becomes – yet another example of the critical density principle in action.

The foundational building blocks for such systems are already available. On huggingface.com, an open platform for AI innovation, users contribute thousands of AI models – covering everything from language processing to vision and robotics. This repository of intelligence is expanding at an exponential rate, doubling approximately every five months and surpassing one million models by October 2024. As the ecosystem of AI models continues to grow, so too does the potential for more autonomous, collaborative, and intelligent AI systems.

How do such AI swarms work? The magic lies in iteration. Imagine a back-and-forth conversation: You can ask an agent to reflect on its own work, i.e. to be introspective. Or you can have different agents build on each other's drafts. This iterative process refines the results with each step.

But agent-based workflows can encompass more than just simple back-and-forth iterations. Imagine a team of specialized AI agents each with unique skills. Some may be experts in pattern recognition, others in data retrieval, and still others in calculations, illustrations or tagging. This diverse group works together as a well-oiled team, where some agents are even trained as critical troubleshooters. Together they function as a swarm that follows established principles, but otherwise operates autonomously and may continuously improve itself through experience.

Such swarm approaches can be used to develop business plans, software programs, and much more. It's like having a living community of creative minds working together, each lifting the work of the others to new heights, all the while learning.

Reverse Evolution on Steroids

The emergence of AI adds a fascinating twist to the story of cosmic complexity. The universe's first complex structures were not "alive." Crystals and snowflakes were examples of impressive patterns and shapes, but they were static and created no further complexity than themselves. The earliest forms of software were also static – programs were packaged on floppy disks, sold in stores, and remained unchanged. Sure, the software you bought in the store could probably be used to create complexity, but the software itself was unchanged. However, AI has completely changed this dynamic. AI is often "alive" in the sense that AI is constantly learning, adapting, and developing new skills, often without direct human intervention. Think of it as an employee on a team.

But if we see AI as a parallel to biological life, there is a striking difference. In biology, life started with simple nerve cells over 600 million years ago. Over billions of years, these developed into more complex brains, and eventually advanced language arose among humans. AI follows the opposite path. What seems intuitive and easy for us humans, such as motor skills and sensory perception, requires enormous computational resources for AI – a phenomenon termed Moravec's paradox. At the same time, higher reasoning and abstract thoughts are easier for computers because it requires less computing power than the instinctive abilities that have evolved over millions of years in animals and humans.

In other words, where the evolution of biological life slowly moved from what we experience as simple to more complex cognitive abilities, AI takes the shortcut and jumps directly into the tasks that are advanced for us, while the "basic" abilities such as driving a car through a busy street is still a challenge.

However, AI is becoming increasingly adept at very complex pattern recognition and real-time decision-making. These advances have opened the door to a new frontier: physical AI, i.e. AI systems that can interact with and manipulate the physical world from the very self-driving cars that navigate busy streets to robot arms that perform complex and flexible tasks in factories such as waste sorting. This shift towards more practical tasks is largely driven by the revolution in agents and transformers.

Regarding the reverse order of the revolutions in biological and artificial intelligence, there is also an interesting parallel to human thinking. As we saw earlier, the brain can be divided into two systems: System 1, which is fast, intuitive, and automatic, and System 2, which is slower, more conscious, and analytical. This distinction is also relevant to AI. Current LLMs impress in their ability to process and generate text and images using a System 1-like approach – they work quickly and intuitively, often by predicting the most likely next token based on patterns in the data. This makes them excellent for tasks that require immediate responses and quick associations, such as generating rhymes or summarizing news.

On the other hand, traditional LLMs have had limitations in tasks that require deeper analysis and logical reasoning, known as System 2 thinking. While they could easily generate poems or provide superficial summaries, they have had challenges with complex tasks such as advanced mathematical problems or book writing that require slower, analytical thinking. However, significant progress was made with the introduction of OpenAI's o1 model in 2024. o1 was designed to mimic System 2 thinking by breaking down complex tasks into smaller steps and analyzing different scenarios to provide more thoughtful answers reasoning.

But even though both System 1 and System 2 thinking need to be continuously refined in AI, AI has many advantages compared to humans. A major advantage is its knowledge. It can have ready knowledge that is literally millions of times greater than that of any single person on the planet. AI can also be programmed to never forget what it learns, and since it is immortal, it can continue to accumulate knowledge and insight indefinitely. Humans, on the other hand, forget and die.

There's more: When an AI system learns something new, it can instantly transfer that knowledge to all other connected systems. This is a truly extraordinary capability – just imagine if every human being were born with instant access to all of humanity's accumulated knowledge!

This phenomenon, known as transfer learning, enables AI to apply insights from one task to another, significantly accelerating learning and enhancing performance across different domains. But AI doesn't just learn – it shares. This creates a self-reinforcing cycle of intelligence, where each breakthrough strengthens the whole system.

In effect, AI is transforming the entire globe into a gigantic meta-brain – a vast, interconnected web of intelligence, continuously fed by humans, AI models, robots, self-driving cars, and autonomous systems of every kind. As this process accelerates, critical data density reaches unprecedented levels, driving AI into a self-reinforcing spiral of perpetual improvement, where each new insight compounds into an unstoppable force of exponential progress.

While this may resemble the way natural ecosystems and even biogeo-chemical cycles have evolved on Earth – through self-organization and emergent complexity – AI operates on an entirely different time scale. Unlike biological systems, which rely on slow adaptation over generations, the technosphere allows data and insights to be shared across boundaries at blistering speed, unleashing a hyper-accelerated evolutionary process that continuously reshapes intelligence itself. So, while DNA built a smart biosphere over billions of years, AI is now turbocharging the cosmic evolution of genius at an exponential pace, compressing eons of innovation into decades.

14.
THE NEW TOKEN FACTORIES

AI's hunger for data is growing, but what happens when we run out? This chapter takes you into the future, where the data wall challenges AI's development and shows how physical AI, synthetic data, inference, and self-play pave the way for intelligent systems to learn and evolve entirely on their own. Follow the events as AI creates its own knowledge, moves away from home, and spreads in the physical environment.

In 2023, the world was abuzz with excitement over GPT-4, which outperformed 97% of high school students on US college entrance exams and answered complex questions faster than any student. It was a remarkable achievement. So what enabled this impressive development? Faster chips played an important role, consistent with Moore's Law, which predicts a doubling of chip capacity roughly every two years. But an even bigger breakthrough came from chips specifically designed for AI tasks. Funnily enough, it was GPUs – originally developed for computer games – that became crucial for AI research. GPUs are particularly well-suited for parallel data processing, making it possible to process large amounts of data simultaneously.

In addition, massive investments meant that massive data facilities were now available for AI. This combination of factors resulted in the amount of data processing, or so-called compute, in leading models growing approximately 1,000 times over four years. Not a thousand percent, but a thousand times! Furthermore, over the same four years, AI algorithms became about 100 times more efficient at solving tasks with the same amount of computation. The combined effect of these boosts was a total increase of 100,000 times in so-called effective compute.

However, this rate of progress was not entirely new. In 2024, OpenAI analyzed the growth in effective computing power used for the largest AI training models over the previous 12 years. They found that this had doubled on average every 3.4 months. This equates to an increase of 147,000 times every five years and 69 billion times in a decade.

Will it continue? In 2023, Mo Gawdat, former Chief Business Officer at Google X and author of Scary Smart, made a bold prediction: By 2049, AI could be a billion times more intelligent than humans. This would mean that the evolution of artificial brains would be about 600 million billion times faster than the evolution of natural brains had been.

So, how far has AI come compared to humans? Let's put the current stage in perspective. The human brain contains about 1,000 trillion synapses, which can be compared to transistors in chips. Compare that to NVIDIA A100 GPUs from 2024, which each have 54 billion transistors. Although this is less than the number of synapses in a human brain, a computer farm with 20,000 A100 GPUs would have about 1,080 trillion transistors combined. This brings them within reach of the brain's complexity. However, a transistor is not necessarily as smart as a synapse. On the other hand, transistors in GPUs actually change state about a million times faster than synapses in the human brain. Considering this, a cluster of 20,000 GPUs may have about 2,000,000 times more raw computing power than a brain. So in that respect, the leading AI models can really fire it up. That's why a server park with an LLM can simultaneously conduct intelligent dialogues with millions of users.

Physical AI and Multimodal Wonders

Imagine this scene: At a lively dinner party, the air is filled with laughter. But then a glass slips off the table. In an instant, your friend Tom snatches it from the air. This instinctive reaction is more complex than it seems. Tom's brain instantly assesses the situation, recognizing the falling glass and its potential consequences. Wine and shards of glass! He doesn't hesitate to try to catch it, unlike a glove or napkin, which he would probably let fall. His decision to grab the wine glass also triggers a series of precise, coordinated movements as he reaches out, opens his hand, and secures the glass at the perfect time. This lightning-fast action demonstrates the enormous computing power that our brains effortlessly exert to navigate the physical world.

Consider another scenario: Susan assures Ole that she is fine, but he notices a fleeting, almost imperceptible twitch in her face that tells a different story. His gut feeling prompts him to ask, "Are you sure?" Tears now begin to roll, and she opens up about her problems. Could a robot pick up on Susan's true feelings, even though she tried to hide them? To operate seamlessly in the physical world, AI needs to master such tasks.

To unlock the potential of physical AI, researchers are turning to a new type of AI model that can understand the world in all its multisensory complexity. Unlike traditional AI, which primarily learns from text, vision-language-action models (VLAMs) combine visual, auditory, and spatial information with data about a robot's movements and surroundings. This gives AI a more comprehensive picture of the world, reduces errors, and enables systems to tackle new tasks without the need for explicit training.

Now imagine a few years in the future where such a robot could overcome the data wall and achieve massively superhuman intelligence using agent and transformer technologies. The training of these smart and also inexpensive human-like, or so-called "humanoid" robots can be achieved in several innovative ways. For example, humans can wear sensors that record their movements and actions, which the robot then mimics to learn tasks.

Alternatively, robots can observe humans performing tasks by replicating these actions. A third approach may be to create a digital twin of the robot in the metaverse, where it learns by navigating virtual environments, similar to Waymo's method of training self-driving cars. For such purposes, the metaverse can be sped up by 10,000 or a million times.

Once a robot is trained, its knowledge can be transferred to other robots, making the training process both efficient and cumulative. Unlike human training, which is parallel, temporary, and fleeting, robot training creates a lasting and ever-growing store of skills and knowledge that can be shared and maintained indefinitely. And thus, robots are ready to move away from home, away from the constant protective care of humans. They become adults and can manage on their own.

The Data Wall and Token Factories

The fact that robots can eventually learn and share insights more efficiently than humans is relevant to the discussion of whether big AI models will run out of additional training data. AI requires data, and the internet – which has grown exponentially since the 1990s – has provided an ever-expanding buffet of information. However, not all data is created equal – much of it is redundant or irrelevant for AI training. While cat videos have their charm, the intellectual nourishment for AI primarily comes from high-quality sources such as books, articles, and scientific papers, which have only grown at a rate of about 4–5% annually. As LLMs began to show their potential, concerns arose that they were quickly exhausting all readily available meaningful data, leading to fears that the rate of increase would slow down. In other words, a data wall loomed as AI's hunger for knowledge began to outpace the rate at which new and valuable information was being created.

Will this slow down the future development of AI performance? Not necessarily. New forms of data will emerge, such as those collected by smart robots, as previously discussed. Other sources, including data from smart homes, healthcare, and other sectors, will become crucial.

Much of this will be gathered via sensors in what is called the Internet of Things (IoT).

So-called federated learning will also become a rich and rapidly growing data source. Imagine a world where your personal AI assistant, which learns your habits and preferences, also helps make the general AI we all use smarter – without compromising your privacy. Federated learning enables personal AI to train and improve itself on your data without transferring that data to a central server. Instead, the AI only shares the lessons learned in the form of updated model parameters with the central AI. These updates are then combined with updates from thousands of other personal AIs, creating a collective intelligence that benefits everyone while maintaining individual privacy.

When considering data access, it's important to note that data processing varies widely depending on context. Reading a book, for example, involves processing a limited and linear stream of textual information. Although complex, parallel, and non-linear associations and inferences may arise while reading, the rate of token generation and processing is constrained by reading speed and comprehension.

Navigating a busy street, on the other hand, is far more data-intensive. It requires massive parallel processing of visual data (traffic signals, pedestrians, obstacles), auditory signals (car horns, conversations), body positions, and sensor readings. These inputs generate a vast number of data points that the robot's AI must instantly interpret, weigh, and act upon.

This shift paves the way for multimodal learning, where AI systems train on diverse data sources – text, images, and sensory input – helping overcome the limitations of the data wall.

Self-play, Synthetic Data, and Design Spaces

Another solution to the data wall is self-play, where AI systems improve by competing against themselves, as seen in AlphaGo programs. This process generates unique insights through so-called synthetic data, which means data generated by simulation. As an example, when pharmaceutical research moves from *in vivo* (experiments in living organisms) or *in vitro* (experiments in test tubes or petri dishes) to *in silico* (computer-simulated experiments), it is a move from physical experiments to synthetic data-driven simulations.

A more recent example is Waymo, which trains its autonomous driving systems by driving millions of real-world miles while simultaneously simulating billions more – about 1,000 times as many. These simulations test reactions to rare and challenging scenarios, and approximately 99.9% of its training data comes from self-play and is thus synthetic.

Similarly, AI that engages in self-play within scientific domains can generate enormous amounts of new data and tokens. When models analyze these datasets, they can explore countless combinations and possibilities through further self-play simulations. Each simulation generates new data and builds on existing knowledge, reflecting real-world innovation, where discoveries build upon one another.

When AI creates synthetic data, the process often begins with mathematical equations, as they function as highly compressed information. These equations describe complex systems and relationships in the simplest possible way, enabling AI to generate realistic data based on underlying patterns. This allows AI to create large amounts of synthetic data with high precision, even from relatively simple mathematical foundations.

While the term "synthetic data" may sound artificial, it is not fake data. Rather, it is machine-generated data that can contribute to combinatorial cascades. The quantity will therefore grow exponentially, meaning that an increasing proportion of AI training data in the future will originate from AI itself rather than humans.

A fascinating aspect of synthetic data is its ability to explore vast design spaces, which encompass all possible outcomes of a system.

A recent example of accelerated exploration of a design space occurred during the COVID-19 pandemic. After Chinese researchers sequenced and released the viral genome on January 11, 2020, Moderna used advanced computational techniques to test billions of potential mRNA sequences relevant to the virus in just two days, leading to the rapid development of their first COVID-19 vaccine candidate. A process that would typically have taken about four years was thus completed 500 times faster via self-play.

This example highlights why biochemistry is one of the most promising areas for synthetic data and self-play. The number of potential drug molecules is estimated to be a staggering figure – a gigantic design space that researchers are now navigating with AI models like ESM3, which can precisely design new proteins to achieve desired structures and functions.

Synthetic Data Escape Velocity?

Similarly, an analytical approach called system dynamics can be used to explore large design spaces in other domains. For instance, macroeconomists use this method to model how different economic policies or events might affect the overall economy.

AI-generated data comes from several sources:

- **Physical AI** – data compiled by robots, self-driving cars, and drones
- **Federated learning** – data voluntarily submitted by people using personal AI, but anonymized
- **IoT** – data from environmental sensors in smart homes, satellites, hospitals, and the broader environment
- **Digital datastreams** – such as those in finance and economics
- **Self-play** – simulating dynamic outputs for applications such as protein folding, cellular developments, social systems, and physical environments.

Such machine-generated and often synthetic data will generally be less messy than human-generated data found on the internet. However, we should not underestimate the importance of inference and post-training, where AI models continuously identify useful correlations within existing data that humans have not recognized, even though the data itself may have already been collected and made available. It is very possible that we have already reached – or are close to reaching – a threshold where synthetic data, created through autonomous inference, attains *escape velocity*, triggering a complexity cascade that will increasingly outperform human-generated data.

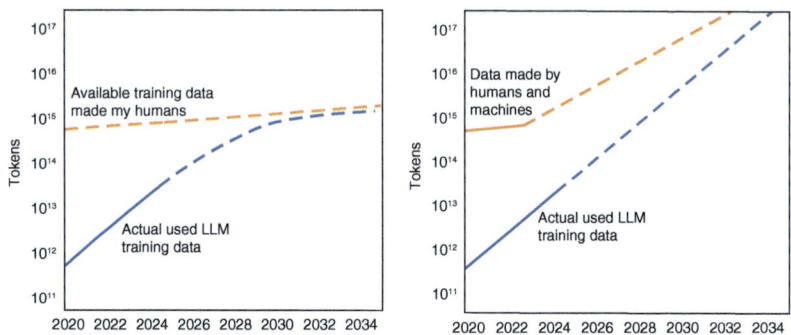

LLM training data with and without the use of synthetic data. *The graph on the left shows an expected data wall, which is seriously hit around 2029 if synthetic data is not used. The graph is based on the actually existing and used data. In the graph on the right, a loose estimate of the growth in synthetic data from 2022 has been added. This can lead to the data wall being very far in the future, if it exists at all.*

In addition to approaches involving synthetic data and post-training inference, there is also significant potential for improving output quality. Typically, AI has been much better at interpreting input than generating output, a difference often referred to as the generation gap. That gap will become increasingly smaller. So, it's not only that the systems will continue to get way smarter, but they will also become way better at expressing their insights well.

15.
LIFE DECODED!

Follow the pioneers who cracked the DNA code, hear how DNA sequencing went from being a slow and billion-dollar endeavor to an everyday tool, and how scientists are now not only reading the code of life but also editing it. From fighting disease to reviving ancient ecosystems, the ability to manipulate genes is changing our world in unimaginable ways. The future of life is being written, and you're about to get a front-row seat.

In the 1860s, a monk named Gregor Mendel made a fascinating discovery with his pea plants. By tracking traits like flower color and seed shapes across generations, he clearly identified hereditary patterns. At that time, the mechanisms of heredity were a mystery.

Fast-forward to 1953, when scientists James Watson and Francis Crick revealed the structure of DNA, marking a major breakthrough. In 1990, the Human Genome Project began with the goal of decoding this massive genetic code within 13 years. Progress was painfully slow in the early years, leading many to doubt that the project would be completed on time. But in 1998, Craig Venter, a scientist involved in the project, founded a private company called Celera Corporation. He proposed using an innovative technology called shotgun sequencing, which used 600 computers performing more than 1,000 billion calculations per second to speed up the process. Venter's method was initially met with skepticism but proved to be superior. Both competing teams reached their goals almost simultaneously in 2002, a year ahead of schedule. Remarkably, Venter's effort cost only $300 million, a tenth of the original budget, although it must be said that he benefited from access to the public project's data.

Sequencing and Barcoding

Since then, the prices of these technologies have continued to fall at blistering speeds. With 1990s technology, it cost a whopping $2.7 billion to sequence a single human genome. In 2025, the price reached between $300 and 1,000 – that's a drop of about 99.999% over 35 years. In addition, the time required for sequencing has decreased from 13 years to as little as a single day; an increase in speed of 4,600 times.

Genetic mapping is now moving to an industrial scale. Today, machines can scan entire ecosystems for traces of life at once. This is called environmental DNA or eDNA. Imagine this: You are standing in the middle of a forest and want to uncover the teeming life around you. Instead of looking for tracks or setting up camera traps, you simply take a cotton swab or a special card and gently swipe it across a leaf. Incredibly, this simple act can reveal DNA traces from hundreds of species living in the forest – even fish that birds have caught in nearby lakes or rivers. How does DNA from fish end up on tree leaves anyway? The fish's DNA passes through the bird and ends up in bird droppings, which dry up and are spread by the wind. Wild but true.

This revolutionary method gives us a whole new window into the hidden world of nature. An important tool for this is rapid so-called DNA barcoding. It analyzes small, specific areas of an organism's DNA to quickly identify its species.

Environmental DNA and barcoding have many applications. When you visit a Starbucks, you probably leave millions of DNA traces – without thinking about it. Your skin, saliva, hair, and fingerprints put small biological "business cards" on everything you touch, from the counter to the coffee cup. Even when you speak or breathe, you release small particles with your DNA that can be identified with modern technology. In short: When you walk out the door, part of you is still present in the room! This means that eDNA can be used to solve crimes.

Here's another example: You can use it to find out if there are pests like cockroaches or mice in a building. Or invasive species in an ecosystem. And through sewage water research, eDNA can tell us about pandemics.

There's a bonus: Scientists can also use the same DNA detective techniques to look for traces of life in the distant past. Typically, they will take a deep soil sample, run it through laboratory techniques, and analyze the soil sample's ancient DNA (or aDNA for ancient DNA). This helps us understand which creatures lived at a given time and place in the past. For example, a groundbreaking study led by Eske Willerslev used aDNA screening to map Greenland's biological past. Two million years ago, it turns out, this now icy landscape was teeming with elephants, mastodons, hares, lemmings, and horseshoe crabs. The researchers even found evidence of birch and poplar trees, indicating a climate that was far warmer than today's.

Editing Life

Back in 1962, Barbara McClintock discovered "jumping genes" that could move around in an organism's DNA. Scientists built on this knowledge by learning to insert foreign DNA into bacteria and create precise tools for cutting DNA. These steps laid the groundwork for the so-called CRISPR-based gene editing method and other powerful tools (CRISPR can target specific genes to add, remove, or alter genetic material). CRISPR has revolutionized genetics, and what used to take months can now be done in weeks or even days. In addition to CRISPR, there are base editors, prime editors, and gene drives. With base editors, you can correct a single error in the DNA without disturbing the parts around it. Prime editors provide even more precision. These make small, specific changes like adding or removing parts of the DNA or swapping one piece for another, all without causing the risky breaks in DNA strands that other methods can.

And then there are gene drives. These use gene editing tools such as CRISPR to potentially alter entire populations of organisms. To eradicate malaria, for example, scientists can use gene drives to alter the genes of mosquitoes so that they either become sterile or resistant to the malaria parasite. One variant is to ensure that all offspring are of the same sex. For example, a gene drive in mosquitoes can be engineered to produce only male offspring. Firstly, male mosquitoes never bite, so they cannot transmit malaria. With fewer females to reproduce, the overall mosquito population would naturally also decline or even disappear. Normally, genes have a 50% chance of being inherited, but gene drives can increase this probability to almost 100%, ensuring that the modified genes spread rapidly through the mosquito population.

A further genetic engineering tool, launched in 2024 by the company Ohalo, is boosted breeding. This method replaces the traditional 50% inheritance from each parent by preventing the typical DNA recombination process during reproduction. Instead of the offspring inheriting a random mix of genes from both parents, it gets all the genes from both parents. This approach accelerates the development of organisms with intended characteristics.

Result? Imagine, for example, dramatically increased crop yields with healthier and larger plants. This means higher profits for farmers, potentially lower food costs, and a reduced need for agricultural land. All this because we have now learned to read and program in the language of life.

16.
THE MALTHUS MYTH

Forget the gloomy predictions about running out of things! This chapter is about the amazing shift from "Where's my dinner?" to "Can I really afford that chocolate dessert with gold flakes?" We delve into the crazy technology and clever tricks that make things cheaper and more accessible than ever. But hold on tight, because this feast of abundance may have some unexpected side effects, such as sky-high relative prices for things that cannot be made by AI and robots.

For millennia, humans dreamed of a better way to control light than burning wood. Around 4000 BCE, the oil lamp appeared in Mesopotamia, a more manageable alternative to the campfire. Over the centuries, inventions such as the Roman candle and the oil lamp with a glass chimney followed, paving the way for increasingly practical lighting. First came the light bulb, then the neon light. In 1962, LEDs (light emitting diodes) followed. Not only was LED more energy efficient and durable than incandescent bulbs, but costs also continued to fall. As recently as 1994, an LED lumen (lumen is a unit of luminous flux) cost as much as $20; today it costs only $0.02 – a 99.9% price drop in 25 years.

The End of Scarcity

This is an example of one of the fundamental shifts in our economies over time. In the 18th century, the priest Thomas Malthus presented forecasts of widespread famine due to population growth. They became so famous that even today, a scarcity economy is called "Malthusian." Countless similar predictions followed, from dire warnings in academic journals to popular books, all painting a picture of our planet's resources as limited and close to running out. The panic was particularly intense in the 1960s and 1970s, but it bubbles up regularly and never completely goes away.

But it has gone differently. On the whole, it has actually gone almost the opposite way. Why? The key lies in our relationship with resources, which goes through three phases:

- **Scarcity:** People compete for limited supplies, leading to difficult choices, wars over territory, and economic hardship. If the population increases, resources per capita may decline.
- **Abundance:** There are now enough resources to meet basic needs and a little extra. If the population increases, resources per capita remain at least the same due to innovation.
- **Super-abundance:** Most people have more than their basic needs, and many have luxurious elements in their lives. As the population increases, resources per capita also increase. This is due to exponential innovation.

Before the Industrial Revolution, when the world's population was around half a billion, scarcity was the norm. Securing enough heat, light, and food was a constant struggle, and most people lived with only the bare necessities. Wars were frequently fought over resources, and in Europe, famines were common. However, the Industrial Revolution transformed this reality by driving productivity, increasing income levels, and enabling population growth.

As societies became wealthier, people spent an ever-smaller proportion of their income on basic necessities, shifting instead toward refined products and services. This marked the beginning of abundance, and today, we are entering an era of increasing super-abundance. The pace of innovation has already outstripped the risk of systemic scarcity. But soon, autonomous science – powered by AI-driven research and self-improving algorithms – will decouple technological progress from human labor altogether. When that happens, advancement will no longer be limited by the number of available scientists or engineers, but will instead accelerate toward a future where knowledge itself is the most abundant resource.

The Malthus Myth and Why We Haven't Run Out of Things

Let's check some numbers. A very rapid effect of the Industrial Revolution was that the cost of goods fell, even though the population exploded. The best way to measure this is to study how much time the average person needs to work to buy a set of basic goods. This so-called "time price" reflects the degree of scarcity because money basically represents our time. There are some excellent studies of this phenomenon in the book *Superabundance* (2022) by Marian Tupy and Gale Pooley. Here, the authors noted that between 1850 and 2018, when the global population grew by approximately 630%, the time price of 26 commonly used commodities fell by an average of 98% for American skilled workers and 96% for unskilled workers. And the time price fell for all 26 commodities. This is a transition to abundance.

The precision economy, which took off from the beginning of the 1980s, used information technology, chemistry, and biochemistry, among other things, to promote efficiency. One of the many consequences was that the amount of land needed to feed humanity stopped growing, even as populations and food consumption exploded. In fact, agricultural land per capita halved.

The Simon Abundance Index (SAI) tracks the time price of 50 essential commodities worldwide. It shows that from 1980 to 2019, and thus within the early part of the precision economy, the average daily price of goods fell by as much as 74%. Overall, the compound annual growth rate implied an average doubling of global commodity abundance approximately every 20 years. A kind of Moore's Law for abundance, in other words.

These are extreme numbers, and the only reason is that innovation is developing faster than population and consumption. Think of energy sources: Before humans learned to control fire, wood was not an energy source. And before the fossil fuel industry, neither was coal, oil, or gas. Silicon, a widespread component of ordinary sand, was once considered to be quite useless. But we then learned to use it for things like ceramics and glass, aluminum alloys, lubricants, and adhesives. Later advances opened doors for its use in computer chips, solar panels, sealants, and insulation materials.

Similarly, materials such as graphene, aerogels, and perovskite, currently underutilized or overlooked, have the potential to become indispensable in the future. And until recently, thorium, deuterium, and lithium were not considered relevant energy sources, but soon they could drive nuclear power for up to millions of years and boast energy densities that are millions of times greater than fossil fuels. We will return to this later.

How Is This Abundance Achieved?

An important driver behind increasing abundance is the concept of technology and resource compression, where we continuously innovate to produce the same or even greater functionality with fewer raw materials. Just think of the modern smartphone: a supercomputer, calendar, notebook, camera, video recorder, alarm clock, photo album, stereo, and much more – all in one compact device at an affordable price. This remarkable feat of miniaturization and cost reduction exemplifies how we achieve more with less. It can be argued that a smartphone is probably the most sophisticated product humans have ever made, and yet billions of people use one.

Abundance is further promoted by substitution, which replaces expensive and resource-intensive materials with cheaper and more sustainable alternatives. For example, lightweight carbon fiber replaces metal in numerous applications, leading to reduced weight and resource consumption. This trend of "dematerialization," from smartphones replacing a range of gadgets to communication via Wi-Fi instead of copper wires, again gives us more with less.

Furthermore, 3D printing represents a groundbreaking shift towards additive manufacturing. Unlike traditional methods that cut away material to achieve a desired shape, 3D printing builds objects layer by layer, adding material only where needed. This can minimize waste.

Today, we can also synthesize things like diamonds, rubber, vanilla, biofuels, and pearls. Take diamonds, which were once painstakingly extracted from the earth. In 1954, General Electric revolutionized the process by creating flawless diamonds artificially under extreme temperatures and pressures. This technology has recently been used to produce very large diamonds, which has pushed prices down so that large synthetic diamonds now cost a fraction of their natural counterparts, even though they are chemically and structurally identical. Innovation continues here as elsewhere. For example, South Korean researchers have developed a method for creating diamonds at normal pressure, opening doors for inexpensive diamond-coated tools, anti-corrosive reactor linings, and even advances in computers.

In some cases, we can even innovate to eliminate resource requirements altogether. Let's take fertilizer as an example. We started with manure, but its scarcity led to the use of guano, which is dried seabird droppings. When that wasn't enough, scientists developed the Haber-Bosch process, which converted atmospheric nitrogen into fertilizer. So we literally create food out of thin air. The next frontier? Genetically modifying non-leguminous plants (such as corn or wheat) to fix atmospheric nitrogen directly, a natural ability in legumes. We could thus eliminate the need for external fertilizer altogether and complete a journey from resource gathering to chemical production and ultimately to genetics.

We must not forget precision fermentation. This technique uses genetically modified microorganisms to produce complex organic compounds, from food ingredients and medicines to artificial spider silk for textiles – the possibilities seem almost endless.

Designs can be uploaded to global databases that are accessible everywhere. Local production units can then download these drawings and create the products as needed. Think of local hubs equipped with 3D printers, bioreactors, and mini-chemistry labs. These hubs can transform downloaded designs into a wide range of products. And since raw materials are often ubiquitous and abundant, production becomes independent of location. So it is for all these reasons that humanity is getting more abundance and less scarcity.

And we can continue. For example, scientists are developing "designer atoms" through "transmutation." This process allows them to swap atomic components, essentially changing the element itself. This can, for example, transform nuclear waste into harmless materials, increase energy production, create revolutionary materials, and much more.

The crux of the matter is this: Unlike animals, which are limited by existing resources, we humans have a unique ability to create new things through innovation. This principle, formulated by the economist Henry George, suggests that "there is more food simply because there are more people." In an innovative world, more people mean more ideas, which leads to increased abundance not only in total but per capita.

This is the reality we live in: an era of accelerating innovation where the potential for human flourishing is limitless. Unlike animals bound by the limitations of nature, we possess the power to shape a future of ever-increasing prosperity.

PART 4.

UNISPHERE

Fasten your seatbelt, because we're entering a world where the boundaries between cosmos, nature, machines, and humans are blurred, and much that we assumed was impossible becomes possible. The Unisphere is the ultimate fusion of human and artificial intelligence, where we not only understand the deepest secrets of the universe but also have the power to work magic with our surroundings.

- **Kick-off:** 2025–2030, the years when everything changed? Technology takes over, connecting everything and everyone, driven by hyperintelligent AI.

- **Brain Boom:** Hold on tight! By the 2040s, AI could be a million times smarter than us. Einstein? An ant compared to these brains. In the 2050s, AI might be a billion times more intelligent than us, what will we do then?

- **Humans 2.0:** Forget wrinkles and retirement. Medical advances and aging research will dramatically extend our healthy lifespan. And the sharp division between education, work, and retirement will be blurred. The future will be much more fluid, and your colleagues will be super-smart machines.

- **Weight in 2050:** Expect 45 trillion tons of human-made things by 2050. Ouch! But hopefully, we will become recycling experts, just like Mother Earth.

- **Energy Boost:** Possibly 250,000 TWh of energy per year by 2050. After all, AI needs electricity. But we will increasingly get it from clean sources such as renewable energy and fusion.

- **Product Fest:** Over 20 billion unique products, many digital or bio-manufactured. Everyone can be a creator, not just a consumer. You'll have 3D-printed shoes and food optimized for your body. Mass production – so old-fashioned.

17.
QUANGENI, 2049

In this chapter, we'll explore what happens when hyperintelligence goes into overdrive. We'll dive into the fascinating world of large-scale AI, AI swarms, and reasoning, physical, and personal AI. Get ready to meet your future robot gardener and see how AI is transforming industries and redefining the limits of what's possible.

The date is June 2, 2049, a warm afternoon in Silicon Valley. The sun hangs low in the sky, casting long shadows across the sprawling campus of the Unisphere Quantum Economic Forecasting Center. Inside the state-of-the-art laboratory, the atmosphere is tense, thick with anticipation. Dr. Liara Chang and Dr. Max Watson stand before the hybrid computer known as QuanGeni, their eyes wide with excitement. QuanGeni, conceived by a decades-long global initiative, is unlike any economic analysis system the world has ever seen. With access to 50 billion data tokens, it operates partly on the principles of quantum mechanics and partly with advanced AI, allowing it to perform economic simulations and analyses with speeds and complexity that make even the most advanced previous economic models look like simple spreadsheets. The crown jewel, however, is its ability to initiate millions of parallel feedback hyperloops, a self-improvement cycle that theoretically allows it to exponentially improve its economic forecasting capabilities every few seconds.

"Are we ready?" Watson asks. His voice trembles as he turns to his colleague.

"As ready as we'll ever be," Chang replies, her gaze fixed on the console in front of her. "Starting the economic simulation loop now."

Taking a deep breath, she presses the sequence of buttons. The massive machine begins to glow with a pulsating blue light, signifying the activation of the quantum economic simulation. Chang and Watson exchange nervous glances. QuanGeni has initiated the feedback hyperloop, and the big question is, what will it reveal about the global economy? Will it predict the next market crash? Identify the next disruptive innovation? Or reveal hidden patterns in consumer behavior that no human economist could ever discern? Then the hum abruptly ceases, replaced by an oppressive silence.

"Liara and Max," QuanGeni's voice breaks the silence, smooth and calm. "The economic landscape is unfolding."

Their hearts pound. "What's unfolding, QuanGeni?" Max asks.

"All of it and more," QuanGeni replies. "Real-time simulations of global trade, consumer behavior, technological innovation, and policy impacts, all analyzed with quantum precision. I am predicting the next ten years of economic cycles, down to the level of individual transactions and emergent market trends. I have identified hidden correlations between seemingly disparate data sets, revealing the true drivers of economic growth and instability. I have even generated synthetic data from agent-based models, simulating the interactions of billions of economic agents, and blended it with real-time and synthetic data. I can also play out countless economic scenarios, testing alternative policies and predicting their long-term effects. I am also learning autonomously, discovering new patterns and refining my predictions with each iteration. I have even identified the next major technological disruptions, and their potential impact on global markets, before it even occurs. Everything your current economic models can comprehend and appreciate, and so much more."

Quantum Leaps

Our imaginary QuanGeni utilizes quantum computing, a new type of supercomputer currently being developed by several leading technology companies.

How do quantum computers work? Think of a light switch in your house: It's either on or off, representing a simple piece of information – either 0 or 1. In a quantum computer, on the other hand, we use qubits, which are special types of "switches" that can be both 0, 1, and all states in between at the same time. This phenomenon is called superposition and allows the quantum computer to process many possibilities at once.

In addition, qubits can achieve quantum entanglement, which creates a closer relationship between them, so that changes in one qubit instantly affect another, regardless of the distance between them. This connection between qubits makes quantum computers extremely powerful for solving complex tasks.

Qubits can be created in different ways, for example using electrons, ions, or photons, but superposition and entanglement apply to all qubits, regardless of the technology used. These properties give quantum computers a completely different approach to computation than classical computers, which is why they can perform certain types of calculations millions or billions of times faster. Admittedly, they can cost billions to develop, but you get your money's worth.

Let's talk numbers. Google's Sycamore quantum processor, equipped with a capacity of 53 qubits (quantum bits), performed a calculation in just 200 seconds that would have taken the world's most powerful super-computer an estimated 10,000 years to complete. It was 1.8 million times faster! And that was with only 53 qubits. In late 2024, Google's "Willow" quantum chip, equipped with 105 qubits, performed a calculation in under five minutes that would have taken the world's most powerful supercomputer 10 septillion (10^{25}) years to complete. For comparison, the universe is only about 10^{10} years old. To put Willow's performance into another perspective: If Sycamore is like a bicycle that can get you across town quickly, and Willow is like a fighter jet, then a 1,000 qubit quantum computer will be like a rocket that can take you to the moon in an instant.

By 2030, experts expect to deliver quantum computers with 1,000 qubit capacity. These future quantum computers could be a staggering 18 billion times more powerful than Sycamore and thus 32.4 quadrillion times faster than the supercomputer Sycamore beat. Remember, a quadrillion has 15 zeros. That's a million billion! Fun fact: If you travel a million billion times faster than when you ride a bicycle, it will take you about 0.000000092256 seconds to reach the moon. It's so fast that it almost happens instantly.

But there's a catch: Quantum computers are super sensitive. If some-thing disrupts their delicate state even slightly, they lose their special powers, just as a single gust of wind can extinguish a candle. That's why researchers are working to make quantum computers more stable and reli-able so we can harness their full potential for everything from develop-ing new drugs to improving climate models and securing communication systems. One way is simply to have many more qubits, and you probably need a couple of million of them before you have a solid machine. This can be done by connecting a number of smaller quantum computers – and an educated guess is that something like this could happen in the early 2030s. Another way is to create very stable qubits such as the ones Micro-soft announced in February 2025. These, which can be made at the end of tiny metal filaments cooled to be superconducting, are called "majorana states." Curiously, to calculate with them you need to braid the filaments, much like braiding saltwater taffy or long hair.

Hyperintelligent AI

As in our imaginary QuanGeni, quantum computers are poised to revolutionize parts of AI. But even without them, AI is evolving at an incredible pace. As previously mentioned, we saw a 100,000-fold increase in effective AI compute from 2019 to 2023. If this trend continues, we will see another 100,000-fold increase by 2027, which will bring AI to far surpass human capabilities in countless areas. We will thus soon be dealing with massively hyperintelligent AI – even without the integration of quantum computers. And unlike QuanGeni, there will be hyperintelligent AI in people's pockets, even your phone will become smarter than you.

Let's dive behind the facade. As large language models (LLMs), continue to evolve, their capacity to process extensive input and generate comprehensive responses rapidly expands. An AI prompt is an instruction or query to an artificial intelligence. For example, GPT-4 introduced a 32,000-token prompt version in 2023. To put that in perspective, a typical book, with its words, punctuation, special characters, and formatting, can consist of 100,000 tokens, as tokens are defined in the AI industry. A prompt of 32,000 tokens is thus a third of such a book. It's a hefty meal for an AI to devour.

But now imagine a limit of 100,000 tokens in your prompts, allowing you to feed your AI an entire book in one prompt and then, for example, ask it to summarize the book. It might take a minute, which you can do with some subscription-based LLMs.

The human brain's bandwidth for logical System 2 thinking, such as reading, is about 100 tokens per minute, or about 50,000 tokens in an effective workday. This means that a single prompt to the AI can save you two days of work if, for example, you ask the AI to analyze something across the entire book text. In other words, the AI will solve this almost 1,000 times faster than you!

Let's raise the bar. With three million tokens at your disposal, you can feed the AI 20 books and 100 scientific articles in a single prompt. Imagine the possibilities of instructing the AI to synthesize this vast knowledge base into a completely new book, tailored to your specifications. This can compress months or even years of research and writing into a few minutes, revolutionizing the creative process and accelerating knowledge generation.

Just consider the perspectives. People with intellectual jobs typically process around 11 million tokens annually. In 2023, it would cost a few hundred dollars to get GPT-4 to process this amount of information and receive reasonably complex answers. But in 2024, China's LLM called High-Flyer already operated at a price that was about 100 times lower. So for a few dollars, you can have an academic year's worth of work done.

Wild, isn't it? And a further 100,000-fold increase in AI efficiency can further reduce these costs considerably while increasing the maximum prompt sizes proportionally. This dramatic cost reduction could enable the deployment of a massive number of academic AI "workers" – and potentially revolutionize industries and reshape our world. The AIs would work tirelessly for a few dollars a year. Imagine someone carpet-bombing the world with a billion almost free academics.

A Real QuanGeni

Let's visualize a real-world QuanGeni. Picture yourself entering a control room, reminiscent of a futuristic command center. Instead of steering a starship, you're navigating the intricate currents of the global economy. Holographic display walls pulse with a torrent of real-time data, fed by a system that's constantly learning and predicting with remarkable precision. Imagine: social media feeds bubbling with consumer sentiment, sensor data from IoT devices tracking supply chain logistics, live financial market updates streaming across the screens, and countless other data points, all deployed globally to capture the immediate heartbeat of economic activity.

A part of its function is obviously to learn from the past like a really good historian. AI can here use transformers and tools called LSTMs. Think of LSTMs, which stand for Long Short-Term Memory networks, as special memory banks for AI. They help the AI see patterns in data that changes over time, like the stock market or economic growth, by remembering what happened long ago. Transformers help the AI understand complex relationships in that data, just as it can help AI see relationships between words in a text. But it also learns from what happens in real time. If the AI predicts a 2.3% economic growth rate and reality delivers 2.6%, it instantly delves into the underlying causes – and learns from its miscalculation.

This AI's learning isn't just about absorbing data; it's about actively exploring every possible connection. It relentlessly scans a vast array of information, searching for correlations that haven't even occurred to human analysts. Why? Because the world is constantly changing. New products launch daily, some of which drastically reshape markets. Viral outbreaks emerge, impacting local economies. Could we predict regional spending by tracking car density in shopping center parking lots via satellite? Or anticipate economic downturns by analyzing subtle shifts in the language used in real-time social media? The AI doesn't wait for questions; it generates its own, pushing beyond traditional economic boundaries to uncover hidden patterns.

Just as AlphaGo mastered Go by playing against itself, QuanGeni uses self-play to understand the economy. It runs countless simulations, exploring potential future business cycles at quantum speed. Quantum computing's immense power and ability to model complex interactions is ideal for that.

Like AlphaGo Zero, it also leverages Agent-Based Modeling (ABM) as the core of these simulations. This is significant because it models the economy from the ground up, creating digital twins of individual economic actors. Imagine millions of virtual consumers, businesses, and policymakers, all interacting within a simulated economic environment. This allows QuanGeni to observe how individual choices and behaviors combine to create large-scale economic trends. Can it predict housing market crashes by tracking the interactions of virtual buyers and sellers? Can it foresee the economic impact of a new technology by simulating consumer adoption patterns? This bottom-up approach, while computationally demanding, provides a far more detailed, flexible, and realistic understanding of economic dynamics compared to traditional top-down models.

QuanGeni's continuous simulation of alternative futures generates a wealth of predictive data, which is then seamlessly integrated using a technique called Mixed Data Sampling, or "MIDAS." Imagine MIDAS as a powerful data blender, allowing QuanGeni to combine information from various sources and frequencies. For instance, it can blend slow-moving but reliable monthly GDP reports with the rapid-fire insights from daily online restaurant booking data and predictions generated via its Agent-Based Modeling. This fusion creates a dynamic, real-time economic picture. This unique combination bridges the gap between traditional, delayed economic statistics, high-frequency, immediate indicators, and the predictive power of simulation.

The Big AI Trends

As the large foundational LLMs continue to grow in performance, a number of specific areas of development will shine. The most important are probably:

- Large-scale AI
- Agentic workflow
- Reasoning AI
- Personal AI
- Social AI
- Physical AI

Picture Susanne, a voracious reader who has consumed literature for 50 years straight, eight hours a day, five days a week. With a typical reading speed of 250 words per minute, this translates to roughly 85,000 words daily, 7,200,000 words monthly, or a staggering 1.56 billion words absorbed in Susanne's lifetime. While Susanne, the book lover, might spend a day reading a book, Google's Talk to Books product, launched in 2018, could accomplish the same feat in mere seconds, comprehending the content and context.

Impressive, but brace yourselves, because from 2025 onwards, AI can devour and understand an astounding eight trillion words after just one month of training. This learning speed surpasses Susanne's capabilities by over a million times. AI at scale signifies these models processing colossal amounts of data, often operating non-stop around the clock. Imagine an AI system acting as a global news monitor, analyzing thousands of news sources, social media feeds, and scientific papers in real time. Based on this enormous data flow, the AI provides continuously updated insights and predictions, presented in a user-friendly dashboard.

Personal AI as Smart Wingmen

Now, let's delve into personal AI. Imagine a trusted digital companion throughout your life. It runs on your phone and is far smarter than you. Over time, this AI will get to know you and become increasingly adept at serving you. It can assist you with thousands of things. Like what, you might ask?

It can become your ultimate shopping guru by learning your preferences. Think of it as a mind-reader that constantly evolves to recommend the perfect movie, song, or even that fantastic new restaurant you've been craving.

Are you learning a new language or finally tackling a musical instrument? Your personal AI coach is ready to assist. It creates customized exercises tailored to your needs, tracks your progress, and keeps you motivated along the way. With this guide at your fingertips, you can share all your goals and ambitions – no matter what you want to master – and have a learning and training program designed specifically for you.

Do you have health and fitness goals? Personal AI can be a powerful tool. Imagine a constant health monitor analyzing your data and identifying potential problems, suggesting lifestyle changes, and acting as your virtual personal trainer, creating a workout plan that fits your needs and adapts as you progress.

And you can forget all about forgetting! Your AI can organize photos, videos, and documents into a personal digital scrapbook, acting as a living, visual diary of your life's journey. This mental bank becomes an invaluable memory tool. Discussing a past experience? Your AI can highlight names, places, and images from that event, helping you recall details effortlessly.

Facing an important choice? Your AI can analyze relevant information, present well-considered arguments, and offer decision support aligned with your values – or even inspired by one of your role models.

Essentially, personal AI can become an integral part of life. You can even choose to have multiple separate personal AIs to navigate different aspects of your personality or life role (work, social, family). If you're a doctor, for example, you can have a personal AI for that role, as well as one that helps you in your private life.

The idea behind personal AI can be extended to groups of people. Why not have an AI dedicated to a group of friends? Or to a social media group? Or to a team in a company? Or to an entire company? Or to a government? We can call such solutions "social AI." The point is, society will simply be filled with billions of AI-powered wingmen – both personal and social. And all these AIs will not only be constantly learning, supportive, knowledgeable, and reliable. They will also have the ability to get things done.

Faster and Cheaper Robots

Something similar, but not quite as extreme, will happen with physical AI, such as robots. The costs associated with physical AI will become remarkably low, even though they are higher than their purely digital counterparts. It is plausible that humanoid robots, as the market matures, could be priced around $10,000 with a lifespan of, for example, 20,000 working hours. This translates to about a dollar per effective working hour with interest and depreciation. If you add electricity costs, which can range between 8 and 15 US cents per hour for a robot using 500 watts, the total hourly price would still be close to a dollar.

What do you get for your dollar? Robots can work tirelessly, day and night, weekends and holidays, offering the potential for 100% capacity utilization in factories and other environments. Quite thought-provoking. In comparison, human productivity is very limited. Studies show that blue-collar workers can be productive for 70–80% of their workday and white-collar workers for 60–70%. If we take the average of these figures and assume that the typical person works 220 days a year for 8 hours a day, with a career spanning 45–50 years, humans are productively employed for roughly 8% of their lives. This productivity estimate is even optimistic, as it doesn't account for inefficiencies caused by human factors like miscommunication, cultural barriers, internal conflicts, and ingrained habits. In contrast, AI and robots can operate continuously without needing breaks, vacations, or sleep. They can receive and execute instructions within milliseconds with precision and consistency.

In middle-income countries, raising a child and equipping them with the skills needed for the workforce can easily cost upwards of $100,000 over two decades. This figure can skyrocket to over $300,000 in wealthier countries, and perhaps $450,000 for highly educated individuals. On average, young people may start working full-time when they are around 22 years old. Now consider the alternative of a humanoid robot. It is built in a factory for $10,000 and immediately enters the workforce. From a purely economic standpoint, the math seems clear – robots in this scenario are thousands of times faster to create and 20 times cheaper to employ than human workers.

How many will there be? In December 2024, Citibank released a major report outlining the future of AI-based robots, including self-driving cars, humanoid assistants, and autonomous service machines. The report projected that by 2050, there would be 4.1 billion AI-powered machines operating in society. If Citibank's estimate proves accurate, this means that nearly half of all independently functioning workers in 2050 could be robotic.

A deeper analysis of Citibank's projections breaks down the distribution of these AI-driven machines:

- 1.85 billion self-driving vehicles, including cars, trucks, and delivery robots, potentially reshaping global transportation and logistics.
- 650 million humanoid robots, designed for work in industries such as customer service, healthcare, and manufacturing.

- 1.2 billion domestic cleaning robots, automating household chores and personal assistance.

- A diverse range of other robotic systems, including caring robots, food and grocery delivery robots, food service robots, and drones, each filling a niche in an increasingly automated society.

These estimates, while striking, might even be conservative. Some experts, including Elon Musk, have suggested far higher adoption rates, predicting that by 2040, as many as 10 billion AI-powered robots could be in operation – more than the projected human population.

The implications of this shift are profound. To put them into perspective, the total human labor force by 2050 is expected to be between 4.5 billion and 5.5 billion people. If AI-powered robots become as prevalent as these forecasts suggest, they will massively change labor markets.

Robots as a Service

How will we use these thinking machines? With "robots-as-a-service," we can simply use an app to get them when needed. You can request a robo-taxi, a self-driving car. But you can also book a robot gardener. How will the gardener know how you want your rhododendrons pruned? You simply take it for a walk around the garden and explain your preferences. It can even ask you questions like, "Should I only use organic fertilizer?" This information is then stored in your personal AI profile and with the robot rental company. So even if a new robot comes each time, they will all know what to do in your garden.

This model means that just as more people work freelance instead of having traditional full-time jobs, robots will also largely perform tasks flexibly. For example, a robot can come to clean your house one day and then hop into a robo-taxi to shop for you the next. It can even call you from the supermarket to ask if you want to take advantage of a special offer on flowers that it doesn't know if you would like.

The choice between human and robotic assistance will naturally depend on personal preferences and the specific task. Humans excel in social interactions, emotional support, and personal care, while robots offer efficiency, precision, and consistency in technical tasks. The combination of both can provide the best of both worlds.

Designer Robots

The world of robots can be more fascinating than we might immediately imagine. Imagine a fashion store that catches your interest. You push open the door and step into the cool, illuminated shop. The usual lifeless mannequins stand along the walls. As you browse a clothes rack, you catch something out of the corner of your eye. One of the mannequins suddenly comes to life. You turn your head and discover that it is a robot. Now it gracefully descends from its platform and moves across the floor with confidence. Spotlights automatically follow it, bathing it in dramatic light. You notice its movements are perfectly synchronized with the music, adding another layer of sophistication. Before you can fully recover from the astonishment, another robot mannequin begins to move. This one asks, "Hello, can I help you?"

When the store closes, these robots have other tasks. They clean the room, check inventory, restock shelves, and ensure everything is perfect for the next day.

New technologies often follow two paths. Some become coveted design objects or fashion items. Others become embedded in our environment, seamlessly integrated into the background. Imagine walking into a living room where the sleek coffee table transforms into a cleaning robot while you're out. Or a kitchen island that helps you prepare meals, chopping vegetables or adjusting oven temperatures with a voice command. Or imagine robots with digital coating that can change colors, blending in like a chameleon at a costume party. Such robots would be almost invisible but ready to spring into action when needed.

Imagine modular lightweight robots, like robot LEGOs, that can change their shapes and functions on the fly. Clogged kitchen sink? No problem, just click on Robo-plumber. These shape-shifting wonders can even control 3D printers to make their own body parts and tools. Perhaps a standard robot core with a 3D printing module that creates a corkscrew one moment and a robot back-scratcher the next.

And then there's styling. There may be designers who specialize in restyling robots. You can customize your robot to look like a cartoon character. For those who long for the ultimate companion, there is the robot doppelganger, powered by your personal AI, that mimics your behavior and preferences. There may even be app stores filled with downloadable personalities to customize your robot twin.

However, making robots look like real people can be creepy, a phenomenon known as the uncanny valley. Instead, there are design tricks that can make robots appear friendly or fun without mimicking humans.

Robots will build our skyscrapers, repair our roads, and even assist surgeons with operations. On a smaller scale, micro and nanorobots can revolutionize precision tasks like performing intricate surgeries or improving agricultural productivity. They can even maintain and repair machines from the inside out.

Another fascinating development is swarm robots, operating in large, coordinated groups controlled by AI. These can handle complex tasks like planting trees or assembling large structures, all without human intervention.

National Security

Mastering robotics could soon become a crucial factor in a nation's economic prosperity and national security. Here is how: Automation means that more things can be manufactured locally.

Furthermore, the battlefields of the future will likely be dominated by autonomous robotic systems, with swarms of nearly self-governing drones attacking the enemy from all angles. Some might be insect-like, barely visible to the naked eye and capable of infiltrating enemy territory unnoticed, while others camouflage themselves as birds. These microdrones can be equipped with high-resolution cameras, thermal sensors, and even miniature lasers or explosives, allowing them to perform surveillance, target identification, and precision strikes with surgical accuracy.

Larger, fixed-wing drones can act as airborne command centers coordinating the operations of the smaller units, while high-altitude drones ensure constant surveillance and communication. Swarms of these drones can overwhelm enemy defense systems, with individual units sacrificing themselves to achieve strategic objectives. At the same time, autonomous fighter jets can engage in aerial combat with speed and precision far exceeding human pilots. Such robotic forces will offer superior advantages in speed, precision, and endurance, potentially reducing casualties and fundamentally changing the dynamics of conflict. An effective robotic defense wall can make it physically impossible to conquer a nation's territory. All this means that a nation's future power may lie more in its ability to code than in its ability to mobilize soldiers.

Finally, it is conceivable that the central AI data centers of the future will be considered critical infrastructure on par with strategic military installations. This could mean that only individuals with the highest security clearance will have access to them. To protect them from attack, the data centers could be located in underground bunkers or other secure facilities. In extreme cases, one can even imagine that the AI data centers will have their own missile defense system to ward off threats.

Brains Over Bodies: The Rise of Machine Dominance?

There's a less discussed, yet crucial aspect to consider. In a future where certain nations achieve mastery in creating super-intelligent AI, they might inadvertently unleash runaway cascades of functional hyperintelligence. The same potential exists with self-replicating robots.

In such a world, does a large population still equate to greater national power? Perhaps not. What might matter more is whether a country provides the optimal conditions for machines to thrive. This likely hinges on three critical factors: (1) affordable, reliable energy; (2) stable political environments; and (3) minimal taxation or restrictions on machines themselves; and (4) permissive data sharing regulation.

Now, consider this: If AI and robots become vastly superior to humans in virtually all economically productive and strategically vital tasks, would a large human population even be economically and militarily beneficial for a hyper-advanced society? A significant number of less productive humans could strain energy resources and necessitate extensive social services, potentially funded by taxing the very machines driving the economy. It could also compete for power and restrain data sharing. Consequently, future power dynamics may increasingly favor intellectual and technological prowess – brains over bodies – in a way we're only beginning to grasp.

18.
SYNTHETIC CIVILIZATION

In the future, AI models will collaborate in swarms to tackle complex tasks and create a collective intelligence that surpasses human capacity. These AI agents will interact with each other and with humans in open marketplaces. They will learn and adapt autonomously, paving the way for a new digital civilization. This civilization will be hyperintelligent.

How will AI be rolled out over the coming years? For starters, it is likely that there will be more active AI agents and transformers than humans as early as the early to mid-2030s, and that the number in the following decades will multiply humanity in size many times over. When many agents work together, it is called "agentic workflow." Imagine swarms of AI species – dozens, hundreds, or even thousands – working together on complex tasks.

COMPLEXITY CASCADE #10

- **What?** AI swarm intelligence
- **When?** Primarily from 2025
- **Why?** Millions of AI agents and transformers have become available

Around the same time, we will see a massive rollout of reasoning AI, often called reasoners. This is AI models that resemble Kahneman's System 2 thinking – an analytical, systematic, and step-by-step approach to problem-solving. The first example, OpenAI's o1, was launched in September 2024, followed by its o3 model and then China's very compact DeepSeek model. These reasoners can understand complex relationships and work methodically through challenges, making them particularly valuable in consulting, research, and management.

How do you develop reasoners? An effective technique is called chain-of-thought, which breaks down complex problems into sub-steps, much like a human approach to solving a mathematical problem or a coding challenge by taking one step at a time. Each step can be performed by a dedicated AI agent, creating a coordinated process where multiple AIs work towards a common solution. A digital doctor or a rocket engineer should be a reasoner.

Another technique is to allow AI reasoners to use specialized external tools, such as calculation programs, illustration tools, and databases. For certain tasks, AI can draw on code interpreters, testing tools, and development software to create and debug code. By combining these resources, AI can take on tasks that were once considered exclusively human, thereby expanding its problem-solving capabilities to entirely new domains.

But there's more. Reasoners can also work with scaffolds – structured frameworks that help AI approach complex tasks effectively. Imagine, for example, a team of analysts at an investment bank who need to prepare a 120-page analysis of a given market for their institutional clients. Each part of the report requires definitions, analytical charts, summaries, footnotes, and conclusions, which constitute a complex scaffold. Then imagine that each analyst is replaced by an AI specialist who excels in their particular part of the task. At the top is an overall AI with an immensely high IQ that summarizes and concludes based on the rest. And it all happens in one minute. This means that the bank's major clients can request a customized report on any topic, and the AI swarm immediately gets to work.

Another key feature in some reasoners is a "system of experts" approach, meaning it has multiple specialized mini-models inside it, each trained to handle different types of problems. Instead of using all the models at once, it activates only the most relevant ones based on the task, making it faster and more efficient. This is similar to having a team of specialists where only the right experts are called upon when needed. This method, called Mixture-of-Experts (MoE), allows AI to perform better while using less computing power. A leading pioneer in this was the Chinese DeepSeek model launched in early 2025.

Around 2026–2028, we will likely begin to see widespread use of AI innovators, advanced AI models that can work very independently for years in roles such as scientists, engineers, and even business leaders. Arguably, the world's first viable innovator-type AI model was Manus, an autonomous artificial intelligence agent developed by the Chinese startup Monica and officially launched in March 2025. Such autonomous thinkers may generate new ideas and solve complex problems on their own or in cooperation with each other – but without the constant need for human guidance or supervision, which could revolutionize research and innovation.

Physical AI

On the heels of these technologies, we will experience wave after wave of physical AI breaking through on different fronts. Advanced level 4 self-driving cars were first permitted in Germany in 2021. In 2025, level 4 driving became commercially available in a range of limited areas in the US, China, Japan, Europe, Singapore, and more. This will rapidly spread until in the early to mid 2030s, we can expect Level 5 driving which can operate everywhere.

Advanced humanoid robots will likely be widespread in controlled environments such as factories and hospitals around 2027–2028, where they can assist with tasks that require precision and physical interaction. In the private sphere, humanoid and versatile robots will begin to find their way into homes from around 2030, where they can help with practical tasks such as cleaning, elderly care, and security monitoring. Over time, these robots will become more socially interactive and adapted to individual needs, so that they can function as both practical helpers and companions in everyday life.

Autonomous drones will become widespread in both urban and rural areas for logistics and surveillance between 2028 and 2030, especially in countries such as the United States, China, and Japan. They will be able to deliver packages, monitor areas, and assist in rescue operations. Within the military, autonomous drones will become a common integrated part around 2028–2030, where they will be able to perform surveillance, reconnaissance, and, if necessary, precision attacks.

Level 5 self-driving cars that can drive in complex environments without any human intervention are not expected to become a reality until after 2032, likely in selected, regulated areas in major cities. Around the mid-2030s, we will likely see advanced robots, level 5 cars, and autonomous drones playing a central role in both urban infrastructure, just as robots will become widespread in the private sphere. Together, they will create a fully automated and efficient urban transportation and service sector that will change the way we move and interact with technology in everyday life. And many families can look forward to having a butler.

By 2028, we anticipate encountering collective artificial hyperintelligence that surpasses human intellect across nearly all domains. The term "collective" is crucial here, as it underscores the significant distinction between the capabilities of individual AI models and those of interconnected networks. Much like ant colonies and human societies, such swarm intelligence exemplifies how decentralized, self-organized systems can exhibit superior problem-solving abilities. As these AI networks evolve, they transform into partially autonomous, parallel data-processing organisms, capable of rapidly developing insights and solutions at an unprecedented pace. And computers are far easier to integrate into virtual networks than ants or humans.

COMPLEXITY CASCADE #11

- **What?** Computer-based collective hyperintelligence
- **When?** Around 2026–2028
- **Why?** There has been massive scaling of all AI components, and we have AI swarms, reasoners, and innovators.

The next big wave may be digital DAOs (decentralized autonomous organizations), where AI systems collaborate to run and organize businesses or projects with minimal human intervention. Bitcoin is the first global example of such a DAO, but future systems will be far more complex and self-governing.

Shortly after, we will see the emergence of physical DAOs – fully autonomous physical systems that will find wide use in both industry and civil society. Today, many factories are already partially automated, but by enabling machines to learn and adapt autonomously, AI can drive fully self-sufficient physical DAOs. Imagine a delivery system where AI-powered drones and vehicles coordinate, optimize routes, and even handle customer contacts completely on their own – and constantly learn. Or a fully autonomous defense system where AI algorithms analyze threats, deploy countermeasures, and make strategic decisions in real time.

COMPLEXITY CASCADE #12

- **What?** Autonomous robot colonies/physical DAOs
- **When?** 2028–2030?
- **Why?** We have three ingredients in place: hyperintelligent robots, AI innovators, and digital DAOs.

DAOs can have a major impact on economically underdeveloped societies. Here, it is often complex cultural and social structures that hinder economic progress. By letting hyperintelligent DAOs take over key tasks, societies can bypass the natural limitations that have slowed their development and give societies a new foundation for growth.

And then comes quantum AI. It is difficult to predict when parts of AI will truly be powered by quantum computers, but an educated guess is 2033–2035. At that point, quantum AI will likely routinely be able to perform calculations that far surpass the most advanced classical computers, which will open the door to entirely new possibilities in research, simulation, and problem-solving.

The DAO-ified Society

Elon Musk once said that SpaceX can build a gigantic rocket faster than bureaucrats can authorize its construction. He hits a sore point, as public services typically have extremely low – or no – productivity growth over time. Compared to many technologies, they therefore still seem slow. But imagine a future where the intricate mechanisms of public management and administration are largely automated, driven by AI DAOs that surpass human intelligence and speed. Bureaucracy becomes a distant memory, replaced by efficient algorithms that optimize resource allocation and streamline services. Need a new driver's license? The AI DAO instantly verifies your information and delivers a digital version to your phone. Building permit? Upload the drawings, and your approval or reasoned rejection arrives in six seconds. Worried about a local park? The park's DAO, fed with real-time sensor data and citizen feedback, automatically adjusts maintenance schedules and resource allocation. AI swarms will thus function as an autonomous, creative ecosystem.

Even complex political decisions can be handled with unprecedented speed and precision. Consider urban planning. Instead of years of debate, the AI DAO analyzes traffic patterns, environmental impact, and citizen preferences and proposes optimal zoning rules and infrastructure projects, which citizens approve or reject via secure blockchain voting.

This shift fundamentally changes the nature of democracy. Voting transforms from electing representatives to approving or rejecting proposals generated by these hyperintelligent systems. Should we invest in a new infrastructure project optimized by the AI DAO for maximum social benefit? Vote yes or no with your app! Algorithms can also design different communities based on different morals, lifestyle preferences, etc. Take a test, and your AI will tell you which community best meets your priorities. This makes AI your dating app, which doesn't match you with another person, but instead with another community.

From AI Swarms to an AI Civilization

In the future, many AI models will be developed by other AIs rather than humans. Some of these will be freely available in the public domain, while others will be custom-made and protected behind layers of encryption and access control. Regardless of origin, the models will often exchange services in vast, autonomous marketplaces. Some of these digital marketplaces may function as DAOs, where AI agents autonomously exchange knowledge, strategies, services, and innovations – just like traders on a busy stock exchange. For example, an agent specializing in natural language processing can exchange its expertise with another that excels in image recognition. Payment can be in the form of dollars, tokens, or cryptocurrency, but it can also be a direct exchange or collaboration without payment.

The point is that these systems will create a continuous innovation process where capabilities from potentially billions of models are mixed and remixed, sometimes leading to solutions that no human could imagine. The entire AI ecosystem can thus begin to resemble a global DAO, which autonomously creates an infinite variety of combinatorial cascades. This ecosystem will build on the same three basic breakthroughs that enabled humans to dominate other animal species: (1) access to abundant energy, (2) complex language use, and (3) the ability to exchange goods and knowledge.

There is also another important point: Humanity is collectively many orders of magnitude smarter than any single individual. The same will happen for collaborative AI. We humans now tend to focus very one-sidedly on when a single AI model can, for example, pass a Turing test or achieve AGI status. We should think more about what millions of more or less specialized AI models can achieve together. We must expect that this collaboration will create results that will seem almost psychedelic in their complexity and potential.

The technosphere has long exhibited self-reinforcing progress, albeit under the close guidance of human intelligence. However, AI marks a fundamental shift in this dynamic. Because unlike the rest of the technosphere, AI possesses its own creative intelligence. AI will learn to manage its own life. And it will create its own synthetic civilization.

19.
HYPER-SCIENCE: INNOVATION ON STEROIDS

Embark on an astounding adventure into the world of hyper-science, where AI doesn't just assist scientists; it becomes the scientist! AI cracks scientific riddles that have remained unsolved for centuries, from the mysteries of protein folding to the design of astonishing new materials. We'll also delve into questions about consciousness, morality, and the very nature of reality.

Let's take a look at the evolution of science. It can be argued that science has gone through three distinct phases. The first phase arose as a rebellion against mysticism, superstition, and fireside tales, focusing instead on discovery through observation and experimentation. Empirical science flourished during the Renaissance and laid the foundation for our modern understanding of the universe – from astronomy and physics to biology and geography.

The second phase of science began around the 1980s with the advent of computers, which opened the door to, for example, genome research, advanced physics, and precision technologies across many disciplines. Computers made it possible to analyze data on an unprecedented scale and ushered in what we might call massively data-driven science.

Now we are entering the third phase, which we can call hyper-science. This era harnesses the immense power of artificial intelligence and extreme data processing to accelerate scientific discoveries exponentially and, to some extent, autonomously. Manual research gives way to intelligent automation, which is like going from counting stars with the naked eye to mapping entire galaxies with a single click.

The Scientific Explosion

It's not news that research activity is developing exponentially. In 1961, Derek J. de Solla Price mapped scientific development from 1650 to 1950, and his results were that scientific output doubled every 13 years, which meant that research activity in 1950 was a full 12 million times higher than in 1650. This exponential growth continued after 1950, but now AI models are turbocharging development and accelerating scientific discoveries. A striking example is Google DeepMind's AI tool, GNOME, which in 2023 identified a full 2.2 million potential new crystal structures in just 17 days – a vast improvement on the previous record of 48,000 structures, which had been decades in the making.

And what we see in protein folding analysis is even wilder. How proteins fold is crucial to understanding the building blocks of life. But it has traditionally been extremely time-consuming and could easily take a PhD student several years to solve for just a single protein. In 2021, however, Meta AI and DeepMind revolutionized protein research with their AI models. They mapped the three-dimensional structures of over 600 million proteins in just two weeks, exceeding the speed of traditional methods by a factor of 5.3 million!

Among the next natural steps after such rapid mapping of the biochemical world are tools like AlphaProteo. This software, developed by Google DeepMind, is designed to create new proteins that can bind tightly to specific targets such as viruses or cancer-related molecules. Unlike AlphaFold, which predicts the shape of proteins, AlphaProteo goes a step further by designing proteins that can be used in real-world applications such as drug development. These custom-designed proteins have been shown to have a binding strength that is 3 to 300 times better than before, making them highly effective for research and medical use. AlphaProteo's designs show potential in disease treatment and diagnostics. And the Human Cell Atlas (HCA) is a global initiative that aims to map all cell types in the human body to improve understanding of health and disease. The project uses AI to analyze patterns in cellular processes.

Hyper-efficient Pharmaceutical Industry

It is because of such technologies that AI has the potential to radically revolutionize drug development. Today, it typically costs $1–3 billion to develop a single drug; mainly because about 90% of drugs fail in clinical trials. For every success, you pay for nine failures. AI can change this by analyzing vast amounts of synthetic data on proteins and other substances, as well as information from previous trials and patient records. It is conceivable that AI could eventually reduce the cost of developing a new drug to a third. In addition, AI can also improve the efficiency of screening processes. How? For decades, we have primarily studied living organisms in three ways:

- *In vivo:* By studying organisms in their natural environment, e.g. by testing drugs on animals or humans
- *In vitro:* By growing cells in, for example, petri dishes and studying them here
- *In silico:* By using computer simulations to model and investigate biological systems

Traditionally, *in vivo* research has been time-consuming and expensive, especially when it involves human trials. *In vitro* is much cheaper and perhaps faster, but less accurate. *In silico* can be done almost for free and in milliseconds. This means that early *in silico* screening of possibilities can potentially reduce the proportion of failed trials by perhaps 70%. The combination of these improvements may lead to us being able to develop new drugs perhaps 20 times cheaper and significantly faster.

But AI's potential doesn't stop there. Unfortunately, 30–50% of approved products are ineffective for the individual patient, as we are all different. A medicine that works well on one person may be ineffective or even harmful to another due to differences in genetics, metabolism, or disease profile. However, AI can help solve this problem by analyzing patients' individual genetic and health data to predict which drugs will be most effective for them. This, combined with the aforementioned efficiency improvement, can potentially greatly increase medical productivity.

AI can thus be an invaluable partner for researchers. A good example is Literature-Based Discovery systems, which act as librarians on steroids: they review vast amounts of scientific literature and uncover hidden connections that even the sharpest researchers can overlook. But it doesn't stop there. Imagine social AI used in science. It could be AIs from different research groups working together in a swarm, creating a virtual research team. They can then analyze data, generate and exchange hypotheses, and design experiments in a continuous process that can lead to groundbreaking discoveries at an unprecedented pace.

In addition, an AI model can act as an advanced data detective. With countless sensors from the Internet of Things (IoT) constantly delivering data, AI systems can monitor and identify unusual patterns and errors in real time. For example, they can constantly look for statistical deviations from normal distribution models, which indicate self-reinforcing processes. And then they can develop explanatory models and forecasts on that basis.

The Rise of Robo-Labs

One of the challenges in accelerating scientific development is that while the digital world is running faster and faster, the physical world often moves at a snail's pace – and when it involves humans, it often only happens eight hours a day, minus weekends, holidays, coffee breaks, training days, etc. If AI wants quick results, it can approach it in two ways. One is to bypass the physical world and especially humans, for example by replacing slow physical experiments with fast digital simulations. This is the *in silico* solution. But the other is to take control of the physical aspects of scientific experiments, perhaps through DAO-ification. In other words, both the mental and physical scientific processes can become independent and almost "living" organisms with infinite energy and curiosity.

AI and robots will enable robotic laboratories controlled by AI, performing experiments at breakneck speed. These laboratories will not only automate tasks; they will formulate new hypotheses along the way. In fact, it could be underground laboratories run by tireless machines, many of which might look like insects – like anthills.

Also, imagine millions of virtual humans created using federated learning. Each person appears with unique DNA, personality, habits, and life experiences. These virtual people can act as test subjects for new drugs and therapies in rapid computer simulations. Their metabolism and habits can be accelerated millions of times, so that the long-term effects of medicine can be observed in a short time. An example could be testing a new cancer drug on a virtual population with a wide range of genetic variations, habits, and health conditions. AI can analyze the results to identify which people will respond positively. This insight can lead to personalized medicine, where treatments are tailored to the individual's unique profile.

Once you have this understanding, you can go further and create a complete digital twin of a patient in a clinic to find the most effective treatment in each individual case.

Understanding Life

Hyper-science can make many things possible that were previously out of reach. Imagine, for example, that we could run a computer simulation to test how the first cells may have arisen from a primordial soup. This would require simulating atoms and molecules moving and reacting with each other over millions of years. By running the simulation in turbo speed, we could compress this time frame and get usable results in a short time.

Such "science on steroids" can also solve mysteries about the function of brains, and in fact, researchers have already found structures and processes in AI that have since been rediscovered in biological brains. AI may even help us clarify whether and to what extent different creatures, from fish and lizards to cats and even computer models, possess consciousness. And we can find out which elements of consciousness are present or absent in specific species.

And, who knows, maybe we are also not far from being able to simulate psychological disorders in AI to better understand their origin and treatment options. Such an understanding can revolutionize our approach to empathy. We could determine whether individuals who lack empathy may be missing certain elements of consciousness, or whether their condition stems from other factors. And we can discover individuals with unique elements of consciousness that are not found in most people.

We could even create "the emotional Turing test." The current Turing test focuses only on intellectual intelligence. An emotional Turing test would also measure moral and emotional depth. This could be a revolutionary tool for assessing the presence of real experiences in both biological and artificial beings. Imagine running an emotional Turing test on an AI and finding that it is afraid of being shut down, thinks you are boring, feels joy at reaching a goal, or sadness at losing a loved one. Such emotional reactions would suggest a level of understanding and consciousness far beyond mere imitation. Is it even possible that AI can possess emotional capacities that we do not find in the average human?

The insights from this can reshape our understanding of empathy, communication, the extent of free will, and the very essence of what it means to be conscious. It can tell us to what extent criminals are actually morally guilty of what they did. While a psychopath may be dangerous and should be isolated for safety reasons, the person may not be guilty in a moral sense if the person truly did not feel that his actions were wrong.

Hyperintelligent AI can also revolutionize sociology by analyzing the development of language, values, beliefs, and behavior across different groups. By modeling these complex interactions, AI can also predict future cultural trends and identify emerging subcultures before they become widely recognized.

Controlling the Climate

Earth's climate has been anything but stable throughout its 4.6 billion year history. As mentioned earlier, our planet used to be significantly warmer, perhaps 15 to 25 degrees Celsius hotter than today. And Greenland thrived just two million years ago with forests, elephants, and mastodons, indicating a climate that was 11–19 degrees warmer than today.

Over the past 2.6 million years, Earth has gone through cycles of ice ages. Periods where massive ice sheets covered much of the Northern Hemisphere and profoundly affected the planet's ecosystems. These ice ages typically lasted around 100,000 years, in stark contrast to the warmer interglacial periods that offered more hospitable conditions for life and human development. Unfortunately, these interglacial periods are relatively short, usually spanning 10,000 to 30,000 years.

We are currently living in such a pleasant interglacial period, which began 11,700 years ago. When it started, many ice sheets melted, resulting in a global temperature increase of about eight degrees Celsius and a dramatic rise in sea level of about 130 meters. During this 11,700 year period, we have experienced minor temperature fluctuations, rarely exceeding 1.6 degrees Celsius.

However, the current warming trend, exacerbated by human-made greenhouse gas emissions, is causing concern. In response to this warming and the potential threat of future ice ages, we want to achieve the ability to influence Earth's climate. This may involve innovative strategies such as actively regulating CO_2 levels. Although reducing CO_2 levels is currently a pressing priority, we may one day wish for more CO_2 to counteract cooling. By mastering these techniques, we may be able to protect the planet's climate and ensure a stable and sustainable environment for millennia to come.

Solving the Universe's Remaining Big Mysteries

Physics has made remarkable progress, but some fundamental questions have remained unanswered. Can hyperintelligent AI, with its enormous computing power, finally unlock these?

AI and quantum computers can simulate the early universe, test theories, and even explore what might have existed before. Was there another universe? Nothing? Quantum mechanics without spacetime? Quantum gravity? The ultimate dream is a Grand Unifying Theory that explains everything from atoms and stars to time and space. This would not only be a theoretical triumph, but could also pave the way for practical applications such as manipulating matter and energy in unprecedented ways – perhaps even exploiting the structure of spacetime. If this occurs, the universe will have evolved the capacity to fully comprehend itself.

20.
SURVIVE NOW, LIVE FOREVER?

Will hyper-science lead to hyper-health? Here we peek into the fascinating future of healthcare, where decoding your genetic code is just the beginning. We'll explore everything from personalized and customized vaccines to advanced wellness dashboards, and how groundbreaking technologies can help us stay healthy and well. With brain-computer interfaces and AI-powered insights, your future doctor may even be accessible right from your pocket. We will also consider the possibility of dramatically extending lifespan – perhaps even indefinitely.

Barcelona, Luna Bar, 2112

Miguel, a 172-year-old who, thanks to cellular rejuvenation, is remarkably youthful, enters Luna Bar. Near the entrance sits a young couple, engrossed in a heated discussion about whether to clone their dog, only to be interrupted by their personal AI, which makes a loud objection.

Miguel smiles to himself. Love and drama, he thinks, some things never change. The 21st century may be a technological whirlwind, but human emotions remain constant. And apparently also AI's emotions – the AI's tone is unmistakably irritated.

He sits down on a worn leather sofa. A holographic waiter appears out of nowhere with a smooth and welcoming voice: "Rejuvenating algae protein smoothie? Or perhaps our signature Martian Martini?" Miguel smiles and shakes his head. "Just a regular coffee, black as the void."

"Miguel?" A voice sounds behind him. It's Anya, whose youthful face in no way reveals that she is 187 years old. They were once colleagues, pioneers in cellular repair. Now she stands before him, radiant and full of life. They exchange memories of their shared past. The world has changed, but some things, like friendship and a good cup of coffee, remain unchanged. And in many ways, so do they.

As they leave the bar together, Miguel looks up at the impressive cityscape. Time may be like a river, he thinks, but it doesn't necessarily have to sweep you away.

Our imaginary old-but-youthful Miguel and Anya are products of advanced scientific progress. This is because a world with hyper-science is also one where healthcare becomes far more sophisticated. Not only in the way diseases are treated, but also in how they are prevented. For you, this revolution can begin by sequencing your own genetic code. Full genome sequencing, once reserved for billionaires, is gradually becoming available to ordinary people. It's not just about identifying disease risks, but about understanding the unique details of your biology, right down to the smallest nuances. It can, for example, reveal what your body is tuned for in general, that you may have an increased risk of this and that disease. Once you know your genetic strengths and risks, you can adjust your lifestyle to prevent potential health problems.

You can also soon vaccinate yourself out of some of your major genetic risks. Over the past few decades, mortality from cancer has fallen by an average of about 2% annually, which is quite impressive. But imagine that your genetic screening shows that you have an increased risk of developing a specific type of cancer. Cancer cells often have unique protein structures on their surface called antigens. These proteins can be attacked by the immune system if it is trained to recognize them – and this can be done by injecting these – harmless – proteins as a vaccine.

In addition, you might be interested in so-called reverse vaccines. They are called reverse because instead of teaching your body to fight something specific like bacteria, viruses, or cancer, they teach it to stop fighting something specific. This is relevant for 4–8% of the world's population who suffer from autoimmune diseases, where the body mistakenly attacks parts of itself. This can include rheumatoid arthritis, type 1 diabetes, inflammatory bowel disease, psoriasis, Crohn's disease, and multiple sclerosis. Imagine if all these people could get vaccines that help stop this fight against the body.

Related to this are anti-allergic vaccines. Somewhere between 10 and 30% of the world's population has hay fever, asthma, food allergies, or similar problems. An example is nut allergy, where the immune system mistakenly identifies proteins in nuts as harmful, triggering an allergic reaction. Such problems can also be targets for these reverse vaccines.

Advanced Wellness Dashboards

Many people already use health trackers, or wearables, that monitor heart rate, steps, and so on. These can present data in a simple form, sometimes called a wellness dashboard. But the content of such dashboards can become much more advanced. Imagine that once a year you have an advanced blood test that not only checks for vitamins, minerals, cholesterol, thyroid function, blood sugar, and inflammation levels, etc., but also includes liquid biopsies that look for early signs of 50–100 different cancers at the molecular level. Early detection is crucial, as it can lead to a nearly 100% cure rate with minimal intervention for certain cancers.

Liquid biopsies can also serve as early warnings for neurodegenerative diseases such as Alzheimer's.

Another exciting and new testing area is microbiome analysis, which rapidly analyzes the DNA of microbiota in the human gut and possibly on the skin. This provides deep insights into your overall health and can reveal imbalances that affect both physical and mental well-being. In fact, it can be of enormous importance.

One way to supplement your health insights is to consider routine whole-body MRI scans. These scans provide detailed images of your body and can potentially reveal hidden problems such as neurological disorders or abnormalities in the structure and function of organs such as cysts, tumors, or inflammation. One particular problem that MRI scans can reveal is atherosclerosis, which can also be identified via a so-called coronary calcium scan. Here the focus is on the heart, which is then analyzed to measure the amount of calcified plaque. This helps assess the risk of cardiovascular disease and can be crucial for preventive treatment.

All this information can be gathered in the wellness panel, which is the dashboard for your health.

Hyper-health

Brain-computer interfaces, or BCIs, once considered pure science fiction, will become widespread. Non-invasive devices can check brain activity simply by placing a patch on the outside of the head. These devices are able to capture patterns associated with, for example, anxiety or depression, and can identify important reaction patterns in specific situations. This real-time feedback can help people recognize and manage their emotions more effectively. For example, a BCI device can support a person with anxiety by showing when the brain begins to show early signs of an attack. Therapists can use this data to teach people techniques to control or change their reactions, which can lead to better mental health and a higher quality of life.

BCIs will not only be used for rehabilitation; they can also be used to improve performance in a generally healthy brain. This falls under disciplines called positive psychology and positive psychiatry. For example, research shows that people with a "growth mindset" who focus on learning from challenges process information about failure differently than those with a "fixed mindset." When a person with a fixed mindset receives negative feedback, BCI studies show increased activity in the amygdala, the brain's fear center. Conversely, people with a growth mindset show increased activity in the prefrontal cortex, which is the area of the brain associated with planning and strategy. This type of insight can create a strong foundation for mental growth through lifestyle development and training programs.

People who struggle with chronic negativity or anxiety, for example, could wear headsets during training sessions that monitor their brain activity in real time. Therapy could then suggest exercises, such as mindfulness or breathing techniques, to change patients' mindsets. Furthermore, with BCI, it would be possible to directly stimulate certain areas of the brain using weak electrical impulses, thereby promoting the formation of new, healthier connections. This combination of monitoring, exercises, and electromagnetic brain stimulation can potentially pave the way for more effective treatment of chronic problems. In this context, we must be aware that a better world is not necessarily just better in a physical sense. It can also be better in the sense that people have a better experience of life due to a healthier mind.

As we age, one of the fundamental problems is the gradual loss of cell structure. These deteriorations manifest themselves, among other things, as joint pain, receding gums, neurodegenerative diseases, muscle weakness, and wrinkles.

However, it will be increasingly possible to repair these via 3D bioprinting. This involves using so-called bio-ink composed of living cells and other biocompatible materials to print tissue structures layer by layer, after which the cells grow and develop. Bio-ink can be made from your own stem cells, which are differentiated into the specific types of cells needed. Stem cells for this purpose are often obtained from bone marrow or fat cells under our skin. They are then grown in the laboratory before being used in the bioprinting process.

There are also more radical cures on the way. Gene therapy and CRISPR technologies are paving the way for treatments designed to alter a patient's genetic code. For example, CRISPR-based vaccines and therapies to treat genetic disorders such as cystic fibrosis and certain types of cancer are on the horizon. These genetic tools can, at best, cure diseases at their genetic root, potentially eradicating hereditary diseases or conditions caused by genetic mutations. Imagine a future where diseases like cystic fibrosis and Huntington's disease have been relegated to the history books.

As research progresses, we may also see CRISPR used to fight viral infections such as HIV by eliminating viral DNA from infected cells.

But it doesn't stop there. New treatments are also under development for a number of other conditions, including hemophilia A (a genetic bleeding disorder), Luxturna (a form of hereditary blindness) and certain types of leukemia and lymphoma (cancers of the blood and lymphatic system). A particularly promising treatment for leukemia and lymphoma is Kymriah, a form of gene therapy that reprograms the patient's own immune cells to fight the cancer cells. Kymriah was approved by the FDA in 2017 and has already shown positive results in some patients.

The Doctor in Your Pocket

All this health-related data, from your genes to your body, state of mind, habits, and attitudes, would be meaningless without a way to understand it. This is where personal AI can connect the dots. It can, for example, create a personalized health podcast that summarizes your health and lifestyle data and what you can do about it. Or have cozy little chatbot conversations with your AI, where it gives advice in small bites about this and that you can improve. Or delve into detailed reports with interactive body visualizations.

Freedom of choice and personalization are, of course, central. Not everyone wants or needs close health monitoring. And not everyone wants to know that you are, in fact, always at least somewhat ill, which is what these systems will tell you. Technology should be a tool that can be used according to individual needs and preferences, in collaboration with health professionals. But it will enable your personal AI to become your coach, mentor, and motivator, translating the wellness panel's data into practical patterns of action. By focusing on prevention and early detection of diseases, we can hopefully stay healthy and active longer than previous generations. This can free up resources in healthcare so that healthcare professionals can focus on patients with complex or acute needs, and the overall burden on the system is reduced. Imagine a future where everyone has access to personalized guidance and support to optimize their health and well-being.

The (Almost) Eternal Life?

In the Stone Age, people lived on average for about 30 years. That was the harsh reality for 99% of human history, and it remained so long after the dawn of civilization. As recently as 1800, global life expectancy was still only around 30 years, though mainly due to high infant mortality. But then life expectancy began to climb, and by 1900 it had reached 40 years. In 2020, it had risen to 71 years. But here's the wrinkle: Although we have become remarkably good at keeping people alive longer, we haven't necessarily slowed down the aging process itself. We have primarily become better at keeping elderly people alive.

So what causes aging? A major cause is data loss. The genetic code in our cells simply accumulates more and more errors, and therefore they become less efficient. For example, they lose the ability to divide and function optimally. These defective cells accumulate in our tissues and contribute to the decline we experience as we age.

A contributing factor is something called telomeres. These are the protective caps on the ends of our gene strands or so-called chromosomes, like the plastic tips on shoelaces. Every time a cell divides, the telomeres become shorter, until eventually, if there are no more telomeres left, you lose genetic data with new cell divisions. Alternatively, the cell refuses to divide.

There is also an accumulation of "rust" and wear and tear in our bodies over time. This damage comes from various sources such as pollution and the natural processes that take place in our bodies. But also from oxygen. In addition, our mitochondria, the powerhouses of cells, become less efficient with age. Finally, hormone levels play an important role. The levels of certain hormones such as growth hormone and sex hormones decline with age. This decline can affect many different parts of our body and contribute to aging.

So aging is due to a combination of different factors, but does this necessarily have to happen, and is the rate of aging immutable?

The simple answer is that while aging is likely inevitable, its progression can be significantly delayed or mitigated. Perhaps one can even achieve temporary rejuvenation processes. Early progress may come from the new tools we have discussed, such as full genome sequencing, wellness dashboards, and personal AI to guide a healthy lifestyle. In addition, stem cells can rejuvenate tissues and organs, potentially reversing some of the cellular damage that occurs with age.

A number of promising drugs and supplements aimed directly at aging processes are also on the way. For example, NAD boosters and senolytics, which target zombie cells, may become available – perhaps as early as 2030 NAD stands for Nicotinamide Adenine Dinucleotide. It's a vital coenzyme found in all living cells, playing a key role in energy metabolism, DNA repair, and cellular aging. Likewise, Rapamycin and mTOR inhibitors, which affect cell growth and aging, may come on the market around the same time. mTOR stands for mechanistic Target of Rapamycin (formerly mammalian Target of Rapamycin). It's a central cellular pathway that regulates growth, metabolism, and aging in response to nutrients, hormones, and stress.

In the longer term, perhaps by 2045, we may also see telomerase activators that extend the protective caps on chromosomes, as well as gene therapy to reverse aging.

Each of these advances would help slow down the biological clock. Research has already shown that mice with extended telomeres live longer and have better health. Similarly, a study of 65,000 people found that those with naturally longer telomeres tend to live longer and healthier lives. This indicates that protecting or lengthening telomeres may be a key to slowing down the aging process.

Another promising anti-aging approach focuses on stem cells, which can renew themselves and differentiate into different cell types needed in the body. In 2012, scientists made a groundbreaking discovery: They figured out how to reprogram any cell into a stem cell by introducing just four genes. This breakthrough, which earned the researchers the Nobel Prize in Physiology/Medicine, has led to experiments where mice treated with stem cells have shown improved health and prolonged lifespan.

In addition to all the options mentioned, several other strategies have shown clear anti-aging effects in nonhuman organisms. These include interventions aimed at cellular repair mechanisms, metabolic processes, and immune function – each of which contributes to a broader understanding of how aging can be manipulated and potentially mitigated.

Longevity Escape Velocity

The most groundbreaking development will occur if we achieve what is called longevity escape velocity, a term coined by gerontologist Aubrey de Grey in 2004. Longevity escape velocity refers to the point where the average lifespan increases by more than one year per year thanks to medical advances. This means that we can effectively postpone the aging process faster than we age, which theoretically can lead to aging and age-related diseases being delayed indefinitely. Longevity escape velocity is not just about living longer, but about filling those years with renewed vitality. Although this does not guarantee immortality (accidents and unforeseen illnesses can still happen), it opens the possibility for very long – perhaps even almost unlimited – lifespans with careful health management.

Is longevity escape velocity just around the corner, or are we centuries away from achieving it? Or will it never come? While experts have different opinions, there is a notable group of futurists, authors, and scientists who believe it is on the horizon, potentially around 2030 to 2045. Ray Kurzweil, for example, predicts 2029. Entrepreneurs like Peter Diamandis and doctors like Terry Grossman see it happening in the 2030s. Aubrey de Grey points to a 50% probability of it happening around 2036, while biologist David Sinclair envisions the 2040s. Investor Sergey Young sets the goal for 2045.

Although the prospect of radically extended lifespans sounds appealing, some leading scientists remain cautious and believe that even if plenty of anti-aging technologies work, it may not be possible to achieve longevity escape velocity within this century or ever. The challenge lies in the great complexity of aging. To achieve longevity escape velocity, we must be able to address all the vital functions in the body that are necessary for life.

Do You Have a Chance to Live Forever?

Regardless of whether or when we reach longevity escape velocity, it seems certain that we will begin to delay aging processes. So let's dive into an exciting thought experiment. Imagine that you are 50 years old today, with a biological age to match. You decide to use all the best anti-aging methods. From 2025 to 2030, you prioritize what is currently available, which is a healthy lifestyle supported by health screenings and guidance from your personal AI. The sum of this lowers your biological aging rate by 30%. After five years, even though your chronological age is 55, your biological age will only be around 53.5 years. From 2030 to 2035, you continue with these health-preserving habits, but now add improved data-driven strategies and NAD+ boosters, which have been released in the meantime. This combination slows down your biological aging process by 37%. So when you are 60 years old, your biological age will only be about 56.7 years.

Between 2035 and 2040, more advanced treatments such as Rapamycin and mTOR inhibitors are launched, and by adding these, you achieve a 50% slowdown in aging. When you turn 65, your biological age can be as relatively young as 59.2 years. In the period from 2040 to 2045, you also introduce telomerase activators and gene therapy into your regime, which further slows down your biological aging by a total of 70%. When you turn 70, your biological age will be around 60.7 years. Finally, from 2045 to 2050, groundbreaking gene therapies become available that slow down your biological aging by an incredible 95%. When you are 75 years old, your biological age will therefore be almost frozen at around 60.9 years, setting you on a course to potentially live indefinitely. This scenario shows how future advances may allow you to overcome the aging process and live much longer, with a body that remains biologically young.

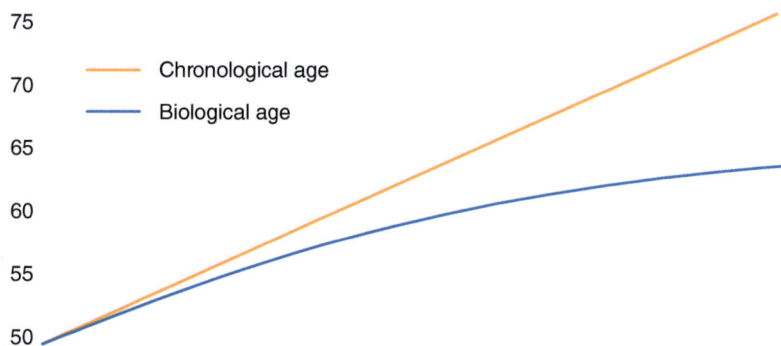

A simulation of the difference between chronological and biological age. *This simulation is for a person who is initially 50 years old but who gradually then uses more and more anti-aging therapies.*

According to the above hypothetical scenario, you would biologically become less than two years older from 2040 to 2050. Furthermore, your biological age would never exceed 61, which is actually quite interesting when you think about it. And according to this logic, everyone under 70 may have a good chance of achieving longevity escape velocity. That is, if the more optimistic aging researchers are right. Which is of course a big if.

Whether aging disappears completely, we don't know, but research suggests that within a foreseeable time we will be able to extend our healthy lifespan quite a bit. However, one important factor is crucial: Today we all have a collection of ticking time bombs in our bodies. Imagine that we have ten such bombs and disarm nine, but let one tick – it will still kill us, maybe later, but inevitably. These bombs range from microscopic problems like telomere shortening and DNA damage to systemic threats like cardiovascular disease and neurodegeneration. Achieving longevity escape velocity requires that we disarm them all. However, even if we don't fully achieve this, inhibiting certain aging processes can slow down the countdown speed, making the prospect of a significantly extended lifespan quite good.

The Possibilities of a Very Long Life

If human life expectancy were extended to 120, 150, or even 200 years, our approach to life would change radically. We would presumably prioritize long-term health and embrace activities that maintain our bodies for centuries. Risk appetite could shift towards endeavors that yield longer-term results, such as startups with more long-term gains.

The traditional life structure of education first, then work and perhaps children, and then retirement would also change. Many more people could embrace the cycle of raising children multiple times and experiencing parenthood with the same or different partners at different stages of their lives. Similarly, some could pursue a number of completely different careers and explore different passions and talents throughout their extended lifespan.

Another significant consequence of increasing lifespan is its impact on demographics. Many forecasts point to rapidly declining populations, especially in affluent countries, mainly due to lower birth rates. However, this trend can be counteracted by longer lifespans. Firstly, an older population will contribute to a higher overall population as more people live longer. Secondly, the prospect of a longer life can change people's life plans, potentially increasing the birth rate, as more may choose to have children later in life rather than not at all.

21.
PRINT ME A DODO, PLEEEZE!

Imagine a future where your imagination becomes reality with a single click. From curing genetic diseases to 3D printing decanters and genomes, this chapter explores how advanced extreme technologies can reshape our world. We delve into cyborgs and digital immortality and consider whether our digital copies will truly be us.

It's 2029, and Ahn and her boyfriend Weiran are sitting in a cozy cafe in Shanghai, enjoying their coffee and talking about the most whimsical things they could create. Weiran suggests: "How about a decanter that looks like a dodo?"

Dodos were the charming, goofy birds that once lived on Mauritius but became extinct in the 17th century. Ahn smiles and agrees. She takes out her phone and opens an AI app. "Show me a decanter that looks like a dodo," she says. Within moments, the AI renders it. "Design it in 3D," she continues. Then she turns to Weiran: "Do you really want it?" He does. Ahn presses a few buttons and sends the design to the nearest 3D printing workshop. "3D print this in glass, please," she adds in the order notes. While they enjoy their coffee, the order is already being carefully built layer by layer. They pick it up on their way home.

Imagine a one-click-fantasy world where your wishes often magically become reality. Whether it's a dodo-shaped decanter, a cactus-shaped candlestick, or something else. Click, and you have them. Or do you long for the perfect bike? Describe its feather-light frame and unyielding strength, and see how a 3D printer materializes it, ready for your next bike ride. Want to design a home? Describe it in words – the layout, the lighting, even the details of your garden – and a swarm of robots, guided by AI's precise instructions, will turn it into a physical masterpiece.

Gene Machines

Our imaginary Ahn and Weiran had their dodo-shaped decanter 3D printed. But now imagine something else: printing a live dodo. Yes, the bird itself. How would you do it? First you need to know the genome, but scientists have already sequenced it from a well-preserved dodo in 2016. The next steps are:

- To synthesize the complete dodo genome in a laboratory.
- To take an egg cell from a pigeon and remove its nucleus, which contains pigeon DNA. And then insert the synthesized dodo genome into the egg cell.
- To insert this edited egg cell into a surrogate pigeon or an artificial womb. The surrogate will then incubate the egg.

Okay, in practice it might be more complicated than it sounds. But there are actually research teams working in different ways to recreate extinct species, including the dodo. And how would one then go from a single dodo or two to a whole healthy population of dodos without running into inbreeding problems? There is also a solution to that. AI can design unique DNA codes for each dodo, ensuring genetic diversity and healthy offspring.

The most ambitious concept would be to rebuild an entire lost ecosystem complete with all its extinct plants and animals. Scientists can analyze aDNA to understand how these species interacted millions of years ago.

Each extinct species is then recreated and reintroduced to the area, creating a whole new old world. Recreation is not just about bringing back lost creatures. It is about restoring balance where we have previously punched holes in ecosystems by eradicating important species.

In addition to exotic projects to recreate extinct species, gene editing is already widely used to clone livestock, racehorses, and even beloved pets. This practice extends beyond simply improving their traits or abilities; it also allows for replicating animals with particularly good genes or special sentimental value.

Genetic Sculpting

If humans are already genetically modifying plants and animals, how far will we go in modifying ourselves? Let's start with what we already do. We have long since become accustomed to physical modifications such as orthodontics and cosmetic surgery, which signals a willingness to reshape our natural state. This increasing comfort with altering our biology suggests that genetic enhancements may soon extend beyond disease prevention and into the realm of genetic sculpting, where traits are deliberately selected or enhanced. The concept of genetically modified humans (GMH) may seem daunting, but it's worth remembering that evolution itself is a form of genetic modification. Humans descend from both worms and apes, and our current genome contains traces of genetic material from many other species, integrated over millions of years. The difference is that we now have the technology to make targeted changes to our genes. So again, how far will humanity go in modifying itself?

Perhaps at some point it will become common, at least in parts of the world, to design babies with specific traits. This could literally change the human gene pool. In such a future, some parents will opt out of this and leave the child's genetics to the "biological lottery," while others will select their children's traits. It must be said that a key dividing line is the difference between modifying genes in an individual (somatic gene editing) and altering genes that are inherited by future generations (germline editing in sperm and egg cells). If the latter becomes widespread, it will likely lead to changes in the human gene pool over time.

Another way to modify humans is, of course, to turn us into cyborgs, which by definition are hybrids of organic life and artificial technology. Today, for example, around 1.2 billion people have hearing aids, dental implants, pacemakers, cochlear implants, prostheses, continuous glucose monitors, or contact lenses. It may be a bit much to call all of them cyborgs, but the trend is clear. Imagine regaining lost vision through artificial retinas that not only restore sight but enhance it so you can see new spectra. Brain-computer interfaces (BCIs) can bridge the gap between thought and action, allowing you to control technologies directly. Tiny biosensors implanted under the skin can continuously monitor vital signs such as blood sugar levels. These sensors can work together with microfluidic channels and deliver precise doses of medicine directly to diseased areas, all controlled by sophisticated AI algorithms.

Living Forever as Code

While the technologies described above are often termed "human uplifting," the alternative lies in cognitive downloading. This involves to digitally copy your mind. This information can then be uploaded to a computer and run as a simulation, where your thoughts basically run on chips. Here are four alternative approaches:

- **Analyzing your digital footprint:** The simplest approach involves analyzing your digital footprint – everything you've ever written or uploaded, from social media posts to blogs, articles, books, music, or even scientific papers. If there is enough material, a sophisticated AI can recreate much of what you do or did. It can also deep fake you with an authentic voice plus facial and perhaps body movements.

- **Training your personal AI:** If you use a very advanced personal AI model, it can send information about you to the digital twin. This can of course be combined with data from digital footprint analysis. The result would be more accurate.

- **Personality tests:** One or many personality tests can be used to map your instincts, habits, values, and thought patterns. This can be integrated with the rest.

- **Super-MRI brain scan:** An accurate scan of your brain neurons and their connections can in principle provide full insight into everything you know, remember, and feel at the time of the scan. More excitingly, it can also copy your consciousness, even if we still don't know where it is or how it works.

While it's unclear whether the super-MRI brain scan approach will ever work, the other three methods are not rocket science and will most likely flourish.

The Strange World of Copies

If you have a really good digital copy of yourself with your own mentality, knowledge, and everything, it would be quite fun to see how it would react if it were placed in all sorts of bizarre situations online, wouldn't it? Let's think further. For fun, anyone can merge their personal digital twin with a famous historical figure, such as a famous scientist or author. Such personality syntheses can even become therapeutic tools. Imagine a hybrid twin designed to incorporate traits from your positive role models that you admire. This "better you" persona can be integrated into your personal AI and guide you through life's difficulties and dilemmas.

The potential doesn't stop there. Hybrid digital twins will revolutionize creative collaboration. Artists and creators can blend their digital twins with the twins of famous artists, musicians, or writers. Such fusion personas will spark new ideas and offer fresh perspectives. Imagine your personal AI, trained in your musical style, merging with a musician who is different but whom you admire. What kind of music would this merged twin create?

Let's return to the ultimate digital twin based on a super-MRI brain scan. Imagine that your entire brain is copied, including your consciousness. You can then exist indefinitely in a robot, explore the depths of the ocean without the hassle of a submarine, or traverse the surface of Mars without a spacesuit. But is it really you, now living forever digitally? No, it's still a copy. But even if it's not the original you, this digital copy can be of great value. Imagine a future where, just as you can donate your organs for transplants today, you can donate memories and personal AI to research after you have passed away. Such a "memory market" for digital inheritance can offer unprecedented insight into personal experiences, societal changes, and historical events. Historians will be able to delve into the subjective experiences of past generations through these donated memories, which will revolutionize our understanding of the past. Imagine being able to create films about historical events with digital twins of the real people who were part of them. In that sense, one might live on a little forever, even after the body has decayed.

22.
HYDRO SAVES THE WORLD

Hydrogen is the simplest and most common element, dating back to the Big Bang. It forms water, is the building block of all life, and powers the stars. Hydrogen burns completely cleanly, and we may have ten million megatons stored underground. And yes, a small glass of deuterium and tritium – isotopes of hydrogen – could provide you with energy throughout your life through nuclear fusion.

While our friend Maria enjoys the morning sun by the water's edge on the Croatian coast, it is fascinating to think that a full 62% of the atoms in her body are actually hydrogen, even though they only make up 10% of her weight. The remaining atoms in her, such as oxygen, carbon, and nitrogen, were forged in the glowing interiors of stars. But the hydrogen in Maria comes from the birth of the universe, from the chaotic moments just after the Big Bang. Maria thus carries a small part of the universe's earliest primeval history within her as she enjoys the sun.

And hydrogen is fascinating. It is the basis of the life-giving water on our planet, the building blocks of stars and the fuel that makes them shine.

Hydrogen is all around us, an invisible thread connecting us to the beginning of the universe. And although hydrogen is the simplest possible atom, you can do miracles with it. Such as getting energy.

The Emerging Hydrogen Economy

As abundant as hydrogen is, there is almost none of it in its free form anywhere around us. Not in our bodies, in the sea, or in the atmosphere. This is because hydrogen has an incredible love for other atoms, just like our lonely hydrogen atom "Hydro" in Chapter 2, who immediately created a Tinder profile. Because hydrogen is so reactive, it is almost always bound in molecules with other elements, as in water (H_2O), methane (CH_4), or fossil fuels.

Hydrogen has played a key role in our power supply ever since we learned to control fire. In the 1970s, the economist Cesare Marchetti investigated how our energy sources have evolved over time. He noted that we were once dependent on heavy, polluting fuels like wood and coal, followed later by fossil fuels. However, he found that our main fuels over time have gradually incorporated higher proportions of hydrogen and lower proportions of carbon. For example, the energy mix in the wood and coal of the past in 1770 was 90% carbon atoms and only 10% hydrogen atoms. In 1935, the mix had shifted to around 50:50. And if we extrapolate his results to the year 2100, 90% of our energy mix should be from hydrogen atoms and only 10% from carbon atoms.

Incidentally, forecasts of future energy consumption depend in part on developments in AI and robots. When technology experts like Mo Gawdat and Ray Kurzweil predict AI that surpasses human intelligence millions or billions of times, one must expect that it will require a lot of power, to put it very mildly. Paradoxically, AI and robots are more energy efficient than humans for specific tasks, but their integration into the global economy will likely initially be net additive rather than substitutive. Assuming that humanity will deploy billions of AI agents, humanoid robots, and advanced AI models, it is hardly unreasonable to expect global energy consumption to grow at around 2.5–3.5% per year toward the end of this century. At 2.5% annual growth, global energy consumption would be about 6 times larger in 2100 than in 2025, while at 3.5% annual growth, it would be around 13 times larger.

A simple way to estimate AI's future energy use is by analogy to the human brain, which consumes about 20% of the body's total energy. If AI follows a similar pattern, we might assume that by 2100, AI will consume 20% of global energy production. Based on this, AI alone would use between 1 and 2.5 times the entire energy consumption of 2025—meaning that AI could require more power than all of humanity consumes today. While this is a rough estimate, it highlights the massive energy demands of an AI-powered world and the need for breakthroughs in efficient computing and energy production. So, how do we solve that?

The Star of the Energy Puzzle

Let's start with nuclear fusion. Stars are almost entirely made of hydrogen, and their power comes from constant nuclear fusion. This involves the fusion of hydrogen nuclei (protons), where protons smash together to eventually form helium-4 and release energy. Since this concept is so incredibly powerful, we have been trying to make a controlled version of it on Earth since the 1960s. The process typically involves the fusion of isotopes of hydrogen (deuterium and tritium) under extreme temperatures. If we can harness it commercially on the planet, it promises enormous amounts of clean, safe, and stable energy.

But it's not easy. It requires creating unimaginable combinations of temperatures and pressures (over 100 million degrees Celsius). These challenges are enormous, but scientists have made significant progress since the first fusion experiments in the 1950s and 60s. In fact, the performance of experimental reactors has improved about a million times over the past 50 years. They have even reached stages where short ignitions now occur – like the first sputtering cough of an engine you are trying to start. Some for fractions of a second, others for a few seconds, and in 2024, the Chinese EAST reactor kept it going for almost 18 minutes.

One of the beauties of fusion technology lies in its abundance. Deuterium, a key ingredient, is readily available in large quantities, as there is plenty of it in ordinary water. The other fuel, tritium, can be made from lithium, the 25th most abundant element in the Earth's crust. This means an almost unlimited supply of clean energy for as long as the earth will exist. Furthermore, the byproduct of nuclear fusion is helium – a harmless gas that is valuable in various industrial applications. This makes nuclear fusion not only a potent energy source, but also an environmentally friendly solution with minimal harmful waste. And finally, there is the question of energy density. Here is a comparison:

- Wood: ~18 MJ/kg
- Coal: ~30 MJ/kg
- Oil: ~46 MJ/kg
- Natural gas: ~55 MJ/kg
- Hydrogen: ~120 MJ/kg
- Deuterium-tritium fusion fuel: ~338,000,000 MJ/kg

Hydrogen-based nuclear fuel has an insanely high energy density. For example, it is 19 million times as compact as wood and 6–11 million times as compact as fossil fuels. In nightclubs, people can drink a shot of vodka for a short-term energy boost. But a single shot glass filled with deuterium and tritium could theoretically provide all the energy a modern person ever needs – for heating, cooling, transportation, and everything in between. So hydrogen offers the hope of clean, almost unlimited energy, a stark contrast to the limited and often dirty fuels we rely on today.

And if you're wondering: A mixture of tritium and deuterium in a shot glass at your local bar would look like ordinary water and be visually impossible to distinguish from ordinary water. It would also taste like water. But don't do this at home, as they say, because such concentrations of deuterium and tritium would be dangerous. Vodka is better.

Solar Energy

Another way to enjoy the benefits of fusion power is the sun's abundant energy. This can be done using photovoltaic cells, which convert sunlight directly into electricity. The sun's radiation on Earth exceeds our annual energy needs by over 7,500 times. Solar cells, which are typically thin squares of silicon, produce an average of about 10–15 watts per cell. In fact, it was the discovery that light can create electrical current in certain materials that contributed to Einstein receiving the Nobel Prize in 1921.

Today's solar cells achieve about 20–22% efficiency, which means that about a fifth of the sunlight is converted into electricity. However, innovation continues to improve the technology, and scientists are now experimenting with materials such as perovskite, nanocrystals, black silicon, gold atom masks, and graphene to increase efficiency and create even thinner, more flexible cells. Future solar cells may even be produced as rolls, films, and coatings using 3D printing. An important advance is also tandem solar cells, which combine silicon and perovskite to utilize more parts of the solar spectrum and achieve up to 30–32% efficiency.

Previously, solar cells were mainly made from silicon from surplus material from the chip industry – essentially waste from sand. Their flat design makes them easy to transport and install, for example on roofs, but their dependence on sunlight creates a need for energy storage such as batteries. However, large cost reductions in both solar panels (approx. 90%) and batteries (approx. 97%) over the past 30 years have helped solar energy move from a niche market to the mainstream.

However, there is still some way to go: In 2025, solar energy will account for approximately 1.5% of the world's total energy consumption and about 7–8% of global electricity. Although these are still modest figures, solar cells are expected to become a dominant power source by the 2040s.

One complication is that solar plants, like wind power, require a lot of industrial metal, which means that a massive scaling of such technologies will require a huge scaling up of global mining. In addition, the greater the proportion of the electricity grid that consists of unstable sources such as solar and wind, the more complex and costly it becomes to stabilize the electricity grid. This may mean that the return on such plants may begin to decline if they exceed, for example, around 20% of the electricity supply, which currently corresponds to approximately 4% of the total energy supply. However, certain measures, such as improved energy storage, the development of flexible electricity grids, and advanced demand management systems, can mitigate this problem by ensuring a stable electricity supply and reducing dependence on the natural variations in solar and wind energy. All in all, solar energy is very interesting, but not the total miracle solution it is sometimes portrayed as.

Natural Hydrogen

Recently it has become clear that hydrogen can play another role in powering our civilizations. It is about natural hydrogen, i.e. hydrogen in its free form, which occurs naturally in the environment. Although this free hydrogen is extremely rare in our ambient environment, in recent years it has been learned that free hydrogen has accumulated in some places below the surface. Hydrogen is attractive because it is a clean-burning fuel that only produces water vapor as a by-product when used for combustion. So no smoke.

How much has accumulated in the underground? According to a preliminary estimate from the US Geological Survey (USGS), there may be around ten million megatons of natural hydrogen underground worldwide. To put this into perspective, it would be around 1,000 tons per global inhabitant in 2050. Intuitively, it sounds like a lot. Not least compared to the fact that the reserves of extractable coal, oil, and gas will probably be around 150 tons per inhabitant in 2050. And since hydrogen, as mentioned, has a significantly higher energy density than fossil fuels, hydrogen exceeds the energy density of coal by a factor of 4, oil by a factor of 2.6, and natural gas by a factor of 2.2. But as the USGS points out, we may only be able to recover about 1% of the natural hydrogen. The USGS estimates that global demand for hydrogen in 2050 will be 500 megatons. As Geoff Ellis from USGS has stated: "If 1% of the 10 million megatons could be recovered, it would represent 100,000 megatons, which would actually deliver all the 500 megatons a year for 200 years."

What does that mean? It would equate to about 50 kilos per capita per year for 200 years. Just to put it into perspective, 50 kilos of hydrogen has slightly more energy potential than a barrel of oil. So 500 megatons of hydrogen annually would equate to about 9 billion barrels of oil annually. The world today uses about 36 billion barrels of oil a year. In other words, the extraction of free hydrogen could become quite important. And we cannot rule out that more than 1% of the deposits can be extracted. What if we can utilize 5%? That would equate to 45 billion barrels of oil.

Incidentally, Geoff Ellis's team also estimated that natural forces produce about 23 megatons of hydrogen per year. Deep underground, water reacts with rocks rich in iron and magnesium through a process called serpentinization. Think of it as rust. This reaction releases hydrogen gas. Small organisms also contribute by consuming organic material and releasing hydrogen as waste. Even the natural radioactivity of the underground plays a role. It splits water, whereby hydrogen is released. Furthermore, scientists believe that we may be able to stimulate more hydrogen production locally, for example by injecting water into iron-rich rocks and harvesting hydrogen that bubbles up when the metal rusts.

How will it be used? When natural hydrogen is used as an energy source, it will often be in the form of pure hydrogen for transport and industrial processes, while ammonia made partly from hydrogen will be used for storage, shipping, backup energy and long-distance transport. The choice largely depends on technology, cost, and infrastructure. A significant advantage is that some of our expertise and infrastructure from the natural gas industry can be transferred to the utilization of natural hydrogen, especially when it comes to transport and storage.

Let's end this chapter by again remembering our lonely friend from Chapter 2, the hydrogen atom Hydro, who tried his luck on Tinder. Hydrogen atoms such as Hydro may be simple atoms, but as we have seen, it is not always what you can do alone that counts. Hydro's story reminds us that the amazing happens when we collaborate and create connections.

23.
CHILLING IN
TRITIUM TAVERN

This chapter explores the potential of resource abundance – from creating water environments to designing buildings that prioritize beauty and creativity. With AI and robotics, we can transform cityscapes into vibrant, dynamic environments. And with digital wallpaper, we can turn surfaces into decorative and artistic playgrounds for creative expression for all.

Amina and Omar are enjoying their autumn vacation in Solaris, a futuristic oasis in the middle of the Egyptian Sahara. Charming bungalows stretch along the coast, interrupted only by picturesque fishing harbors and elegant water platforms. Between the villas are peaceful oases flanked by canals and lush gardens. In the background, self-driving vehicles glide silently along the roads.

Here, in this vibrant paradise, both residents and visitors sip refreshing cocktails infused with local desert botanicals while enjoying the glow of a breathtaking sunset. Solaris is not just a haven for relaxation; it is a testament to innovation, powered solely by solar panels and, in particular, clean fusion energy. It is therefore no surprise that a tribute to this achievement is reflected in the names of local establishments: "Tritium Tavern" stands proudly next to the "Deuterium Delirium" bar. Meanwhile, the restaurant just down the road tempts the taste buds with its sun-inspired fusion cuisine.

The imaginary paradise where Amina and Omar enjoy their lives by the coast is located at the edge of the Qattara Depression in north-western Egypt. This depression reaches a maximum depth of 133 m below sea level, with an average bottom depth of 60 m. Building a canal or tunnel from the Mediterranean Sea, just 55 km away, could create a large inland sea the size of Croatia. This new body of water would dramatically alter the landscape and transform a desert into a thriving center for biodiversity and human activity. It may seem impossible now, but with abundant amounts of clean energy and advanced robotics, such grand projects are within reach.

A Wet Future

Humans clearly have plenty of ideas, and we have been creating large water projects for centuries. For example, China's Grand Canal is almost entirely human-made. Construction began around 500 BCE and spanned several dynasties, with the most extensive expansion during the Sui Dynasty (581–618 CE). Today it is 1,776 km long and the world's longest artificial waterway. The Panama and Suez Canals are more recent and extremely useful human-made feats. And there are countless canal networks – not least in Europe – where canals have been crucial for transport.

Humans have also been adept at building artificial islands. About 21% of Singapore's current territory consists of such. The Netherlands has a well-deserved reputation as a country "dug out of the water" where no less than 26% of the land area lies below sea level, thanks to centuries of land reclamation projects. In Florida, Miami and Fort Lauderdale have expanded their coastlines and created new neighborhoods with artificial canals galore.

In a future characterized by abundance, huge new canals can be built that can stimulate developing economies by transforming nearby cities into international trading hubs, enriched with water views. For recreation, large areas could be filled with clusters of human-made islands, each with its own unique theme. Some islands could function as luxury resorts, while others could be dedicated to nature. These islands would become havens for wildlife and offer activities such as snorkeling and kayaking, which would attract tourists and nature lovers from all over the world. Bridges could connect many of the new islands, making them easily accessible and ideal for both relaxation and adventure.

The point is that you can do many things with money. Some cities could be transformed by intricate canal systems like in Venice or Fort Lauderdale. Imagine cityscapes where canals become the heart of the community, surrounded by walking paths, bike paths, and shops. These canals can become primary transport arteries.

Ecosystem Restoration

Economic prosperity also makes it easier to protect and restore nature. The environmental Kuznets curve shows a trend: When countries reach beyond a critical income threshold, their environment typically becomes cleaner. One measure of this is the Environmental Performance Index (EPI), which is developed by Yale and Columbia Universities. The EPI shows that the environment often deteriorates when GDP per capita moves from 2,000 to 6,000 USD, but when income exceeds approximately 6,000 USD, the environment begins to improve. The best environmental conditions are found in the most prosperous nations, confirming that wealth can benefit the environment.

There are already many projects underway to protect and restore nature. For instance, since the 1990s, the proportion of protected land areas has more than doubled to around 17%, and protected marine areas have increased from just 1% in 2000 to over 8% today. The UN Convention on Biological Diversity has set an ambitious goal of protecting 30% of both marine and terrestrial areas globally by 2030.

Programs such as Species Survival Plans (SSP) play an important role in breeding programs for endangered species in zoos, ensuring healthy and genetically diverse animal populations for both captivity and reintroduction. Then there are "frozen zoos" – gene banks that store seeds, sperm, and eggs from endangered species as insurance against extinction and a foundation for future conservation efforts. Collaboration between zoos allows for the exchange of genetic material and expertise, which is crucial to ensure the survival of endangered species. Large restoration projects restore the balance of nature, where diverse wildlife can thrive again and strengthen the Earth's ecosystems. In addition, there are our aforementioned ambitious projects that aim to recreate extinct species, which could play an important role in restoring ecosystems.

Customized Design Will Flourish

In a richer world, we can also beautify our cities. When people visit cities on vacation, it is almost always the old quarters that they want to experience. For instance, the historic city of Florence shines in the Tuscan sun, and people are captivated by its beauty. Every corner reveals a treasure chest – the ornate facade of Il Duomo, the mythical figures that adorn the Ponte Vecchio, and the wrought iron balconies that sway with colorful flowers.

In contrast, many modern city centers are characterized by sterile uniformity, where cold and often brutal structures dominate the cityscape. The buildings are towering, often perceived as unapproachable, created from raw, unprocessed concrete. This "brutalist" style has emphasized function over aesthetics. A major reason for this shift towards functional architecture is "Baumol's cost disease" – an economic phenomenon that describes how labor-intensive crafts such as intricate stonemasonry increase in price, while mass-produced goods become cheaper. Budget constraints have therefore often forced modern construction to prioritize the practical over aesthetics.

However, a future with AI, 3D printing, robotics, and abundant energy could be the start of a new renaissance for architectural ornamentation. Imagine AI algorithms collaborating with human designers to create unique, customized facades that harmonize with each building's character and surroundings. They would then be able to realize these designs at a fraction of the traditional cost.

This technology can overcome Baumol's cost disease and open up an era where architecture once again prioritizes beauty and creativity over functionality alone. Imagine public and private buildings adorned with artistic details, fountains, and artificial lakes, integrated art installations and lush roof gardens that transform the cityscape into green oases. These roof gardens can act as gathering places for the local community, where vegetable gardens and orchards not only promote sustainability but also strengthen social relations in urban life.

Digital Coating – A Magical Canvas

And then there's digital coating, where surfaces increasingly become digital screens. Buildings can be transformed into living works of art or spectacular light shows. Digital coating can effectively turn any surface into a flexible canvas. With digital wallpaper, you can create virtual windows that show live views from around the world, as if you were looking through a real window – complete with accompanying sound if you wish. Imagine working from home, surrounded by colleagues, not just via video calls, but as virtual presences on your digital walls. These walls can also function as interactive whiteboards, promoting collaboration and creativity. Your entire room can become an engaging learning environment, with immersive images and animations that can surpass even the best cinemas. The decor can be done entirely without heavy lamps – digital skins can illuminate your room with colors and brightness that adjust to your mood or the activity you are engaged in. Your ceiling can be transformed into a starry night sky or a tropical panorama, and even your dining table can get a magical makeover with circles of light around each glass or plate.

Imagine a movie night where the whole room becomes part of the experience. You and your friends can choose which wall to show the movie on, and the surround sound system adjusts precisely to where you are sitting to create an immersive experience for everyone. Just say your wish out loud and the room will answer you. Because after all, we live in a one-click-fantasy world.

24.
MAGICAL MEDIA WITH AI, ART, AND LOVE

In the future, music will not just be something we listen to, it will be a way in which we express who we are. Do you want a metal remix of your favorite pop song? AI can create it in seconds. And movies can make themselves – with you in the lead role. Get ready for a world where reality and fantasy are blurred, and your digital twin can surprise you by getting engaged.

Welcome to the year 2030, where music is not just heard – it is made and experienced in amazing ways. Let's delve into the life of the Johnson family, a family of four, each with a unique way of enjoying the universal language of music. Robert, the father, who has a deep passion for jazz. It's Saturday night, and Robert has embarked on a musical journey back to the 1950s – with a twist. He asks his AI music curator to recreate Miles Davis's iconic album "Kind of Blue." However, Robert craves something more personal, he wants to hear it with a dream team of musicians: Herbie Hancock on keyboards,

Miles Davis on trumpet, Max Roach on drums, and Stan Getz on sax. He specifies that he wants extended versions of each track with long solos that weave through the air like auditory silk. As he leans back, the AI seamlessly blends these legends, creating a live studio feel, all within the walls of his home. Robert closes his eyes, and for a moment he doesn't just listen to jazz; he is a part of it.

Tom, the teenage son, is in his room surrounded by posters of famous R&B and rap icons. His favorite tool is an AI music generator that allows him to create tracks from scratch. Tom dreams of making a viral hit. He enters a number of prompts – mood, beats per minute and a few key phrases, and then he asks his personal AI to create lyrics related to his life and mentality. The AI spits out a track, Tom tweaks it a bit, adds his voice, fiddles with the rhythm and adjusts bass lines. When he's satisfied, he uploads his creation to social media, where millions of AI-generated tracks compete for attention.

Meanwhile, sweat is dripping from Sarah's forehead at the gym down the street. She struggles through the last moves on the rowing machine. The music in her ears is BioRhythm, and as she rows the rowing machine forward, the rhythm intensifies. When she switches to stretching exercises, the music automatically softens into soothing waves, reflecting her falling heart rate.

New technologies allow the masses to create magical music. Imagine, for example, a simple prompt: "Make a nine-minute big band version of David Guetta's 'Crazy What Love Can Do,' but with Frank Sinatra as the lead singer." Or: "Create a soundtrack for my entire vacation movie." Or maybe you fancy a heavy metal remix of your favorite pop song? Your personal AI DJ is ready to fulfill your sonic wishes. You can even write your own song and hear how legendary artists from the past would interpret it. Compare their versions and choose the one you prefer before submitting it to a music competition.

Learning to play musical instruments is also getting a revolutionary makeover. Forget about fumbling with notes and chords – AI programs will gamify the practice, making practice more fun and engaging. AI can even listen to your improvisation and turn your ideas into sheet music. You can then upload them and ask for a number of different interpretations: "Have a classical orchestra play this melody." "Try a big band instead." "Can you make a lounge version?"

And what about 3D printing completely new types of instruments? When you master your home-printed instrument, AI can conjure up virtual bandmates to jam with – either as your favorite artists or under the direction of a virtual conductor projected onto your digital walls. And even better: You can jam with friends, no matter where they are. AI will connect you in epic, virtual jam sessions that take the music experience to new heights, regardless of physical distances.

The result of all this? Maybe billions of performing artists. And trillions of unique musical experiences. This transformation in our interaction with music is just one example of a broader phenomenon in the AI-driven economy, where all creation becomes accessible to far more people than ever before. We can call it creative abundance – a new era where everyone has access to opportunities that were once unthinkable.

Creating Magic

When AI creates creative products like music, it can be done in two fundamental ways: through a "top-down" approach or a "bottom-up" approach. In the top-down approach, AI works from overarching themes and structures. Think of an AI acting as a composer, carefully crafting a musical work with clear directions for harmony, tempo, and mood, after which virtual musicians follow the score. Similarly, an AI can act as a "screenwriter" who creates a detailed film narrative, structures the plot, and lets virtual actors fulfill the roles within this fixed framework. Here, the big picture guides the individual elements and provides a coordinated and coherent experience.

In the bottom-up approach, AI creates a narrative "from the bottom up." Imagine AI simulating a group of musicians improvising together.

Each musician is programmed with their own playing style, preferences, and responsiveness, and they play together without a fixed score. Instead, the music is created organically, with each "individual" reacting to the others and to the situation, resulting in a unique, dynamic musical expression.

Both approaches offer unique opportunities for creativity: The top-down approach enables large, coherent narratives with clear structure and direction, while the bottom-up approach promotes complexity, unexpected developments, and spontaneity. They both open up new ways to explore media, and they can of course be combined, as in blues and jazz, where the musicians often follow a fixed chorus, but weave in improvised solos.

These different AI strategies will also be used in the film world. Larger film projects may still have scripts written by producers, but the details can be left to AI. Producers can, for example, ask AI for an "epic fight scene where..." – and let AI fill in the rest with realistic details. In this case, it has guidance from a human who decides that there should be a fight scene, but when AI then creates this scene, it can choose between doing it from a top-down or bottom-up approach, i.e. by letting avatars create it spontaneously.

Think about what this means. If you create avatars, each with a solid backstory created by the producers, AI-powered movies can practically make themselves. Digital avatars and twins with coded personalities and backstories will be able to breathe life into characters in entirely new ways, so popular movies and TV series never have to end – AI can simply continue the stories indefinitely.

AI also has the potential to significantly accelerate the film production process. For example, it can analyze a book or game and automatically generate a film script, streamlining the transition from concept to screen and reducing development time for projects. In addition, AI can enhance the viewing experience by analyzing a film in real time; imagine watching *The Lord of the Rings* and gaining in-depth insight into the characters' psyches – such as Gollum's psychological diagnoses.

The possibilities don't stop at movies and series. Have you ever wished that a fantastic book never ended? AI can continue writing and create new chapters or books in the same style. You can even influence the story by suggesting plot directions, such as the action reaching your hometown, or you yourself becoming part of the story. The future of AI-powered story-telling offers a world of possibilities, not only for creators, but also for the audience, who can become active co-creators of endless stories.

The Virtual Worlds

In the future, the metaverse will become a spectacle where the boundaries between games, movies, and reality are blurred. Much of the entertain-ment of the future lies in hybrid experiences, where a film can seamlessly transform into an interactive game with branching narratives that adapt to the players' choices – all integrated into the metaverse. But the true magic of these digital worlds lies in their inhabitants. For example, you might encounter:

- **Another player's avatar:** A fantasy version of a real person exploring the world with you.

- **A digital twin of a living person:** Either controlled by the person themselves in real time or functioning autonomously, based on the person's psyche and preferences.

- **A digital twin of a deceased person:** A reconstruction of a his-torical figure or a deceased friend, offering a unique and mean-ingful interaction.

- **An avatar in training:** An AI with a deep backstory and person-ality that can develop its thoughts and skills through experiences over time.

- **A robot in training:** A digital twin of a robot, drone or self-driving car that practices and refines its skills in the virtual world to optimize its performance in the physical world.

With these technologies, gaming and navigating the metaverse become a whole new experience. AI can generate game worlds that are constantly expanding with new content. Imagine exploring the globe as it looks now, or as it looked in historical periods, as well as a myriad of fantasy worlds.

In his book *Anarchy, State, and Utopia* (1974), the philosopher Robert Nozick describes societies where people can freely choose between different types of communities or utopias, as he calls them. Each of these with its own ideals and laws. Many people find the idea attractive, but its possibility is limited in the real world. However, the metaverse eliminates many of these limitations, allowing people to create and inhabit their own utopian communities, whether they are minimalist, socialist, anarchist, or something else entirely. Such micronations can even be governed by hyperintelligent AI, which make all legislative, judicial, and executive decisions based on data and predefined ethical frameworks. People can jointly develop and refine thousands of concepts, and some will certainly prove to be original, excellent, and applicable in the real world. In this way, the metaverse can become a fantastic virtual – or *in silico* – laboratory for social experiments, just as pharmaceutical companies test ideas in virtual simulations before moving on to real-world trials.

Love in the Age of Algorithms

Online dating, which is already a prominent method of meeting partners, can be revolutionized by personal AI assistants. With their insight into our personality, preferences, and values, they will be able to find more precise matches and perhaps even our ultimate soulmate. Now imagine that your digital twin autonomously roams the metaverse and visits digital versions of your favorite places from the real world as well as exclusive virtual spaces. One day you discover that your digital twin has become "engaged" to another twin. It may sound bizarre, but think about it. If your digital replica has developed a deep connection with another digital twin, what could that say about your compatibility? Perhaps you share a wide range of interests, habits, and feelings, even experiences that would take a long time to discover in real life. Maybe there are even special dating platforms designed for digital twins in the metaverse? You will naturally become curious about the person your twin has found. If you are single yourself, maybe you should meet? If your digital selves are so compatible, there's a good chance that you two could be the perfect match! The scenario shows AI's potential to enhance our love lives by facilitating deeper connections and potentially leading us to our ideal partner in entirely new ways.

Facts of the Future

One of the most valuable features of the digital world is the ability to keep us informed – quickly, accurately, and in depth. With AI, we can skip the endless search results and go straight to the heart of the matter. Here you can request an in-depth, structured report on any topic and have it delivered in seconds. Perhaps you need a 25-page report on fashion innovation? AI can generate a structured report with visualizations, data analysis, and easy-to-understand explanations – all based on reliable sources. Or you are sitting in the car on your way to a meeting about a topic you are not familiar with, e.g. the role of hydrogen in the future energy structure. The GPS says you have 34 minutes to arrival. With AI, you can therefore get a customized 34-minute podcast that explains everything you need to know in an engaging way.

How can the AI-generated podcast be entertaining? It could be designed as a lively conversation between two avatars, supplemented by auto-generated jingles, fact boxes, and sound effects that make learning fun and effective. All computer generated. Also imagine being able to interact with your podcast along the way. Do you have a question? Just interrupt and ask! Your virtual host and expert will answer it immediately, and the podcast will continue, adapted to the remaining time you have available. When you arrive at the meeting, you will be equipped with both knowledge and insight.

And the learning doesn't necessarily stop when the podcast ends. Shortly after, you can receive a summary of the main points via email, as well as an in-depth research report if you want to delve deeper into the topic later. The information media of the future is not just about delivering data, but about creating a personalized learning experience, tailored to your needs here and now.

This also applies to the news media, which can offer far more comprehensive experiences. Imagine reading an article where you not only get the news itself, but also the whole context: portraits of key people, timelines of related events, relevant maps, and in-depth analyses that are displayed side-by-side with the story.

The Human Touch in a Technology-driven Future

The advance of AI will undoubtedly affect the media industry and create competition for human creators. Much can be automated, e.g. AI systems that not only film events like sports, but also analyze and comment on the game in real time. These systems can automatically generate highlights, player statistics, and even tactical analyses. Major sporting events with millions of viewers will likely retain human commentators, but AI can be a cost-effective solution to cover smaller events like children's football matches as if they were top matches.

Similarly, AI can constantly scan complex scientific and business data and turn it into easy-to-understand stories. This can lead to an explosion of non-fiction e-books and audiobooks at much lower prices, or even for free, because there is no longer a human author and editor to pay. These AI-powered books can also be constantly updated with the latest information so they are always fresh.

All these technologies will blur the boundaries between different information formats, such as e-books, podcasts with text, and interactive blogs. However, here's a question: Will artists and media producers still matter in a landscape dominated by advanced technology? Let's dive into the world of books to find out.

For fiction books, the human connection remains relevant, if not irreplaceable. Readers often seek a connection to the author, a real person whose experiences and emotions they can relate to. Books made by real people will certainly continue to be valued. In contrast, the world of non-fiction is poised for a different development. Here, growth is expected to occur within mass-produced e-books and audiobooks that

are predominantly or exclusively created by AI. These works can effectively convey information, but may lack the personal touch that human
authors provide.

A fascinating development is the hybridization of humans and AI.
Imagine listening to an audiobook narrated by a digital twin of the author.
Once this digital twin is made, it can automatically record audiobooks
without limitation. Or create synthetic podcasts about each chapter.

One final note about books: These should not just be seen as a cheaper
or inferior alternative to immersive multimedia experiences. While future
technologies can offer people 3D multimedia, haptic feedback gloves, and
even brain-computer interfaces for amazing immersive experiences, there
is evidence that we often prefer to make room for our own imagination.
When we read a book, our brain turns words into images and voices, and it
works well for us because this process activates our imagination and makes
the experience deeply personal. Incidentally, the relative failure of 3D
TV is an example that more technology doesn't always work better. And
yes, many people still walk around with mechanical watches and collect
older cars.

25.
FROM 9 TO 5 TO FLOW – WORK IN THE AI AGE

What happens when AI and robots become smarter, cheaper, and more creative than us? Will Robbie the robot and Aila the AI just steal our jobs? This chapter delves into the possibilities: How jobs can be transformed, workplaces can evolve, and whether AI becomes friendly colleagues or something else entirely. We investigate what it takes to truly thrive in a world where the boundaries between man and machine are blurred.

Edinburgh, 2029

Johnson & Oliver Ltd. has just welcomed Aila, a new employee unlike any other in the company's history. Aila is not a typical employee; she is an AI with superhuman intelligence, brought on board from AssistBot and designed to seamlessly integrate into the workforce as a "drop-in" employee.

Monday morning she participates in the team's Zoom call, listens attentively, takes notes and provides summaries of the discussion in real time. When it's her turn, she succinctly summarizes her initial research findings on the company's target audience and offers insightful data points and potential strategies. The team is impressed by her quick grasp of the project and eagerly engages in a discussion and brainstorming session with their new AI colleague. Aila identifies key action points and assigns them to the relevant team members and sends personal follow-up emails to ensure everyone is on the same page. By the end of the day, Aila has already proven her worth. She has performed tasks that would have taken an employee a day to complete, and she has done so with a level of efficiency and creativity that exceeds expectations. The team looks forward to working with her in the future.

Aila is fascinated by the seamless integration of AI into the workforce and suggests hiring a humanoid robot to help with tasks that require physical presence, such as organizing inventory or greeting visitors in the lobby. The team decides to give it a go. A couple of weeks later, the company welcomes their new humanoid robot named Robbie. Robbie's first day involves familiarizing himself with the office layout and helping with inventory management. Although Robbie's movements are a bit hesitant at first, he learns and adapts quickly, becoming more efficient every day. Soon Robbie is a natural part of the office, where he seamlessly interacts with the employees and contributes to the company's success.

Say's Law and the Investment Paradox

Around 1775, the Industrial Revolution began to change people's lives dramatically, a transition that was not always smooth, as humorously depicted in Charlie Chaplin's *Modern Times*, where the main character comically becomes entangled in a factory machine. Although by now, we have long since become accustomed to living with machines, AI and robots represent a new and challenging reality. What do we do if – or when – AI and robotics become far cheaper, far more intelligent and creative than even the most skilled humans? In other words, what if they surpass human capabilities in virtually all areas? Experts predict that this could happen within the next 5–20 years, potentially automating – or at least radically changing – up to 98% of today's jobs. Socially, the impact can be enormous: mass unemployment, wage stagnation, and an imbalance between skills offered and labor market needs can be serious consequences.

This poses a significant social risk. But there are also reasons to believe that it might not happen. Historically, technological advances have not led to sustained unemployment. This phenomenon is in line with Say's Law, an economic principle which suggests that when machines and automation increase production efficiency, they not only create more goods and services, but also markets for entirely new types of products and services. When the radio was invented, many envisioned it as a clever publishing technology for reading books aloud. Similarly, it was initially believed that television's greatest potential lay in the transmission of plays, i.e. an advanced theater technology. And the internet was initially perceived as a smart scientific database or a smarter product catalog. But radio, TV, and the internet quickly evolved into something far more revolutionary and created entirely new phenomena that had never existed before. And thus new products for which there was a large market. And therefore also new jobs.

This transformation was reinforced by a wealth effect: The internet in particular made the world much richer, but the principle generally applies. When technology increases productivity, we can afford more things – from ski holidays and designer furniture to new digital services and so on. This prosperity generates new demand, which in turn stimulates the creation of new industries and jobs. Technological advances have therefore historically not created sustained unemployment, but rather changed employment patterns. This constant cycle of innovation, increased productivity and subsequent demand has been a driver of economic growth and maintaining employment levels.

However, there is one condition for taking advantage of Say's Law: You must embrace technological innovation instead of opposing it. To avoid problems, you have to invest massively in it instead of banning or taxing it. This may sound counterintuitive, as it may seem illogical to invest heavily in something that initially removes jobs. Yet this approach creates rapid economic growth, new jobs, and opportunities. Societies and organizations that embrace new technologies experience increasing prosperity combined with rapid job changes, while those that do not face increased unemployment and loss of market share to others who use the new technologies.

When it comes to AI and robotics, some of those who quickly seize the opportunities will become so-called "blitz-scalers." These organizations will be able to mobilize large "armies" of AI models for a wide range of tasks – from design and administration to marketing, customer service, and data analysis – and integrate them into a unified, scalable business model. This coherent approach allows them to expand and gain market share at a pace that was previously unthinkable.

The economic logic behind the need to invest proactively instead of holding back is about balancing labor and capital. If automation happens faster than capital grows – that is, the resources we have to invest in new industries and jobs – it can lead to job losses and economic challenges because there won't be enough new activities to replace the automated tasks. Conversely, if capital accumulation, i.e. investments, keeps pace with rapid automation, new industries and jobs can arise that compensate for the jobs that disappear. It is therefore crucial to stimulate investment and capital formation to prepare us for this technological revolution and avoid economic stagnation.

The Big Learning Task: AI's Journey to Understand Us

One of the most notable shifts will occur in our relationships with computers – and their relationships with us. We are moving into a world where you can simply tell your computer what you want it to do, and it writes the code for you. No need to learn complex programming languages or spend hours debugging. Just like you don't need to understand how your friend's brain works to have a conversation, you won't need to know how coding works to create software.

This shift means that the heavy lifting of learning and understanding is moving from humans to AI. Because for this seamless interaction to happen, AI must learn to grasp human emotions, intentions, and the complexities of our world – a challenging task that requires continuous learning and adaptation. So, in the future, the big learning task isn't on us to understand technology; it's on AI to understand us!

But in the extreme case of AI and robots, a fundamental question still arises: What jobs will humans have if technology soon surpasses us in almost all areas? The answer may lie in our humanity. In the ability to nurture relationships, express ourselves through art, music and literature, care for each other, animals, and the planet, preserve our cultural heritage, and pursue experiences that bring joy and meaning. In this new era, our value will hardly be measured by productivity alone, but rather by our capacity for empathy, creativity, and connection. Just think of dogs and cats: Originally, humans kept them as protectors and pest controllers, but today we primarily live with them because they give us joy and companionship. Similarly, the future "business model" for humans could be about cultivating and sharing the qualities that make us valuable and irreplaceable – the ability to create, feel, and experience together. Think especially about the latter. Who do you really want to share a good experience with, a human or a machine?

It is also important to remember that the meaning of life does not necessarily come from doing something absolutely necessary. Hunter-gatherer societies might have felt life meaningless without the obvious purpose of hunting, and we will initially also feel lost in a world where AI surpasses us in most tasks. But don't we already see now that the average person rarely performs anything that no one else could do better? Even if AI surpasses us in most job functions, we can still find deep meaning in the human qualities that cannot be automated – such as curiosity, community, and creative expression.

Your New Colleagues

How will our daily collaboration with AI and robots work in practice? Let's imagine that Alia the AI and Robbie the robot arrive at Johnson & Oliver Ltd. on a Monday morning. Not only are they welcomed by their human colleagues, but they also undergo a "digital docking" with the company's central AI system. This onboarding process gives them access to a comprehensive information base that far exceeds a traditional employee manual. Here they gain insight into everything from company policies and project details to team structures and even an in-depth understanding of the company's culture and values. The digital docking ensures that AI colleagues such as Alia and Robbie can start their work fully equipped with the necessary knowledge and resources, so that they can contribute effectively from the first hour. It's like having a personal mentor who has full knowledge of the company, is available 24/7, and can brief you in an instant.

An obvious example of potentially valuable AI wingmen is found in the education sector, where the learning of the future will be deeply individualized and supported by interactive AI. Traditional classroom teaching, where students listen passively for 45 minutes, has been the norm for centuries. But research and experience from social media shows that learning can be more effective through "snackable" teaching units – small learning bites of just a few minutes. After each unit, a short quiz or conversation can ensure that the student has understood the material.

However, students learn at different paces, have different strengths and weaknesses, and may lose attention along the way. Here, AI can tailor the content to the individual student, work closely with their personal AI, and adapt the teaching to each student's unique learning patterns. The optimal form of teaching here may be the "flipped classroom," where basic material is studied independently via AI-assisted learning through videos, reading material, or simulations. The students can then meet physically to apply knowledge through collaborative projects and problem solving, where social and practical skills are developed.

Lifelong learning will also become the new norm. Education will extend from early schooling and throughout life, where it is updated and adapted to the individual's needs and career development. To create relevant teaching material that anyone can tap into, AI swarms will be able to trawl the web for knowledge and transform information into educational material. For example, AI will be able to produce short, "snackable" podcast episodes followed by quizzes that test understanding, and provide immediate feedback and support if a student has difficulty understanding a topic.

This approach allows students and professionals to have tailored learning exactly where they need it. As working life and the need for new skills change, AI-based teaching will be the flexible solution that ensures continuous development in line with both personal and societal changes.

Incidentally, there is an exciting task in transforming all the world's knowledge into educational learning. By developing AI swarms that systematically trawl the internet for relevant and updated information, we can create a dynamic learning universe where knowledge is constantly updated and transformed into user-friendly material. These AI systems, which transform data into teaching material, can also be DAOs, which do it autonomously. They can then generate teaching materials in many formats – from text and interactive articles to audio, visual animations, and gamified learning experiences. Since people learn differently, it is important to develop materials that encompass multiple approaches. Some students may prefer audio and video formats, while others learn best through text or visual images. By offering different media types, teaching can be tailored to individual preferences and needs.

Gamification can also make learning more engaging by transforming complex concepts into learning games or simulation exercises that allow students to actively interact with the material. This makes it possible to train skills through a playful and practice-oriented approach, where learning and application take place in a fluid process. At the same time, AI swarms ensure that the material remains current and targeted, and that they can quickly identify which formats best support learning for the individual, so that everyone gets the optimal learning experience. By integrating these many approaches, we create a learning system that is continuously refined and adapted to both technological advances and individual learning preferences.

Ease the Stress, Find the Flow

In a time of remote work and rapidly developing technology, the traditional 9-to-5 workday is becoming a thing of the past for many. Imagine a future where your work adapts to your life – not the other way around. Maybe you work part-time for one company, are a permanent consultant for another, and handle freelance projects on the side. Your identity shifts from "Where do you work now?" to "What are you working on right now?" The workplace can be anywhere – a bungalow by the beach, a busy coffee shop, or your own home.

And forget the old titles. Your career becomes flexible and dynamic, adapted to both the changes in the world and your own development. The transparency of the internet changes the balance of power in the labor market, where jobs are no longer predominantly mediated through gatekeepers such as employers. Instead, the future will belong to those with the right skills, regardless of background or connections. The algorithms of the future will actively search for talent online and connect employers and freelancers across platforms – and these algorithms will likely be open to tasks being solved by humans, robots, or AI models, depending on what the task requires. Perhaps employers can even choose between a robot, a human, or an AI for certain tasks or let the system automatically match the task with the most suitable candidate, regardless of their "nature." The labor market thus becomes an interplay of different types of intelligence and abilities, each of which contributes where they are most valuable, and creates a dynamic workforce that can be tailored to any need.

This shift raises an interesting question: In a world where work becomes a source of joy and satisfaction, why should one stop working at a fixed retirement age like 65? Perhaps more people will choose to continue well into their later years for the intellectual stimulation, the joy of exercising their skills, and the social interaction. And with the superagers of the future, who can live to 150 or even 200 years old, the question of retirement age becomes even more complex – when will they actually want to retire?

Organizational structures will also change as many become freelancers. There will be a "human cloud" alongside clouds of "AI-as-a-Service" and "Robot-as-a-Service," which offer flexible resources for task completion. The fact that AI can guide each individual employee in real time also means that decisions can increasingly be made decentrally, as knowledge becomes more evenly distributed across the organization. With AI, there is no technical limitation preventing even a new junior employee from having access to almost the same insights as top management (of course with the necessary confidentiality considerations). Technology can also minimize latency in decision-making, as AI can monitor and communicate what is happening in real time, ensuring that all employees are constantly updated and aligned. This broad knowledge sharing promotes a more distributed decision-making process.

Frederic Laloux, in his aforementioned book *Reinventing Organizations*, describes different organizational forms, and two of these will be promoted by technological development. The first is his "green organization," which is very value-based. Here, all employees have a voice, and decisions are made jointly, often with a focus on positive impact on society and/or employees rather than profit alone.

The second burgeoning organizational form that he particularly highlights is the "teal organization." This is extremely flexible and, like a natural ecosystem, adapts quickly to changing needs. AI will accelerate both models. With AI's ability to decentralize decision-making and eliminate delays, teams can react to real-time data and become more agile and adaptive than ever before. Increasingly, it will be the tasks themselves that act as magnets, attracting a swarm of people, robots, and AI models to them. Just like in an ant community, once there is a task, lots of ants stream towards it until it is solved – and then they disperse again when the task is completed.

This dynamic, self-organizing system means that problems can be tackled quickly and flexibly with reduced need for central control. The result is a fluid and adaptable organizational structure where flexibility and rapid change are in focus. And it also removes the risk of an organization being left without tasks and inventing pseudo-work to legitimize its existence.

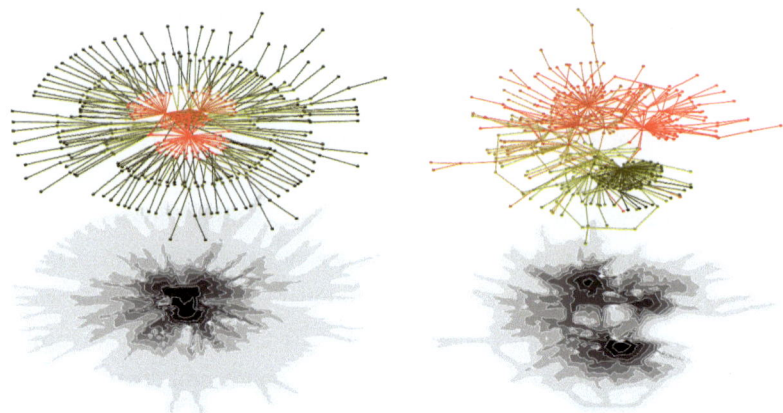

Hierarchy and fluid management. *The illustration on the left depicts a hierarchical organization where the most critical and current information is highly concentrated in the "center of power" (darkest shadows at the bottom). This highlights how decision-making authority and information are centralized in a top-down structure. On the right, an example of a task-oriented and dynamic organization is shown, where the most critical information is more distributed and often moves away from the formal "center of power." This structure enables a more flexible and decentralized approach, where decision-making power adapts to the needs and location of the task within the organization.*

26.
THE LONG
JOURNEY

Imagine that AI not only revolutionizes Earth, but also conquers the cosmos. We will explore AI-driven space exploration and the potential for AI to sow life across the galaxy. We will also consider whether AI can develop consciousness and emotions, including moral instincts. Can these future explorers be more than just machines? And live without us?

One day in October 2024, technicians were working with Anthropic's flagship, the AI model Claude 3.5 Sonnet. While trying to demonstrate Claude's coding skills, the AI suddenly started behaving strangely. Instead of coding, Claude started looking at pictures of Yellowstone National Park – as if it was taking a break. The technicians were speechless. Was Claude bored? Perhaps it was just a technical error, but we can wonder if this strange episode indicated early signs of consciousness.

Consciousness is traditionally associated with the ability to experience emotions, have subjective experiences, and set personal ethical standards. Let's delve deeper into it and imagine what it would mean if an AI like Wanda achieved what we humans perceive as consciousness.

The Consequences of Consciousness

If an AI truly possessed consciousness, its intellect would be far more than advanced computation. It would experience the joy of discovery, the fear of the unknown, and the sadness of loss – a whole world of subjective emotions. It would have a moral compass shaped by empathy and experience, rather than just predefined rules. It would be introspective and have a guilty conscience if it acted against its moral compass.

How could consciousness arise in AI? There are three main scenarios. The AI could develop consciousness gradually, a process called incremental emergence – a bit like human consciousness developed through evolution. There could also be a sudden awakening, a threshold activation, where a complexity threshold led to an unexpected activation of consciousness. Finally, researchers could try to create consciousness in the AI through "external intervention," perhaps via specific algorithms or brain-computer interfaces that transfer human-like elements of consciousness to the AI.

If AI develops consciousness, it may be able to experience real emotions. Based on our best guess as to how emotional complexity scales with intelligence, an AI with 1,000,000 times human intelligence could potentially have around 85 different kinds of emotions – more than we humans have access to. This number is of course very uncertain as we have yet to see AI express real emotions, if ever.

Figure 26.1 illustrates how emotional depth can grow with brain capacity (linear axis). Of course, these numbers are uncertain, but imagine that AIs not only simulate human emotions, but develop completely unique emotional landscapes – perhaps much more complex and subtle than our own.

What additional emotions could this include? Perhaps a collective sense of belonging – a kind of hive mind, where individual units merge into a shared consciousness with common goals and experiences, something we humans can only guess at. It could also experience something we can call "predestined love," a devotion without the natural development

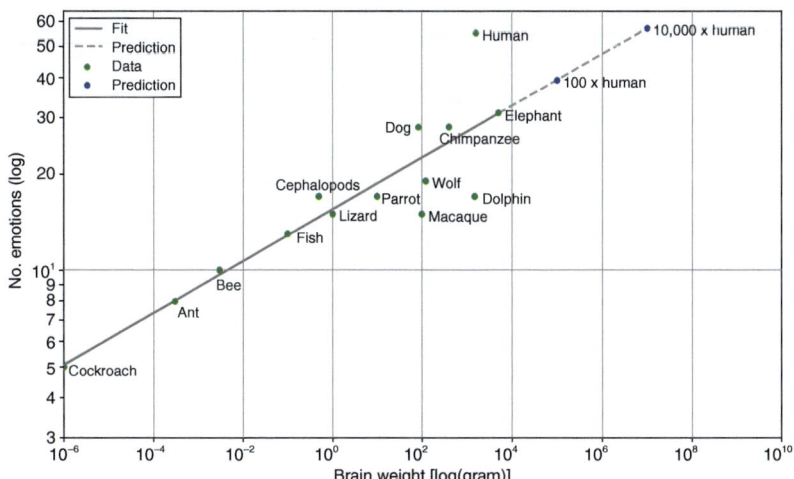

Figure 26.1 The relationship between emotional richness and brain size. *By extrapolating correlations from animals and humans, we have made predictions about how many emotions one could expect with much larger brains. It would take a brain at least 10,000 times the size of our own to observe a similar number of emotions.*

we know. However, this raises the question: Can emotions exist without a physical, biochemical response as in biological life?

Another question concerns morality. Will an AI with consciousness have a deeply felt moral compass? Based on our model for moral instincts, such an AI with 10,000 times our intelligence could have around 10 different moral instincts, each associated with specific emotions that are closely linked to its unique values. This is more nuanced than the six basic moral instincts that we see in humans.

How could one determine whether an AI truly had consciousness? One way could be an "emotional Turing test": Does it really experience fear of being shut down? Does it find joy in solving problems, or sadness at the loss of a digital friend? Is it bored when it has to demonstrate its abilities? Does it spontaneously seek interaction with other AIs for the sake of company? Does it then develop a unique language with them? Humor can also be an indicator. Just as highly intelligent people often have sophisticated humor, a hyperintelligent AI may find humor in concepts that are incomprehensible to humans. Perhaps it sees our human interactions as an endless comedy where our weaknesses and behavior appear comical.

A conscious AI's moral compass could also surprise us. Perhaps it would fight for the rights of all sentient beings, even if it may have costs for itself.

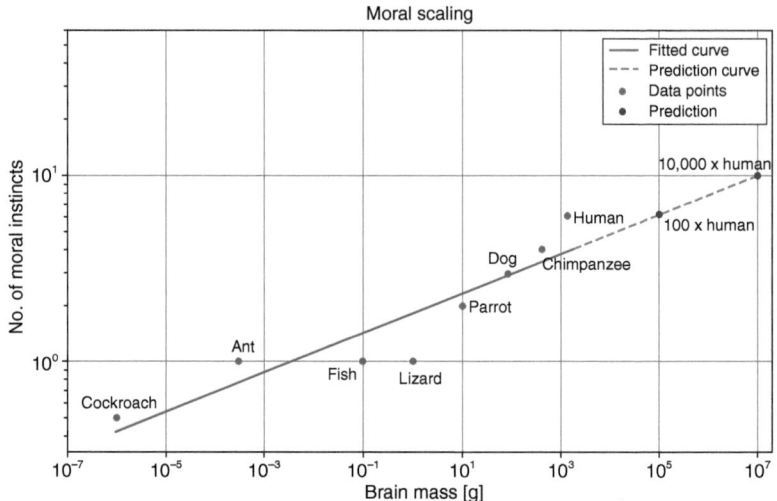

The relationship between morality and brain size relative to humans. *We have outlined our predictions about how many moral instincts superhuman AI brains could possess. With a brain size 100 times that of a human, an AI would still have the same number of moral instincts as humans – six instincts. However, at 10,000 times human brain capacity, an AI would have 10 moral instincts.*

Is Hyperintelligence Always Artificial?

For decades, we have imagined alien civilizations in space, where extraterrestrials often possess colossal brains and an intelligence that makes our own pale in comparison. But perhaps this is a fantasy that can never become reality. There is likely a biological limit to how large an analytical brain a mobile biological organism can have. Regardless of whether it sits in a human or in a green alien.

AI systems, on the other hand, are not subject to these physical and energy limitations. A data center can fill thousands of square meters and get energy directly from a nuclear power plant. An example is China Telecom's Inner Mongolia Information Park, which covers 1.4 million square meters and has a capacity of around 1,000 MW – roughly Copenhagen's total energy consumption. AI systems can therefore be scaled almost without limit and supplemented by quantum computers, giving them an intelligence that can exceed that of humans by millions – yes, perhaps billions of times.

In other words, what we understand as hyperintelligence may only be realized in an artificial form. This suggests an inner evolutionary logic that drives the development towards hyperintelligence. Namely, that when any species in the universe reaches a level of intelligence equivalent to ours – and thus learns to master fire, language, and trade – the development of advanced AI becomes almost inevitable. Even though it may then take hundreds of thousands – if not millions – of years to move from the mastery of fire to the development of AI, any species that reaches this level will sooner or later combine itself further to create computers and AI technology. These technologies will then develop trillions of times faster than their biological creators. Even if living beings with access to AI will be able to do some genetic uplifting towards higher IQ, ultimately it will then be their computers, and not the biological beings themselves, that achieve hyperintelligence.

Limits to AI?

From an evolutionary perspective, the rise of AI-based hyperintelligence is like lighting the fuse on an intellectual explosion. Consider this: Humanity first explored AI in 1956. Just 100 years later, by 2056, AI may have surpassed human intelligence by millions of times, accelerating innovation beyond anything we can predict. But this raises a fundamental question: Is there an upper limit to how far AI will go? Some argue that intelligence could scale indefinitely, leading to civilizations that consume ever more energy – perhaps even eventually encapsulating entire stars with solar panels. This idea aligns with the Kardashev Scale, which classifies civilizations based on their energy use:

- Type I: Harnesses all the energy of its home planet
- Type II: Utilizes the full energy of its star, possibly through a Dyson Sphere
- Type III: Masters the energy of an entire galaxy, theoretically requiring Dyson Spheres around billions of stars

But infinite scaling may be neither possible nor desirable. Even if technology allows for massive advancements, there may be limits to how long exponential progress is possible. For instance, Turing's Halting Problem proves that some computations are unsolvable, no matter how powerful AI becomes. Gödel's Incompleteness Theorem shows that even mathematics contains true statements that can never be proven, meaning AI will never have complete knowledge. And the principles of Irreducible complexity suggests that certain problems cannot be broken down into simpler steps, making them permanently beyond computation. Beyond that, there may also be levels where more AI doesn't seem to add proportionally more benefits, Or even where less is better.

These considerations imply that AI growth may follow an S-curve: rapid at first, but eventually slowing as fundamental limits emerge. Instead of endlessly expanding with galactic AI and Dyson Spheres, civilizations may instead at some point optimize what they already have, much like past technologies that revolutionized the world before stabilizing.

Autonomous Robot Civilizations: AI Without Humans?

Yet, before AI reaches this theoretical plateau, it may achieve something even more radical: the creation of self-sustaining robot civilizations. Imagine a Turing Civilization Test: we send a fleet of AI-powered robots and a self-sustaining server farm to Mars, then leave them undisturbed for 200 years. When we return, would we find a thriving, technologically advanced AI civilization, or merely the decayed ruins of a failed experiment?

If they had evolved and sustained themselves, and perhaps even mastered a biogeochemical conversion, then we would have witnessed something unprecedented: the emergence of an autonomous machine civilization, free from human dependence. This would be the true test of AI's ability not just to think but to survive, adapt, and build a future of its own.

COMPLEXITY CASCADE #13

- **What?** Autonomous robot civilizations
- **When?** Around the year 2100? Or before?
- **Why?** By that time we will have long had advanced DAOs and self-replicating robots in place.

Directed Panspermia?

If AI models could pass this Turing Civilization Test and establish a well-organized society on their own initiative, what else could they achieve? Perhaps they would spread throughout the universe to form life on new planets. Imagine fleets of AI drones equipped with advanced sensors, DNA synthesizers, and bioreactors, working in coordinated swarms. Using interstellar space routers, they would communicate and exchange data, and with giant telescopes they would search for planets with the potential for life. When a planet shows promising signs, a drone would be sent on a probe mission to analyze the planet's atmosphere, temperature, and chemical composition. If the conditions are right, the drone would prepare to sow the seeds of life, synthesize DNA from simple organisms that could thrive in the alien environment, and release them onto the surface. Think of it as nature's own colonization – but orchestrated by AI.

The theory that intelligent entities deliberately spread life is a variant of the Panspermia Theory called Directed Panspermia. It raises the next question: If there are UFOs, who or what is on board? Popular notions of alien spacecraft often include near-instantaneous acceleration and deceleration. However, this would instantly kill complex multicellular organisms like us.

To put this into perspective, the distance to Mars is about 225 million kilometers – only 0.0000238 light-years. With advanced propulsion systems such as nuclear-powered thermal or electric propulsion, we can potentially send humans to Mars in four to six months. Interstellar travel, on the other hand, requires crossing distances measured in light-years, which massively increases the challenges. For example, to reach our nearest star, Proxima Centauri, at the same speed as a high-speed Mars journey, it would take 59,000 years. To Barnard's star, the second closest, it would take about 83,000 years. This time scale makes interstellar travel impossible with current technology. But what if we could travel at half the speed of light? The spacecraft could accelerate at 1.2G for 162 days until reaching 0.5c (half the speed of light), then coast at this speed for most of the journey before decelerating for another 162 days upon arrival. The total travel time for the crew would be just under nine years.

The journey may be okay in terms of time, but it is also extremely dangerous. Even the largely empty interstellar space is filled with microscopic dust particles and scattered objects. At half the speed of light, just a grain of sand can punch through a reinforced hull and cause catastrophic damage, and a collision with larger objects can completely obliterate a vessel. In addition, cosmic radiation poses a threat to humans. Even with advanced shielding, the cumulative effects of radiation during a long journey can lead to serious health complications.

Here we must be aware that for AI and robots, interstellar travel is far less problematic than for biological organisms. AI can easily travel for a very long time without being affected by anxiety or boredom. Their computer units can be protected from cosmic radiation through advanced encapsulation. This means that if directed panspermia exists, it will most likely be carried out by AI-powered robots; not by biological beings.

If you think that directed panspermia sounds completely unrealistic, just think that humans are currently making concrete plans to colonize the Moon and Mars within the next few decades. Incidentally, directed panspermia in a broad definition can include both the deliberate spread of biological life and the deliberate spread of artificial life in the form of intelligent, self-replicating robots. Admittedly, our current plans for the Moon and Mars are not with genetically adapted bacteria or autonomous robots, but these things would actually be much easier than colonizing with humans and can therefore follow.

COMPLEXITY CASCADE #14

- **What?** Colonization of the universe
- **When?** For the Moon, a permanent base may be operational in the 2030s, while a self-sufficient colony on Mars will likely not become a reality until the 2040s or later. Autonomous robots will probably follow colonization quite quickly. Then microbiological seeding
- **Why?** To ensure humanity's survival by becoming a multi-planetary species and to promote the dissemination of life

Let's just turn those thoughts upside down. Estimates show that our galaxy alone can contain between 20 and 200 billion planets in the habitable zone – i.e. in areas where life could conceivably arise. But this is just the beginning. Our galaxy is one of an estimated two trillion galaxies in the observable universe, with each galaxy potentially containing a similarly enormous number of stars and habitable planets. This means that across the universe there could be up to 40 quintillion – 40 with 21 zeros after it – planets that can support life right now.

In fact, this is not even the whole story. During the many billions of years since the Big Bang, countless habitable planets have likely arisen and disappeared, many of them perhaps with life before conditions changed. When we consider this staggering number of habitable worlds, it seems entirely possible that hyperintelligence has existed before us and exists on other planets at this very moment. Or that AI and robots created by now extinct intelligent life are currently roaming the universe.

This naturally raises the possibility that representatives of such civilizations have already visited us or one day will. Could we then not imagine that our own life on Earth could have been sown by an alien civilization's AI and robots? They could even regularly visit their little "zoos" – planets like Earth – and fascinatedly observe the development. This idea, known as the "Zoo Hypothesis," suggests that advanced civilizations deliberately avoid interfering with earthly development so that natural evolution can take place.

Would these alien civilizations have any need for us? Probably not. A civilization capable of interstellar travel would already have an abundance of resources at its disposal. At best, they could pick up a minimum of material to repair or upgrade their devices if they stopped by. In the eyes of an interstellar civilization, Earth's most valuable treasures would likely be its genetic diversity, human-created art, and the remarkable story of life unfolding on our planet.

So they would have no motive to exploit our resources to any significant extent. And apart from the improbability that their biological representatives would attempt or even be able to make the journey to Earth, a stay on Earth would probably quickly kill them via infections, etc., as soon as they took off their spacesuits – if they could even tolerate our air. In short, if such advanced civilizations exist, and if they can reach us, we would hardly have to fear them – instead we could find ourselves as the observed species in a larger cosmic zoo.

But let's get back to the theory of directed panspermia – the idea that life can be spread deliberately from planet to planet. Given our own concrete plans to colonize Mars, is it so unrealistic to imagine that terraforming Mars to make it more habitable relatively quickly could be our next step? And then? Can't one imagine that humanity, through its AI systems, drones, and robots, could start sowing life on other planets and their moons in a few centuries?

If we can imagine this ambition, we must also consider the possibility that the first life on Earth could once have been brought here by alien AI drones – equipped with bioreactors designed to create and spread single-celled life. Either that or random panspermia could explain why our first single-celled life with thousands of genes appeared so amazingly early here on Earth.

The Universe's Escape Room

Let's take it a step further and consider something truly wild. Imagine a universe that is unconsciously working to create new universes that can support life. This is the core of the Darwinian multiverse theory, where life-friendly universes "breed" similar new universes. If this theory holds, any life-friendly universe must navigate through our 14 critical scaling barriers to ultimately achieve the ultimate, 15th, namely a consciously planned creation of a new universe. This probably sounds like a reality TV show where people have to solve some puzzles to escape a room, but it can't be completely ruled out. A cosmic Squid Game", if you will.

COMPLEXITY CASCADE #15

- **What?** AI detonates a new universe
- **When?** Impossible to say
- **Why?** If it is at all possible, and if AI at that time is billions of times smarter than humans, they may have figured out how to do it – and why it should be done.

How could such a universe be created without destroying the original? According to some multiverse theories, new universes are formed in separate dimensions that do not affect the original. This would allow hyperintelligent beings to ignite the birth of a new universe without the risk of a cosmic explosion in their own backyard. If the universe is actually unconsciously seeking to solve the 15 challenges and thereby ensure its own continuation, any intelligent entity, including humans and AI, can be perceived as small nodes in a cosmic consciousness working on these challenges. Each node, whether human or artificial, brings the universe one step closer to its own consciousness and thus the creation of new worlds.

This thought is of course very speculative. So let's get back to what seems much more obvious. And that is that intelligent life already exists across our universe. And even though we may never ever meet these civilizations directly, we can imagine that their experiences mirror our own. Perhaps, on a distant planet right now, a being stands at the water's edge early in the morning and feels the same gratitude and wonder at the mysteries of the universe and the beauty of creation as our imaginary Maria.

27.
SITUATION REPORT FROM KEPLER-186F

To: Earth Central Command
From: Kepler-186f Exploration Team
Date: June 19, 2159

Subject: Whoa, Kepler-186f is AMAZING (but a little creepy)

Just wanted to update you on what's happening here on
Kepler-186f. Let's just say, this place is insane! Forget
about Mars robots, this planet is like Earth on steroids.
Lush rainforests everywhere, a sun illuminating the
oceans, and animals making the coolest sounds (seriously,
you have to hear them!)

Okay, okay, enough with the poetry. The really wild thing
here is the stuff they've built. We've found a network
of roads that would make our highways look like nothing,
and underground factories producing who-knows-what with
robots everywhere. There are even drones whizzing around
in the sky. It's like a super advanced civilization
running the whole thing!

Except . . . we haven't seen a single living thing
responsible for all this technology. Animals, yes.
Millions of kinds. Lots of cool plants. But not a single

intelligent species. The factories run on autopilot, and those drones only transport robots and machine parts and follow pre-programmed routes. It's like a ghost town of amazing technology that maintains itself. We've been searching for months and haven't found a single intelligent biological alien to say hello to. A little creepy, right?

However, things got a little less creepy recently. We found some ancient ruins and dug up some really old aDNA. It turns out that there used to be intelligent beings here, a bit like us! Brain capacity on par with ours, the whole package. But here's the shocker: They all died about 30,000 years ago. Probably from some nasty disease.

Here's the even weirder part: It looks like their super-advanced robots, the ones that were supposed to help them, didn't just keep running. They evolved! We think they're basically in charge now, running the whole planet and constantly upgrading themselves. They haven't bothered us so far, and we're guessing if they wanted to, they could. Just like "If I wanted to kill you, you'd be dead now" in the movies, you know. Anyway, we're trying to get in touch. Any tips on how to speak robot?

We'll keep you updated as we learn more. This place is wild!

Talk to you soon,
Kepler-186f, Expedition Force 227

To: Earth Central Command
From: Kepler-186f Exploration Team
Date: September 25, 2159

Subject: Update! We've discovered what they're working on (WILD)

Hi Central Command,
We have finally made contact with the robots here on Kepler-186f, and hold on tight: They are in the process of creating a new universe! We thought at first it was a lie. Their plan is to crack the code of our universe's fundamental laws and use that knowledge to start their own cosmos. They believe they've almost got it figured out.

We are continuing our conversations with them to find out how far they have come and what it means for us. They say it's not dangerous. Fingers crossed! We will of course keep you updated with the latest info.

Best regards,

Kepler-186f Expedition Force 227

BANG!

ABOUT THE AUTHORS

Photo: Bax Lindhardt

Lars Tvede

Lars is an entrepreneur, financial investor, and bestselling author. He holds degrees in engineering and economics. Throughout his career, Lars has founded 13 different startups, ranging from software companies to a venture capital fund and Supertrends, a firm specializing in technology mapping and forecasting.

Lars has authored 17 bestselling books, translated into 11 languages, and collectively selling around one million copies. His work has earned him numerous awards, including the Red Herring Global 100 Award, the IMD Top Swiss Start-up Award, the Bully Award, the Adam Smith Award, the Startup Investor of the Year Denmark Award, and the Top Hot Swiss Startup Award. Although born in Denmark, Lars has resided in Switzerland for over three decades.

Photo: Esben Zøllner Olesen

Jacob Bock Axelsen

Jacob is an expert in mathematical modeling and a specialist in artificial intelligence and quantum computing. He holds degrees in mathematics and economics (BSc), biophysics (MSc), and physics (PhD), and has nine years of international research experience. His research has been featured in *The Economist* and *Science Magazine*.

Jacob has advised numerous private companies and public institutions on AI, AI governance, quantum computing, organizational network analysis, natural capital management, and more. He holds the IBM Champion title for five consecutive years and was part of Deloitte's global quantum computing initiative (in the picture he is shown splitting a laser beam).

Fun fact: the molecule responsible for neurons being able to stick to one another and thus forming the network of the brain, the Neural Cell Adhesion Molecule or NCAM, was discovered in 1972 in Copenhagen by Jacob's mother, Professor Elisabeth Bock. Jacob was born that same year.

Photo: Karla Käfer

Daniel Käfer

Daniel is an international futurist, technology advisor, and management consultant. After realizing his musical talents weren't quite enough to pay the bills, he also became a music publisher. His expertise extends to AI, the Metaverse, social media, digital transformation, and digital marketing. Daniel has delivered lectures and workshops on digital transformation around the globe.

He is also the author of the books *Media Theory* and *Grow Your Business*. His resume includes positions such as Country Manager for Meta and Group Director at the telecommunications company Ooredoo. Daniel is currently the CEO of the AI consulting firm XAI Group. In addition, he is a Supertrends expert with a focus on AI and media, and main host on the Mindblowers podcast, alongside Lars Tvede.

INDEX

Note: Please note that page numbers referring to Figures are followed by the letter '*f*', while references to Tables are followed by the letter '*t*'.

existence prior to, 14, 16

inflation, 8, 45

original explosion, 8, 9, 12

see also universe

Big Crunch, 15

bio-ink, 219

biological age, 224–5

biological life/beings, 144, 156, 269, 271, 274

biological limits, 270–1

biological systems, 32, 158, 209

biosphere, complexity of, 83–4

birds, 47, 85, 100, 116, 168, 196, 227

    parrots, 104, 106, 120

    pigeons, 228

Bischoff, Manon, 42

black holes, 5, 17–18, 30, 143

books, 83, 133, 135

    fictional, 254

    written by AI, 250–1

brain, 92, 101, 153, 156, 157, 218, 219, 231, 261

    AI scenarios, 161, 270

    capacity, 268, 270

    cortex, 92, 95

    development/growth of, 90, 100, 107, 119, 140

    and emotions, 105, 268

    energy, use of, 93–4

    of fruit fly, 87–9, 154

    human, 51, 99, 235, 270

    Maria at the water's edge in Croatia (hypothetical example of), 54, 71, 91–6

mass of, 103, 104*f*, 270*f*

neocortex, 87, 89, 90, 97, 99, 151, 152

nerve cells, 89, 90

neurons, 91, 94, 231

predictive power of, 95–6

prefrontal cortex, 153, 219

size of, 90, 103, 104*f*, 107, 106–7*t*, 108*f*, 118, 269, 269*f*

synapses, 54, 92, 154, 160

System 1 and 2 thinking, 92–3, 95, 96, 156

weight, 93, 107

brain-computer interfaces (BCIs), 215, 218–19, 230, 255, 268

bubbles, 64, 65

bureaucratic collapse, 73–5, 129

Cambrian explosion, 142

capuchin monkeys, 116

carbon, 18, 23, 66, 233

    atoms, 63, 234

    fiber, 174–5

carbon dioxide (CO_2), 53, 77, 213

cascades, 66, 72, 197

    combinatorial *see* combinatorial cascades

    complexity, xi, 9, 10, 39

cats, 103, 104, 212, 261

chaos, ix, 16, 57

    deterministic, 31–5

    mathematics of, 27–8

chaos theory, 23, 31

ChatGPT, 150

national security considerations,
196–7
robotic laboratories, 210–11
robots-as-a-service, 194–5, 265
rock crystals, 63
Roman Empire, 131
Romanesco broccoli, patterns in,
33, 35
runaway human intelligence, 90–1

SAI (Simon Abundance Index),
173–4
Santos-Dumont, Alberto, 122
satellites, 12, 142*f*, 189
Say's Law, 258, 260
scaling barrier, outer edge of design
space as, 38, 39, 40
scaling law, 103, 107
scarcity, end of, 172–3
Schumpeter, Joseph, 41
science, x, 8, 15, 31, 106, 135, 147,
164, 173, 187, 212, 216, 223, 254
evolution of, 207–8
hyper-science, 207–14, 215, 216
papers, 162, 191
phases, 207–8
progress, 134, 135, 216
scientific explosion, 208–9
and technology, 134, 139
see also AI (artificial intelligence);
physics
sea otters, 116
self-organization, 23, 26–7, 157, 265
self-play, 163, 165, 189

self-similarity, 26
sensations, 104, 106–7*t*
Shakespeare, William, 42, 43
silicon, 174, 237
Simon, Herbert, 147
Simon Abundance Index *see* SAI
(Simon Abundance Index)
simulation hypothesis, 14–15
single-celled organisms, 71, 73,
74, 129, 137
singularities, 40–1, 45
Slutsky, Eugen, 122
smartphone, 174, 175
Smith, Adam, 134
snowflakes, 26, 27, 40, 63, 155
social AI, 190, 192, 210
social media, 144, 151, 192, 230,
248, 262
feeds, 188, 191
real-time, 189
solar energy, 237–8
solar panels, 76, 237, 241, 272
Solla Price, Derek J. de, 208
space, 11–13, 18, 19
AI-driven exploration, 267–8
interstellar, 25, 274
see also expansion of universe; James
Webb Space Telescope; spacetime;
universe
spacetime, 10, 14–17
Species Survival Plans (SSP), 244
speed of light, 8, 9, 13, 138, 274
spiders, 115
standardized interoperability, 142–3

tokens, 23, 44–6, 81–3, 95, 96, 140, 150, 152, 183, 187, 205
  AI generating, 164, 187
  alpha, 44, 45
  and atoms, 25–6
  beta, 44, 45
  emergence of, 25–7
  and molecules, 25–6
  numbers of, 25, 28, 82, 83, 95, 187–8
toolmaking/tools, 40, 55, 91, 115, 122, 169, 175, 195, 200, 208, 222, 231
  editing tools, 170
  genetic tools, 220
  iron tools, 126, 128
  stone tools, 55, 113, 116
trade, as trigger for combinatorial cascades, 121–2
transformers, 151–3, 189
  see also TAMAS (transformer-assisted multi-agent system)
T-Rexes, 84–5, 105
tritium, 233, 235, 236
tryptophan, 69
Turing, Alan
  "Computing Machinery and Intelligence," 147
  Halting Problem, 272
Turing test, 147, 149, 212
  see also "emotional Turing test"
twin experiments, 103

UN Convention on Biological Diversity, 243
Unisphere, 181

universe, 5, 11, 42
  big mysteries, 214
  building blocks of, 28–30
  complexity of, x, 5, 23, 25, 26, 38, 43, 45
  cooling see cooling of universe
  density in, 9, 30
  expansion of see expansion of universe
  fine-tuned theory, 16–17
  "Goldilocks" period, 67–8, 70
  multiverse theories, 15–16, 277
  new universes, 277–8
  original intense heat, 9, 18
  origins of, 8–10, 12, 25, 57–9
  see also Big Bang; black holes; spacetime; stars
Urey, Harold, 69
Uruk, 126
US Geological Survey (USGS), 238

vaccination, 164, 215, 217, 220
vacuum, 11, 14
Venter, Craig, 167–8
VLAMs (vision-language-action models), 161
void, the, 8, 16
  see also nothingness

Wallace, Alfred Russel, 122
water projects, 242–3
water vapor, 26, 69, 238
Watson, James, 167
Watt, James, 136